The Art of Narrative

By the same author

The Pearl: an interpretation (1967)

The Poet Reading to an Audience

Chaucer and the Making of English Poetry

Volume II

The Art of Narrative

❀❀❀❀❀

P. M. KEAN
University of Oxford

Routledge & Kegan Paul
London and Boston

First published 1972
by Routledge & Kegan Paul Ltd
Broadway House, 68–74 Carter Lane,
London EC4V 5EL
and 9 Park Street,
Boston, Mass., 02108, U.S.A.
Printed in Great Britain by
The Camelot Press Ltd
London and Southampton
© P. M. Kean 1972
ISBN 0 7250 3

Contents

Contents

Plates

Abbreviations

CT	*Canterbury Tales* (passages quoted from F. N. Robinson, ed., *The Works of Geoffrey Chaucer*, 2nd edn, 1957, Houghton Mifflin Co., Boston)
EETS	Early English Text Society (O.S. = Old Series; E.S. = Extra Series)
ELH	*English Literary History*
MLN	*Modern Language Notes*
MPh	*Modern Philology*
OED	*The Oxford English Dictionary*
PL	J.-P. Migne, *Patrologiae Cursus Completus* . . . Series Latina
PMLA	*Publications of the Modern Language Association of America*
RES	*Review of English Studies* (N.S. = New Series)
SATF	Société des Anciens Textes Français

The *Knight's Tale*

In the *Complaint of Mars*, Chaucer built up a short *divertissement* around the idea of the planetary gods and, as we have seen, used this framework to introduce the themes of both love and philosophy. In the *Knight's Tale*, an incomparably more ambitious work, he once again put the planets in the forefront of the action, in a symmetrical arrangement in which each planet-god is linked to a figure in the human story. Once again the main themes are love and a philosophical system which embraces love as one of its leading ideas. The result is a poem which, in itself, without taking its context within the *Canterbury Tales* into account, is one of Chaucer's most important works. It is also, at the same time, a work which is very fully integrated into the scheme of the *Canterbury Tales*. We know – for example, from his use of it in the *Troilus* – that Chaucer must have been working on the *Teseida* of Boccaccio, his main source in the *Knight's Tale*, before he devised the plan of the *Canterbury Tales*;[1] but, nevertheless, the version we know as the *Knight's Tale* is thoroughly adapted to the character of the Knight, and, moreover, the intrusion of the teller in his tale is made an important structural device in a way which we must presently examine.

The *Knight's Tale* is an Italian-Latin derived romance – if we are justified in calling it a romance at all, and I think that there is, in fact, something to be gained by using for it a term that would never fit the *Troilus*. Chaucer, of course, knew that the actual story is not to be found in the *Thebaid*; but he would also have recognized that, whatever was the source of Boccaccio's story, the Italian poet drew heavily on this work.[2] Chaucer's own treatment of the story and his very extensive alterations of the *Teseida* have, I believe, two main impulses behind them. In the first place, he shortens and tautens because, no doubt, he prefers a tighter narrative structure, and also because the length of his original would be too great even for the freedom which he allows himself as to size in the *Canterbury Tales*. But he also tightens up the narrative because he is not, like Boccaccio, primarily interested in presenting the episodes of an episodic story. His interest, it is evident, is rather to use the story to develop certain themes, and these are of a philosophical kind. It is also true, I think, that many of his alterations are designed to turn the work away from the world and outlook of the Italian poet and back to those of Statius; Chaucer's more elaborate treatment of the gods, in the course of which he especially develops the figure of Saturn, who plays no part in Boccaccio's poem, points in this direction.[3]

To see how this comes about it will be necessary to look closely at the actual material which Chaucer handles in the tale; and first, at the risk of appearing paradoxical, it must be emphasized that for Chaucer, whatever it may have been for Boccaccio, the story is not primarily one of love in the normal sense of the word. It is, of course, the love story which provides the outline of the plot, but we have only to think of the very different way in which Chaucer approaches both plot and characters in the *Troilus*, where the love story *is* the main interest, to see that something else is in question in the *Knight's Tale*. A good deal is said about love, it is true, but there are no paeans in its praise, and the lovers are comparatively flat, undifferentiated figures,[4] while their lady is notoriously unresponsive to them and remains uninterested in love until the final moment, when at Theseus's bidding she, happily, becomes a perfect wife. While in the *Troilus*, in fact, Chaucer gives us a philosophical treatment of a love story, in the *Knight's Tale* a love story forms the pretext for a philosophical poem. This is, perhaps, one reason for the difficulty, and even the feeling of repulsion, with which this poem is sometimes approached by modern readers. The philosophical ideas are unfamiliar and sometimes misunderstood; and the apparently familiar ground of the love story does not fulfil expectations. To appreciate the poem, and to see what Chaucer is really doing, we must, I think, approach it from the right viewpoint.

I have already indicated something of this viewpoint in speaking of the epilogue to the *Troilus*. There, I have suggested, Chaucer develops a view of the gods, very like that which he would have found in Statius, as, on the one hand, the instruments of a benevolent providence and, on the other, as forces affecting the lives of men in an apparently random and usually unfortunate way – operating, that is (from the Boethian point of view), at the level of fortune and chance, and involving the cooperation of the irrational passions. We have also considered the place of human free will within this scheme. In the *Knight's Tale*, we have the same view of the gods and the same fundamental problem of human responsibility and free will. But, with the much flatter and less detailed presentation of the human protagonists, and the more elaborate presentation of the gods (who do not make a personal appearance in the *Troilus*), the emphasis shifts, from a demonstration of the human problem, primarily through human actions and reactions, to a much more theoretical type of treatment, in which the solution – and indeed all the turns of the plot – is seen rather as the result of the nature of the system within which human beings (free will and all) operate than as deriving directly from individual traits and acts. In fact, to put it shortly, the *Knight's Tale* generalizes where the *Troilus* particularizes; and, in place of the individual, even idiosyncratic, dilemma of the persons in the *Troilus*, we have something much nearer the type-situation of, for example, the morality play, which is devised to set forth general principles in a general way, not to show their particular application.

The formality of the scheme by which human and divine protagonists are coupled suits this purpose but would, obviously, be out of place in a more naturalistically conceived plot. The arrangement is as follows: Theseus corresponds to Jupiter, both as the king whose commands are obeyed by the other characters and as the beneficent force which brings order out of disorder. Egeus, his father, corresponds to the father of the king of the gods, Saturn. The function of Saturn, in the narrative, and his characteristics are somewhat complicated, and we must leave their definition until later.[5] Palamoun corresponds to Venus, who represents love seen first as a destructive force and later as a uniting and saving principle.[6] Arcite corresponds to Mars. Emily corresponds to Diana, the moon, who governs change. Four of these five gods have, further, a special astrological relation to each other. Jupiter and Saturn are, respectively, *Fortuna Major* and *Infortuna Major*, the greatest of the fortunate and unfortunate planets, and Jupiter is, therefore, the only planet which can 'master' Saturn. Venus and Mars have the same relationship, to a lesser degree; they are *Fortuna Minor* and *Infortuna Minor*. Venus, like

Jupiter in relation to Saturn, can overcome the bad influence of her partner in the scheme. Chaucer has thus, through the introduction of Saturn, gained a very simple, clearcut plan of planetary forces.

No such scheme is to be found in the *Teseida*, although the gods are, of course, mentioned by Boccaccio and do, as in the *Knight's Tale*, take part in the denouement. Nor would Chaucer have found it in the *Thebaid*. There, the gods act in parallel to the actions of men – for example, the activities of Jupiter and Juno, Venus and Mars, precede, and cause, the outbreak of war, although this is amply motivated by the human conduct of affairs; but they are not consistently associated with particular individuals. For the actual coupling of human figures with those of the gods, however, Chaucer would only need to turn to the *Aeneid*, where, for example, the affairs of Aeneas and Dido develop as they do because behind each human actor stands the figure of its corresponding goddess – Venus acts for Aeneas, Juno for Dido.[7] Chaucer has only elaborated this scheme to include more characters and to accommodate a more complicated and double-edged view of the gods, which derives in part from Statius and in part, especially in the case of Saturn, from medieval developments in the astrological conception of the planet-deities.

In his analysis of the astrological material of the *Knight's Tale*,[8] Curry states that for Chaucer the motivating force of the story is the 'formative and impelling influence of stars in which his age believed'; that, 'in order to furnish such a motivating force for the final stages of the action, (Chaucer) has skilfully gone about transferring the power of the ancient gods of his sources to the astrological planets of the same name; that the real conflict behind the surface action of the story is a conflict between the planets Saturn and Mars'.[9] These claims, it seems to me, need modifying in two ways. In the first place, as we have seen, the relation of the planets to the individuals is not as simple as Curry here suggests, and, in the second, we cannot so lightly assume a general acceptance of astrological lore. Nor, of course (as Curry himself points out, pp. 149 ff.), can we credit Chaucer with the whole change of gods to planets. This association goes back to the late Classical period – indeed, as we have seen, there are already signs of it in Statius. For Curry, the apparently random and cruel acts of the planetary gods are brought within a more comprehensive philosophical system by Theseus's final speeches and actions, although he considers that the poem offers no final resolution of the philosophical problem. But this resolution is, in fact, implied not only by the philosophical arguments of Theseus's great speech on the First Mover, but by the whole treatment of the gods throughout the poem, which shows them not merely as destinal forces, but also as aspects of the behaviour of the human beings to whom they are so closely linked. Just as, in the *Thebaid*, the infernal deities do not cast a *new* blight on the house of Oedipus, but merely emphasize 'it's *usual* gloom',[10] so Mars does not alter Arcite's character and the actions which spring from it, but merely illustrates and sums up these aspects of his personality – and the same is true of the other human-planet pairs. It is tempting, here, to compare a later, typically Renaissance, formulation of the relationship of human beings to the stars. In the *de Vita Triplici*, Ficino wrote:[11]

> Always remember that already by the inclinations and desires
> of our mind and by the mere capacity of our *spiritus* we can
> come easily and rapidly under the influence of those stars
> which denote these inclinations, desires and capacities.

In fact, it does not seem to me that, in the *Knight's Tale*, we are dealing so much with a study based on the Boethian world-picture, in which the main problem is expressed in terms of the power and influence of destiny and fortune (since this is not necessarily the major implication of the planetary machinery of the poem), as with a development of the theme of the effects on human life of disorder and unreason opposed to an order which extends from the most minor aspects of life up to that unmoved first mover on whom the very principle and idea of order depends.[12] Chaucer, as usual, is unwilling to indulge in didactic comment, which could only appear heavy-handed in a work of this kind; but he does, I think, assume that he shares with his audience a standpoint from which the problems besetting his characters are seen to be capable of solution and, more-over, so organizes the work that it is consistently viewed by the audience from this standpoint. How this is achieved, however, can only be shown by a detailed reading of the poem.

It is obvious that the whole structure of the *Knight's Tale* is built round two focal points within the narrative: these are the pair of lovers (as we have said, distinct, but not strikingly differentiated) and the figure of Theseus. It is also obvious that, if anything in the poem stands consistently for the principle of order, it is Theseus. From the beginning, he is represented as in the fullest possible control of his circumstances and his world. He is lord, governor, conqueror – these terms are constantly used and repeated in the opening lines of the poem. For the Middle Ages, the ruler was invariably seen as, above all, the ultimate source of law and order in the state.[13] There are, I think, signs that the term 'conqueror' had a special sense and was also related in a particular way to the achievement of order. In *Piers Plowman*, Christ is both king and conqueror, and it is explained that it is the function of a conqueror to bring benefits to his people:[14]

> It bicometh to a kynge to kepe and to defende,
> And conquerour of conquest, his lawes and his large.
>
> (B, XIX, 42–3)

In Christ's case:

> And sith he ʒaf largely alle his lele lyges
> Places in paradys at her partynge hennes,
> He may wel be called 'conquerour'.
>
> (56–8)

The same idea, that the conqueror is responsible for bringing benefits not destruction, seems still to be implied in Donne's use of the term in 'The Prohibition':

> But thou wilt lose the stile of conqueror
> If I, thy conquest, perish by thy hate.

Theseus's most recent conquest conforms to these ideas, since it is peculiarly well designed to serve the cause of order, and since he engages on it in a way which is clearly thought of as good:

> What with his wysdom and his chivalrie,
> He conquered al the regne of Femenye.
>
> (865–6)

Without necessarily going as far as D. W. Robertson, who sees in this the conquest of sensuality by reason,[15] it is evident that a realm consisting only of 'Femenye' is incomplete, and so lacking in order. Moreover, Theseus's conquest is so happily concluded that he brings back a bride from the campaign; and this is a further assertion of order, since for Chaucer, as for other medieval authors, marriage stands for order and harmony in human life in a fundamental way, both literally and figuratively – a point to which we must return.

It is in the course of this happy and ceremonial return – 'with muchel glorie and greet solempnytee' (870) – that Theseus encounters the lamenting widows of Thebes, who represent the reverse of his own marriage party and who are the victims of 'Fortune and hire false wheel' (925). They are suffering from the tyranny of a very different conqueror, Creon, 'fulfild of ire and iniquitee', who, far from restoring a happy state of order to the realm by his conquest, has so far insisted on disorder as to have even forbidden the decent burial of the corpses of his victims. The patterning which is so characteristic of the *Knight's Tale* is thus apparent from the beginning – we have the wedding and the widows: the true and the false conquerors bringing, respectively, order and disorder, happiness and misery – a pattern which is carried through to the end, when the funeral is followed by the wedding. In Boccaccio's much longer and more diffuse treatment this symmetrical arrangement does not emerge as significant.

Theseus is moved by this tragic reversal of fortune:

> Hym thoughte that his herte wolde breke,
> Whan he saugh hem so pitous and so maat
> That whilom weren of so greet estaat;
>
> (954–6)

and he loses no time in remedying the situation. He conquers Thebes, kills the false tyrant and gives back to the ladies what is left of their husbands 'to doon obsequies, as was tho the gyse'.

Order and decency are thus restored, but the battle gives rise to a new situation. After it – and we perhaps hear a note of grim professionalism from the Knight – things take their usual course:[16]

> To ransake in the taas of bodyes dede,
> Hem for to strepe of harneys and of wede,
> The pilours diden bisynesse and cure.
>
> (1005–7)

In such a heap of dead bodies are found, still breathing, Palamoun and Arcite. They are brought to Theseus, who, acting with apparent arbitrariness, consigns them to prison forever, without hope of ransom. This act is perhaps more intelligible when we remember that they are Theban princes, a part of the guilty tale of Thebes, a prime instance of wickedness and disorder among gods and men. Theseus here, as at other key-points in the action, is intent on settling the political problem of Thebes – a purpose good in itself and conducive to order, but unfortunate in its effects in the particular case of the Theban princes. There is, too, a sense of fundamental difference between the two princes and Theseus, which goes deeper than the mere ability of the latter to enforce an arbitrary decision. When we read the following lines, we are aware of a basic difference in the destiny of the two parties:

> But by hir cote-armures and by hir gere
> The heraudes knewe hem best in special
> As they that weren of the blood roial
> Of Thebes, and of sustren two yborn.
> Out of the taas the pilours han hem torn,
> And han hem caried softe unto the tente
> Of Theseus; and he ful soone hem sente
> To Atthenes, to dwellen in prisoun
> Perpetuelly, – he nolde no raunsoun.
> And whan this worthy duc hath thus ydon,
> He took his hoost, and hoom he rit anon
> With laurer crowned as a conquerour;
> And ther he lyveth in joye and in honour
> Terme of his lyf; what nedeth wordes mo?
> And in a tour, in angwissh and in wo,
> This Palamon and his felawe Arcite
> For everemoore; ther may no gold hem quite.
> (1016–32)

Palamoun and Arcite are to be imprisoned 'perpetuelly': Theseus, who has only acted in accordance with his function of a worthy conqueror, is to live in joy and honour 'terme of his lyf'. There is nothing to be done about either destiny. In Theseus's case, 'what nedeth wordes mo'; in that of the princes 'ther may no gold hem quite'.

In bringing about the event which starts the story, Theseus acts, then, in an arbitrary way, but in accordance with his essentially benevolent function of conqueror. His action is like those acts of Jupiter which express an ultimately benevolent providence: although they may not be easily understood or immediately pleasing, they are yet part of the total divine scheme. When we come, however, to the catastrophic love which overwhelms Palamoun and Arcite, the emphasis shifts to the lower and more random influences on human life. In lines 1086–91, Arcite blames their imprisonment, not on providence, but on Fortune, working through Saturn and through their personal horoscope at birth:

> 'Fortune hath yeven us this adversitee.
> Som wikke aspect or disposicioun
> Of Saturne, by som constellacioun,
> Hath yeven us this, although we hadde it sworn;
> So stood the hevene whan that we were born.
> We moste endure it; this is the short and playn.'

Palamoun expresses similar ideas in his despairing speech on the 'crueel goddes' (1303 ff.). Now, these are ideas and beliefs which, as we have seen, Chaucer elsewhere condemns as 'filth' and 'ordure', which are contrary to the nobility of man in his possession of free will.[17] These speeches, therefore, are an important part of the statement of the argument of the poem and serve to develop the contrast between Theseus, associated with Jupiter and acting like a beneficent providence, who, as we have seen in the case of the unfortunate Theban ladies, is not in the power of fortune but is able to reverse its bad effects, and the two princes, who are ranged with the lesser, fully planetized gods and who submit themselves, like the beast in the stall in *Fortune*, to their influence. Since, as we have again already seen, it is the passions which are peculiarly subject to the influence of the stars, it is in keeping that the love which comes to the two princes is described mainly in terms of its unbridled, unreasoning and disruptive effect:

> 'Wostow nat wel the olde clerkes sawe,
> That "who shal yeve a lovere any lawe?"
> Love is a gretter lawe, by my pan,
> Than may be yeve to any erthely man;

9

> And therefore positif lawe and swich decree
> Is broken al day for love in ech degree,
> A man moot nedes love, maugree his heed.
> He may nat fleen it, thogh he sholde be deed.'
>
> (1163–70)

So Arcite, using with unconscious irony terms so ambiguous as to be almost riddling. Love seen as the greatest, overriding law, more important than *lex positiva* – law which, in contrast to natural law, depends on human decrees – points forward to the love described by Theseus as the great chain which holds the universe in its place. On the other hand, as Arcite sees it, the love he describes is the cause of a disruption – breaking of the law – which extends through all the orders of society – 'in ech degree'.[18] The image which he uses to bring home his point, of the quarrelling dogs robbed of their bone by the kite (1177–80), reinforces the impression of disorder, and the conclusion he draws is in keeping:

> 'And therfore, at the kynges court, my brother,
> Ech man for hymself, ther is noon oother.'
>
> (1181–2)

It is not only that this describes a state of disorder, but that it places it at the heart of human affairs and human relationships. The king's court ought to be the source of order in human society, and the ties of friendship and brotherhood – Palamoun and Arcite stand in the important relationship of sworn, blood-brothers – ought not to be so easily broken, nor the human 'brothers' so easily debased to the conduct of the wrangling dog and kite.

When Arcite is freed and finds himself in a worse prison than before, since he is even further from his lady, it is Fortune that he blames:

> 'O deere cosyn Palamon,' quod he,
> 'Thyn is the victorie of this aventure . . .
> Wel hath Fortune yturned thee the dys,
> That hast the sighte of hire and I th'absence.
> For possible is, syn thou hast hire presence,
> And art a knyght, a worthy and an able,
> That by som cas, syn Fortune is chaungeable,

Thow maist to thy desir somtyme atteyne.
But I, that am exiled and bareyne
Of alle grace, and in so greet dispeir,
That ther nys erthe, water, fir, ne eir,
Ne creature that of hem maked is,
That may me helpe or doon confort in this,
Wel oughte I sterve in wanhope and distresse.
Farwel my lif, my lust, and my gladnesse!'

(1234–50)

The reference to the four elements and the creatures made of them is significant. This is, precisely, the realm over which love as a universal force has power, as we know from the *Troilus* and are to learn from Theseus's great speech. Arcite, in fact, looks to changeable Fortune, which has power over a love as temporary and changeable as herself, instead of to the stable forces which, under providence, hold all Nature together. This is underlined by the reference to divine 'purveiaunce' which immediately follows. It is a reminder to the reader that Fortune is not all-powerful, although Arcite himself makes no distinction:

'Allas, why pleynen folk so in commune
On purveiaunce of God, or of Fortune?'

(1251–2)

The passage in Boethius's *de Consolatione Philosophiae* which Chaucer is using does make a distinction. This comes in prosa vi of Book IV, and, in the first place, Philosophy points out the difference between Providence and *Fata* (here equivalent to destiny):

'And thilke devyne thought that is iset and put in the tour (*that is to seyn, in the heighte*) of the simplicite of God, stablissith many maner gises to thinges that ben to done; the whiche manere whan that men looken it in thilke pure clennesse of the devyne intelligence, it is ycleped purveaunce; but whanne thilke manere is referred by men to thinges that it moeveth and disponyth, than of olde men it was clepyd destyne. . . . For purveaunce is thilke devyne resoun that is establissed in the sovereyn prince of thinges, the whiche purveaunce disponith alle thinges; but, certes, destyne is the disposicioun and ordenance clyvyng to moevable thinges.'

(IV, pr. vi, 47–65).

11

Secondly, neither Boethius nor any other Stoic-inspired philosopher ever suggested that the kind of goods which Arcite enumerates as deceiving – riches, material freedom – were anything else. Moreover, the reference to the man who 'dronke is as a mous' relates to a passage of Boethius which is about something quite different. The drunkenness which Boethius laments is that which makes man's quest for the sovereign good uncertain,[19] not the search, which Arcite has in mind, for the 'felicitee' which is situated 'in this world'. The passage, in fact, is so framed that it gives a clear picture of Arcite's wrong-headed point of view, and yet ensures that a reader familiar with the philosophical background is all the time clearly signposted to the opposite one.

This speech is balanced by one made by Palamoun, which, again, is based on a passage in Boethius, this time on metre v in Book I. This metre is spoken by Boethius in his own person, lamenting his cruel fate, and to understand its significance we have to read on to Philosophy's reply in the prosa which follows. Arcite's speech is built up from scraps from several different parts of the *de Consolatione*, used in an altered sense, but in Palamoun's speech Chaucer is able to use a consecutive passage, because in this metre Boethius expresses a mistaken and wrong-headed view set up only to be knocked down by Philosophy, who comments dryly:

> 'Whan I saugh the,' quod sche, 'sorwful and wepynge, I wiste anoon that thow were a wrecche and exiled; but I wyste nevere how fer thyn exil was yif thy tale ne hadde schewid it me . . . thow hast fayled of thi weye and gon amys.'
>
> (I, pr. v, 4–11).

Even here, Chaucer has modified his source and has worked in other material. The first part of the speech is closest to Boethius.[20]

> Thanne seyde he, 'O crueel goddes that governe
> This world with byndyng of youre word eterne,
> And writen in the table of atthamaunt
> Youre parlement and youre eterne graunt,
> What is mankynde moore unto you holde
> Than is the sheep that rouketh in the folde?
> For slayn is man right as another beest,
> And dwelleth eek in prison and arreest,

And hath siknesse and greet adversitee,
And ofte tymes giltelees, pardee.
    What governance is in this prescience,
That giltelees tormenteth innocence?'
                                    (1303–14)

The alterations, however, are almost as striking as the likenesses. In the first place, the Creator of the Heavens, the Governor of all things, becomes the 'crueel goddes' in the plural, and the emphasis shifts from the question of guilt and innocence to a comparison of mankind with the beasts. Secondly, Chaucer does not here use the long passage which describes the cycle of time and the seasons. This, as he must have been well aware, in fact belongs to the argument in favour of the goodness of Providence, as is made clear in metre vi, where Philosophy says:

> Signat tempora propriis
> Aptans officiis deus.
>
> (God every several time
> With proper grace hath crowned.)
>   (Loeb trans.)

In fact, Chaucer restricts the speech to the manifestations of the stars and of Fortune and does not make Palamoun, like Boethius, call in question the whole operation of God's providence in the natural world. He thus makes the argument a more trivial one than Boethius's, more obviously aimed at forces far below providence in the Boethian scheme.

He then introduces the image of the slaughtered beast, which has no parallel in Boethius, but which, as we have seen, is used elsewhere by Chaucer as a part of the argument in favour of man's free will and independence of Fortune. This image is carried over into the next part of the speech:

> 'And yet encresseth this al my penaunce
> That man is bounden to his observaunce,
> For Goddes sake, to letten of his wille,
> Ther as a beest may al his lust fulfille.
> And whan a beest is deed he hath no peyne;
> But man after his deeth mot wepe and pleyne,
> Though in this world he have care and wo.'
>   (1315–21)

Here, Chaucer has moved on to Book III, prosa vii, of the *de Consolatione*, in which Philosophy argues that if physical pleasure were man's only good, the beasts ought to be called blessed, since they certainly have no other goal:

> And yif thilke delices mowen maken folk blisful, thanne by the same cause moten thise beestis ben cleped blisful, of whiche beestes al the entencioun hasteth to fulfille here bodily jolyte.

At the beginning of prosa viii, Philosophy concludes that:

> Now is it no doute thanne that thise weyes ne ben a maner mysledynges to blisfulnesse, ne that they ne mowen nat leden folk thider as thei byheten to leden hem.

If Palamoun had understood where true pleasure lay, he would not have envied the beasts. That he does so shows the depth of his error.

To end the speech, Chaucer returns briefly to Boethius for the contrast of the treatment meted out in the world to guilt and innocence, and concludes with Palamoun's application of his arguments to his own circumstances, in which he blames his fate wholly on the activities of the gods – Juno, who is at the bottom of all the troubles of Thebes; Saturn and Venus, who are responsible, on the one hand, for his imprisonment and, on the other, for his painful love (a love which has plunged him in 'jalousie and fere') and who are to be seen acting in concert later in the poem. The whole speech, therefore, illustrates Palamoun's complete submission to Fortune and to the influences of the gods who help to bring about particular events within the transitory world. The arguments are familiar ones, which, in their usual context, either carry the reverse meaning or are only used to be contradicted. As in the case of Arcite's earlier speech, the reader who is familiar with material of this kind will have no great difficulty in seeing what the poet is aiming at and in taking up the position which he is intended to occupy. As we have seen from the treatment of such material in the short poems, there seems no reason to doubt that Chaucer's audience shared with him a knowledge of, and interest in, philosophizing of this type.

This, then, is the situation – the philosophical groundplan – as it is laid out in part i. The end of this part brings us the first of the prosaic, semi-ironical comments which remind us vividly of the presence of the Knight as story-teller and, at the same time, set us at a little distance from the story itself, allowing us the space to look at it dispassionately. As we have seen, the actual style of these comments, like that of many of Theseus's speeches, is in accordance with the methods of earlier romance. Chaucer's innovation lies in the subtlety with which he uses such methods. The Knight puts his question:

> Yow loveres axe I now this questioun:
> Who hath the worse, Arcite or Palamoun?
> That oon may seen his lady day by day,
> But in prison he moot dwelle alway;
> That oother wher hym list may ride or go,
> But seen his lady shal he nevere mo.
> Now demeth as yow liste, ye that kan,
> For I wol telle forth as I bigan.
>
> (1347–54)

We are not only disengaged for a moment from the story. By the posing of the conventional *problème d'amour*, we are also disengaged from any tendency to take too high a philosophical flight. The problems which have been raised are serious ones. The themes of determinism and free will and of order and disorder are fundamental to human life and to human happiness; but, nevertheless, Chaucer has chosen to make them the themes of a tale told for entertainment as well as profit, and therefore demanding more frequent and complex modulations than would be possible, or necessary, in a more single-minded treatise on philosophy. The love story, as has been said, may not be the main purpose of the work, but it is not to be set aside as a mere artificial pretext for the philosophy. The immediate source of disorder in the poem is the disastrous love which falls upon the two princes, and it is in order to ponder the significance of all their frenzied acts and speeches that we need, at times, to set them at a distance. We are not, in this tale, to be too closely involved with what Henry James likes to refer to as the victims bleeding in the arena – towards whom, too, he has much of Chaucer's attitude of compassionate, occasionally half-exasperated irony, and whom he also likes to view through the eyes of an observer only partially involved in the struggle. Chaucer arranges his distancing partly through such an observing figure – that of the Knight – and partly through the figure, to some extent a duplicate of the Knight, of

Theseus, who is not only the observer of the lovers' activities but also the kingly ruler in whom is to be found the ultimate earthly source of order in their world. His down-to-earth comments, therefore, although they may seem intrusive, or even flippant, to some readers, help to indicate a change of focus and to reinforce the effect of the careful organization of the philosophical arguments. They help, in fact, to show the difference between the state of disorder in which the lovers suffer and struggle and that of order within which Theseus operates, and which, though with some loss, he is finally able to impose on the situation.

Part i, then, sets the scene and establishes the basic themes and patterns. Part ii carries on the story and develops the contrast between the lovers and Theseus. This part opens with a description of the 'loveris maladye of Hereos' which afflicts Arcite, and to which is added symptoms pointing to 'manye / engendred of humour malencolik'. Boccaccio also describes Arcite's frantic sorrow and changed appearance,[21] but the medical treatment of the subject is wholly Chaucer's. 'Heroical love' (Burton's term for it) was a well-recognized illness, which was discussed in numerous medieval medical treatises.[22] It was likely, in itself, to lead to madness, but Chaucer suggests that Arcite's mania derives rather from melancholy. This, too, was for the Middle Ages not merely a frame of mind, but a serious medical problem.[23] Melancholy is invariably associated with the influence and characteristics of Saturn, so that, through this description, Chaucer not only establishes the extreme seriousness of Arcite's morbid state, but places it within the pattern of links between the planet-gods and men which is so important in the poem. Arcite shows associations with Saturn in this illness and also in the final one which ends his life, although he dies after expressing his devotion to Mars and placing himself under his protection, and it is to Mars that he corresponds in the arrangement of gods and human beings round which the poem is built. Arcite's association with both the unfortunate planets is important, since it places him in the position, not only of great personal danger, but also of assisting in the ultimate solution. This is because, although the immediate effects of Saturn's power are invariably unpleasant, he is, as we shall see, ultimately, and in his wider operations, a force on the side of order.

At the end of the description, Chaucer emphasizes the results of such an illness, which are to bring disorder to the sufferer's whole nature and constitution:

> And shortly, turned was al up so doun
> Bothe habit and eek disposicioun.
>
> (1377–8)

In the same way the injuries which cause his death bring about a state of affairs in which 'Nature hath now no dominacioun' (2758). Arcite dies, as he had lived, a victim to a state of disorder which is typical of the evil influence of the planets on the natural world and on the physical nature of a man who, through failure to rule his passions, lays himself open to their power.

Part ii also contains several references to the capriciousness and arbitrary character of the activities of the gods. We hear in line 1536 of 'geery Venus', who can overcast the hearts of lovers 'in hir queynte geres' (1531); of Juno (1542) and her ancient enmity towards Thebes. Just as Troy forms a background, of which we are constantly reminded, to the story of Troilus, so in the *Knight's Tale* the background is not Athens, which remains a shadowy city in spite of the fact that almost all the action takes place there, but Thebes and all its evil history. Again, in line 1623, we have the telling paradoxical conceit of 'Cupide, out of alle charitee', as the source, not of love, but of a jealousy which brings about the near mortal combat between Palamoun and Arcite.

The fight between the lovers is described not only in terms of the utmost violence – 'up to the ancle foghte they in hir blod' (1660) – but also with a cluster of the wild beast similes of which Statius is so fond:

> Thou myghtest wene that this Palamon
> In his fightyng were a wood leon,
> And as a crueel tigre was Arcite;
> As wilde bores gonne they to smyte,
> That frothen whit as foom for ire wood.
>
> (1655–9)

Not only are the sworn brothers, like Cupid, out of charity, they are also reduced to the level of savage animals. Nevertheless, although love has brought them to this paradoxical state, they have not lost all

17

their noble and chivalric characteristics. Arcite provides food and arms for Palamoun and is willing to give him the best weapons and take the worst for himself (1614). Chaucer is careful to show that, while the two lovers become the apparently helpless victims of their unrestrained passions, their essential nature is still not necessarily debased.

Theseus appears on the scene in time to stop the fight; he acts, in fact, as Reason to bring under control this particular burst of Sensuality. That Chaucer sees him, however, as something more than Reason is shown by the passage which introduces him. This is the passage on destiny spoken by the narrator, which provides for Theseus the same kind of anchorage in the philosophical ideas of the poem as their earlier speeches do for Palamoun and Arcite. The narrator says 'And forth I wole of Theseus yow telle' and then continues:

> The destinee, ministre general,
> That executeth in the world over al
> The purveiaunce that God hath seyn biforn,
> So strong it is that, though the world had sworn
> The contrarie of a thyng by ye or nay,
> Yet somtyme it shal fallen on a day
> That falleth nat eft withinne a thousand yeer.
> For certeinly, oure appetites heer,
> Be it of werre, or pees, or hate, or love,
> Al is this reuled by the sighte above.
> This mene I now by myghty Theseus . . .
>
> (1663-72)

What is said of destiny is thus linked to Theseus both at the beginning and at the end. He acts to stop the unbridled savagery of the lovers; and rules their passions, just as destiny, the power nearest to God in the chain of influences through which His providence is enacted in the world,[24] rules all human appetites. But, and this must be emphasized, Theseus is not destiny itself, still less providence. He is a man who is able to act because of a chance encounter, not through any share in divine 'purveiaunce', the knowledge which God alone possesses. Since, however, unlike the lovers, he acts in accordance with reason, he naturally has a closer affinity to providence than they can have. Chaucer ensures that the action, in spite of the omnipresent gods, is played out in human terms.

At first sight, with its insistence on the inescapable nature of destiny, this passage bears a resemblance to Palamoun's on the 'eterne graunt', but the likeness is superficial. Instead of the lower, and more random, forces of Fortune or chance governing the accidents of human existence – sickness, adversity, imprisonment – we have a power which, coming nearer to God, has a more profound influence – that is, it operates, in a comprehensive way, on the whole of human feeling and activity. We are, in fact, in the presence of a system, not, as in Palamoun's speech, of a series of random observations. Moreover 'purveiaunce', 'providence', is now in question. The word was not used by Palamoun who only speaks of 'prescience'.[25] This latter, too, belongs to the gods in the plural; it can be thought of in connection with the planetary dispositions, while 'purveiaunce' belongs to God in the singular, who, far from being cruel and regardless of His creatures here below, operates for their good to prevent violence and restore the state of order.

Theseus shows himself as a king both in power – he stops the fight with a word – and in the possession of the kingly virtues. He is merciful and magnanimous, wise and just. More than this, in his long speech on the nature of love, he does two things: he shows us the disruptive and destructive power of love and its lack of sense, or obedience to reason, and he also, through his humorous, matter-of-fact style, helps to reinforce the distancing effect which we have already seen induced by the narrator's comments. It is not only the fight that stops when Theseus calls 'Ho!' The reader, too, pauses to look at the story from a different angle. Theseus thus emphasizes the paradoxical situation to which love has reduced the princes:

> 'Lo heere this Arcite and this Palamoun,
> That quitly weren out of my prisoun,
> And myghte han lyved in Thebes roially,
> And witen I am hir mortal enemy,
> And that hir deth lith in my myght also;
> And yet hath love, maugree hir eyen two,
> Broght hem hyder bothe for to dye.
> Now looketh, is nat that an heigh folye?
> Who may been a fool, but if he love?
> Bihoold, for Goddes sake that sit above,
> Se how they blede! be they noght wel arrayed?
> Thus hath hir lord, the god of love, ypayed

Hir wages and hir fees for hir servyse!
And yet they wenen for to been ful wyse
That serven love, for aught that may bifalle.' . . .
(1791–1805)

But these reversals of the probable and normal order of things are not all. The crowning piece of unreason is that the lovers' passions are operating in a vacuum. This is not yet a mutual love, leading to a union in which both parties cooperate to produce a new order and a new wholeness:

'But this is yet the beste game of alle,
That she for whom they han this jolitee
Kan hem therfore as muche thank as me.
She woot namoore of al this hoote fare,
By God, than woot a cokkow or an hare!'
(1806–10)

This sums up what has already been implied concerning love of this kind; and, at the same time and with a vengeance, it cuts the lovers and their problems down to size. We are dealing with serious problems and with important topics, but neither in the heroic nor in the romantic manner.

Theseus's common sense is not harsh, nor yet wholly unsympathetic. He too, in his time, has been a servant of love, and therefore, with royal magnanimity, he offers the lovers pardon, provided that they swear friendship to him and:

'That nevere mo ye shal my contree dere,
Ne make werre upon me nyght ne day.'
(1822–3)

Theseus's concern, in fact, is to use this disorderly, individualistic love to further the establishment of a general state of peace and order: he is, once more, primarily concerned with the political problem of Thebes. He also offers to take their individual problem in hand. Their position is, as he points out, a fundamentally unreasonable one:

'Ye woot yourself she may nat wedden two
Atones, though ye fighten everemo.
That oon of you, al be hym looth or lief,
He moot go pipen in an yvy leef;
That is to seyn, she may nat now han bothe.'

(1835–9)

He proposes to resolve this dilemma by arranging matters so that:
'ech of yow shal have his destynee / As hym is shape' (1842–3). There
is, in fact, nothing to be done but to submit to the 'ministre general'
of God and to await the outcome of divine 'purveiaunce'. Theseus is
not, it must be emphasized, removing or affecting their freedom of
will. Each remains at liberty to withdraw and to cede Emely to the
other, now or at any time in the story.

Theseus makes a somewhat subtle distinction between this general
submission to destiny and the operation of Fortune in the tournament
which, he proposes, is to settle the matter. He undertakes to give
Emely 'to whom that Fortune yeveth so fair a grace' as to gain the
victory. In this he speaks accurately, since at the level of the tournament, the destinal decree will be worked out through the apparently
random operation of Fortune. This also prepares the way for the part
played *in propria persona* in the tournament by the capricious planet-
gods, who, as in Arcite's speech (1086 ff.), are, in certain respects,
hardly distinguished from Fortune.

Part iii is largely taken up by the development of the theme of the
gods, through the long descriptions of their temples and the prayers
offered there. But, just as the gods (whether they are thought of as
pagan deities or planets) act under the ultimate control of Provi-
dence-Jupiter, so the whole elaborate setting of their temples is
shown to be part of Theseus's ordering of the situation and arises
through his plan to resolve the lovers' problem.

The temples form part of the edifice constructed to hold the lists
for the tournament, and the whole structure is presented to us as an
expression of Theseus's ability to achieve a perfectly ordered arrangement. Chaucer introduces the description as a matter of importance:

I trowe men wolde deme it necligence
If I foryete to tellen the dispence

21

Of Theseus, that gooth so bisily
To maken up the lystes roially,
That swich a noble theatre as it was,
I dar wel seyen in this world ther nas.
(1881–6)

The adverb 'roially' and the epithet 'noble' – a word, as we have
seen, which carries important connotations for Chaucer – imply an
activity which is both serious and typical of Theseus's kingly nature.
This 'noble theatre' is circular:

The circuit a myle was aboute,
Walled of stoon, and dyched al withoute.
Round was the shap, in manere of compas,
Ful of degrees, the heighte of sixty pas,
That whan a man was set on o degree,
He letted nat his felawe for to see.
(1887–92)

The actual lists, which Chaucer does not describe in detail, would be
marked off by barriers and would run across the circle, as we
presently learn, from west to east. Chaucer has departed from
Boccaccio in causing Theseus to build the theatre specially for this
occasion. In the *Teseida*, the theatre is already in existence, and in
describing it, with its marble walls, seating formed from stone steps
and two gates, Boccaccio probably had an actual Roman amphi-
theatre in mind. He certainly does not, as Chaucer does, depart from
the Classical model by incorporating temples in the structure.[26] By
these two innovations – the description of the actual erection of the
theatre and the incorporation of the temples – Chaucer, as we shall
see, alters the meaning of the whole episode and uses it not only to provide a brilliant description of an artifact, very much in the traditional
manner of romance, but also to further the exposition of his plan of
linked planet-gods and human protagonists.

There are few medieval romances, either in French or English,
which lack a passage of description of some splendid building or work
of art in which the writer dwells on all the details of ornamentation.[27]
Chaucer, therefore, in bringing together in one splendid passage the
temple descriptions and that of the theatre, was no doubt catering

for this taste. He was also writing for an audience which, in the London of the second half of the fourteenth century, could actually see buildings of unsurpassed splendour and workmanship around them.[28] His approach to his description, with its emphasis on method and good workmanship, is appropriate enough to a Clerk of the Works, but it also recalls that of Chrétien de Troyes in *Cligès*, a romance which makes exceptional use of architectural description. Chaucer mentions the craftsmen who work on the theatre in the following order: men 'that geometrie or ars-metrike kan', that is the architects responsible for the plan and basic structure;[29] 'portre-yours', painters; and 'kerveres of ymages', sculptors. The whole passage is one of hyperbole – no man skilled in these ways was absent from the building. Chaucer may, in writing in these terms, be think-ing of the actual assembling of a swarm of workmen on one of the great building projects of his own day. The romances, less realistic-ally, tend to concentrate these three essential functions in one man. Thus Cligès's servant John is famous 'for the works which he has made and carved and painted',[30] but even in real life the range of the medieval architect tended to be greater than his modern counterpart. Villard de Honnecourt, for example, made architectural, decorative and sculptural working drawings, and painting and sculpture were often practised by the same man.[31] The formula of praise which Chaucer uses to sum up the excellence of his theatre is a traditional one, used of John's work in *Cligès*. Chaucer says:

> And shortly to concluden, swich a place
> Was noon in erthe, as in so litel space,
>
> (1895–6)

and of John it is said 'there is no land where he is not known . . . there are no arts however diverse, in which anyone can vie with him'.[32] Once again, this formula could also be used of real-life artists. Froissart used it of André Beauneveu, who was employed by the Duc de Berri; and Thomas Walsingham, a monk of St Albans, used it of Matthew Paris.[33]

Chaucer thus prepares his audience for a description in the best of taste, in terms of both romance and real life. But, in so far as we have seen Theseus enacting a providential rôle on earth, parallel to that of Jupiter in heaven, it seems likely that there are other and wider implications to a building activity which unifies the conflicting planetary powers within an all-embracing circular scheme. The same division of the work of building into architectural and decorative is used in accounts of the activities of the divine Architect in the creation of the world. This plan is followed, for example, in the very influential *Hexameron* of St Ambrose. Here the work of creation is divided into two on the basis of Genesis 1:1–2: 'In the beginning God created heaven and earth. And the earth was void and empty', and Genesis 2:1: 'So the heavens and the earth were finished, and all the furniture of them' ('et omnis ornatus eorum'). These two passages gave St Ambrose the formula 'to create, and afterwards to beautify', which enabled him to compare God to the good architect who 'lays the foundation first, and afterwards, when the foundation has been laid, plots the various parts of the building, one after the other, and then adds thereto the ornamentation'.[34] That the created universe was circular, like Theseus's theatre, or rather formed a perfect sphere, hardly needs illustration. The whole principle of the concentric spheres leading up to the *primum mobile* depends on this idea, which was an important part of the cosmology of both Plato and Aristotle. The idea of God as an arithmetician and geometrician derives from Wisdom, 11:21: 'thou hast ordered all things in measure, and number, and weight'. This leads to the familiar motif of visual art of the creative hand of God holding the compasses – the tool also used to identify human architects in painting and sculpture.

The order which Theseus imposes through the circle within which he brings the temples of the gods, even though it may be comparable to that imposed on the universe by its divine Architect, remains, it is clear, of a strictly subordinate kind. The immediate purpose of the building is conflict, although it is hoped that a solution will arise from the meeting of the lovers in the lists. Moreover, in the descriptions of the temple decorations, the sinister, adverse and apparently discordant activities of the planet-gods are stressed. Theseus's achievement, by means of which the planets can work towards a final solution, is, clearly, essentially an earthly one in its limitations and its need to accept all the anomalies which belong to the world of change: once more he is like, but not identical with, providence. Nor is the element of discord absent from the world of the planet-gods: the conflict in the lists only echoes the conflict between Venus and Mars, while the impression that the cruel and irrational attributes of the gods actually belong to them, and are not merely due to the human viewpoint, is confirmed by the effect of Saturn's speech, in which he characterizes himself in terms similar to those of the temple paintings (the work of human hands). Order is finally achieved only when the different planes of disorder, among gods and men, are brought under the influence of something which transcends both – when, in fact, the ultimate ordering force exemplified by the chain of love in Theseus's speech in part iv, is brought to bear.

The three temples – of Mars, Venus and Diana – are brought, as we have said, within Theseus's circular scheme. Saturn and Jupiter are not included, although Saturn is given a self-descriptive speech which runs parallel to the descriptive decorations of the temples. In so far as Jupiter is identified with a providential power above the minor gods, with which Theseus and his architecture are also associated, he is as much outside the scheme as Theseus himself. In so far as he is a planet-god, his function, as we shall see, is closely linked to, and even overshadowed by, that of Saturn. Theseus, we are told at line 1902, built the temples 'for to doon his ryte and sacrifise', but in point of fact we do not see him using them. It is only the lovers and their lady who each offer up prayers at the appropriate altar. The tournament is not initiated by any general ceremonial directed towards the gods. The day before, it is true, is spent by the whole company 'in Venus heigh servyse' (2487) – but this is a somewhat ambiguous activity.

In his descriptions of the decoration of the three temples and in Saturn's self-characterizing speech, Chaucer utilizes the tradition known as 'the Children of the Planets'. This takes the form, in visual art, of a representation of the planet-deity, at the top of the picture, presiding over a crowded composite scene below, in which all the various human accidents and occupations that can be ascribed to the influence of the planet in question are depicted.[35] It is, obviously, from such sources that the unheroic element comes in, for example, the list of catastrophes caused by Mars – the cook scalding himself with his own ladle, the baby eaten by the sow and, possibly, the carter run over by his own cart.[36] Chaucer, however, blends the Children of the Planets scheme with another. The fact that he is describing actual temples demands that the gods should be shown not as inhabiting the heavens, but as presiding over their altars. Thus, Venus and Diana appear in typical scenes: Venus rising out of the water[37] and Diana equipped for hunting and standing on a crescent moon, like the Lady of the Apocalypse. Mars is actually given a temple within a temple, because here Chaucer follows, in part, the long description of Mercury's arrival at the house of Mars in the *Thebaid*, VII, 40 ff. Chaucer thus preserves the ambiguity of his lesser gods, who remain part planet, part deity, although in other respects in these passages he tends to heighten the impression that we are dealing with astrological forces.[38]

The effect of the Children of the Planets material is to emphasize the way in which the gods are implicated in the details of human life, down to the most trivial and unpleasant accidents. This is, of course, not incompatible with the view that their influence stops short of the soul; it does, however, significantly link the providential scheme to the apparently random operation of chance in the world, just as lines 1663 ff. link Theseus and his chance appearance in the grove to 'the purveiaunce that God hath seyn biforn'. It is, too, this kind of random, undeserved and apparently malicious operation of chance which gives rise to the darker view of life expressed in the lovers' speeches. The descriptions of the planetary activities and influences do much to reinforce, and even to justify, their point of view, and thus play an important part in the overall balance of the poem: we are not, in fact, to see Arcite's tragedy as in any sense unreal. On the other hand, a more complete and unbiased view of the planets sees them working towards joy as well as woe, while an even more profound and philosophical perception places them as a part of the whole providential design for good. The parts of the descriptions which are more appropriate to the temples as Chaucer found them in his Italian or Classical sources, on the other hand, work in a grander manner to support the more heroic elements in the narrative. In these passages, in fact, as everywhere in the *Knight's Tale*, Chaucer is careful to modify a romantic-epic set piece by bringing it into relation with the actual and everyday, without, however, allowing the epic character to be entirely lost.

In the case of Venus, it is hardly possible to give her much variety in the events she controls or to distinguish the more commonplace, everyday ones, but her activities are brought within the scope of Theseus's humorous, deflating comments on the love story by the narrator's summing up:

> Lo, alle thise folk so caught were in hir las,
> Til they for wo ful ofte seyde 'allas!'

> Suffiseth heere ensamples oon or two,
> And though I koude rekene a thousand mo.
>
> (1951-4)

Mars, as we have seen, has his curiously unheroic accidents, and Diana has the lifelike representation of a woman in childbirth before her:

> But for hir child so longe was unborn,
> Ful pitously 'Lucyna' gan she calle.
>
> (2084-5)

Saturn's influence is as wide as his course: he causes unromantic and unheroic stranglings and hangings,[39] revolts on the part of the peasants,[40] treasons and secret poisonings,[41] and diseases and pestilence of all kinds;[42] the unfortunate miner and carpenter are coupled with 'Sampsoun shakynge the piler'.

The influence of the four gods is described in every case, as unfortunate. In the case of Mars and his 'sory place', there are no mitigating circumstances, unless we can take the phrase 'the infortune of Marte' (2021) as suggesting that the planet could have another more fortunate aspect. In fact, this could be brought about, and is, as the story develops, by conjunction with Venus. As Saturn says:

> 'Though Mars shal helpe his knyght, yet nathelees
> Bitwixe yow ther moot be som tyme pees.'
>
> (2473-4)

That Chaucer sees the denouement in terms of a conjunction of Mars and Venus is shown by the concluding lines of part iii:

> Now wol I stynten of the goddes above,
> Of Mars and of Venus, goddesse of Love.
>
> (2479-80)

Venus is shown surrounded by unhappy lovers, as is the Venus of the *Parlement of Foules*. The emphasis is all on

> The broken slepes, and the sikes colde,
> The sacred teeris and the waymentynge,
> The firy strokes of the desirynge
> That loves servantz in this lyf enduren.
>
> (1920–3)

There is no indication that she can also stand as Venus-Cytheria, as a force tending to peace and harmony. She seems entirely in keeping with the view of love as a destructive force on the side of disorder which is emphasized throughout the early parts of the *Knight's Tale*. It is only when we come to Theseus's speech that we realize that Venus can have a more fortunate aspect and can see love as a principle or order, working to bring about a new unity in which the problems of the poem are resolved in the final marriage of Palamoun and Emely.

Diana is the moon and the avenger of unchastity, but she has a wider function too. She is triple Hecate:

> Hir eyen caste she ful lowe adoun,
> Ther Pluto hath his derke regioun
>
> (2081–2)

and Emely speaks of 'tho thre formes that thou hast in thee' (2313). Moreover, she is also Lucina, who presides over childbirth, which prepares us for her rejection of Emely's plea 'noght to ben a wyf and be with childe' (2310). It is significant that in the *Paradiso* the sphere of the moon is occupied by the blessed souls of those who have had, for good reason, to break vows of chastity, not by those who preserved them.

Saturn is Chaucer's addition to the company of the gods – a fact which suggests that he regarded him as of particular importance in his conception of the story. The series of misfortunes over which he has rule are unmitigatedly sinister. Nevertheless, 'al be it that it is agayn his kynde', he is finally seen as a supreme force working towards order and unity, when he intervenes after such serious conflict has broken out between Venus and Mars that Jupiter is unable to compose it:

> Til that the pale Saturnus the colde,
> That knew so manye of aventures olde,

Foond in his olde experience an art
That he ful soone hath plesed every part.
As sooth is seyd, elde hath greet avantage;
In elde is bothe wysdom and usage;
Men may the olde atrenne, and noght atrede.
Saturne anon, to stynten strif and drede,
Al be it that it is agayn his kynde.
Of al this strif he gan remedie fynde.

(2443–52)

The list of typical Saturnian accidents which follows shows that
Saturn's means to this end are unlikely to be pleasant and may
indeed seem as blindly cruel and capricious as the acts attributed to
the gods by Palamoun. Nevertheless, it is clear that, seen on a higher
level, his action is designed to bring order out of disorder. We may be
reminded of the dual aspect of Fortune explained by Philosophy in
Boethius's *de Consolatione*[43] and hymed by Dante in the *Inferno*:

> Vostro saver non ha contasto a lei:
>   questa provede, giudica, e persegue
>   suo regno come il loro li altri dei. . . .
> Quest' è colei ch' è tanto posta in croce
>   pur da color che dovrìen dar lode,
>   dandole biasmo a torto e mala voce;
> Ma ella s'è beata e ciò non ode;
>   con l'altre prime creature lieta
>   volve sua spera e beata si gode.

> (She is past your wit to understand; but she
> Provideth, judgeth, governeth her own,
> As the other Gods do theirs in their degree . . .
> This is she who is cursed without a cause,
> And even from those hath maledictions got,
> Unjustly, of whom she should have won applause.
> But she is in her bliss, and hears them not.
> In chime with the other primal creatures glad,
> She turns her sphere and tastes her blissful lot.)

(VII, 85–96; Binyon trans.)

It would, I think, be possible to account for Chaucer's treatment of
Saturn as a force for ultimate good on this basis – simply as an

instrument of a benevolent providence. But the way in which he introduces the god, with the emphasis on age and wisdom, shows that there is rather more to it than that. Chaucer, in fact, appears to know the tradition of Saturn as wisdom and also as Chronos, time. The idea of a good Saturn, and indeed the idea that all the planets were essentially good, since they were part of a descending scheme originating in the divine source of all goodness, is ultimately neo-Platonic. It was elaborated, in slightly different ways, by Plotinus and Proclus.[44] Transmission of these ideas to the later Middle Ages is mainly through a source well known to Chaucer: Macrobius in the *Saturnalia* and the *Somnium Scipionis*. Macrobius treated the gods as names for the planets – that is, as fully and unambiguously astro-logized. Although this process had begun with the neo-Platonic writers, especially with Proclus, their main interest was in the formulation of a philosophical system rather than a cosmological one. Chaucer, therefore, in retaining (in part from his immediate source, the *Teseida*) so many of the characteristics of the gods as against the planets, is actually, though no doubt unwittingly, going back to a stage which lies behind Macrobius.

The relevant passages on Saturn from Macrobius are from:
1. The *Saturnalia*, I, xxii:[45]

Saturnus ipse, qui auctor est temporum et ideo a Graecis inmutata littera Κρόνος quasi Χρόνος vocatur, quid aliud nisi sol intelligendus est, cum tradatur ordo elementorum, temporum numerositate distinctus, luce patefactus, nexus aeternitate conductus?

(Saturn, who is the author of time and is therefore called Kronos by the Greeks, that is, with a change of letter, Chronos (time) – how else is he to be understood but as the sun, through which the ordering of the elements is brought about, separated by appropriate numerical intervals, and made manifest by light, a bond made fast to eternity.)

Elsewhere, in the *Somnium Scipionis*, Macrobius refers to the 'unbreak-able chain' ('mutuatus insolubili inter se vinculo elementa devinxit', I, vi, 24) by which the elements are bound and which, according to the *Timaeus*, depends on the numbers three and four. This is the chain which Chaucer attributes to love in Theseus's speech and to Nature in the *Parlement of Foules*.[46] For Macrobius, the bond of the elements is especially associated with the planetary movements and spheres, a fact which may throw some light on the transition in the *Knight's Tale* from the planet-gods as prime movers in the love story in parts i–iii to, in part iv, the Aristotelian unmoved first mover which initiates their, and all other, movement and which is also the *'amor che muove il sole e l'altre stelle'*.

2. The *Somnium Scipionis* which also has an important passage on the planets, including Saturn:

> Hoc ergo primo pondere de zodiaco et lacteo ad subiectas usque sphaeras anima delapsa, dum et per illas labitur, in singulis non solum, ut iam diximus, luminosi corporis amictitur accessu, sed et singulos motus, quos in exercitio est habitura, producit: in Saturni ratiocinationem et intelligentiam, quod λογιδτικόν et θεωρετικόν vocant; in Iovis vim agendi, quod πρακτικόν vocant; in Martis animositatis ardorem, quod θυμικόν nuncupatur; . . . desiderii vero motum, quod ἐπιθυμητικόν vocatur, in Veneris; . . . φυτικόν vero, id est naturam plantandi et augendi corpora, in ingressu globi lunaris exercet.

> (By the impulse of the first weight, the soul, having started on its downward course from the intersection of the zodiac and the Milky Way to the successive spheres lying beneath, as it passes through these spheres, not only takes on the aforementioned envelopment in each sphere, but also acquires each of the attributes which, by approaching a luminous body, it will exercise later. In the sphere of Saturn it obtains reason and understanding, called *logistikon* and *theoretikon*; in Jupiter's sphere, the power to act, called *praktikon*; in Mars' sphere, a bold spirit or *thymikon*; . . . in Venus's sphere, the impulse of passion, *epithymetikon*; . . . and in the lunar sphere, the function of molding and increasing bodies, *phytikon*.)

> (I, xii, 13–14)

This passage describes a neo-Platonic descent of the soul through the spheres, acquiring, as it becomes further and further separated from the divine, characteristics in each, ending with the one which, Macrobius says, is furthest removed from the gods, since it relates to the bodies which are the prisons of souls on earth.[47] Chaucer certainly makes no explicit use of this journey through the spheres, though he does use the idea of descent (and ascent) in Theseus's speech on the Prime Mover (2987 ff.). Nevertheless, as we shall see, he certainly presents us in this poem with a Saturn and Jupiter who represent theory and practice and with a Venus who, clearly, stands for the impulse of passionate love, which, with the cooperation of a Diana who presides over childbirth, can find issue in marriage and, presumably, the increase of mankind. Macrobius's description of the activities proper to the lunar sphere are very suggestive of Nature's labour in her forge in the *Roman de la Rose*, where she propagates all natural beings including man – a similarity which is unlikely to have escaped Chaucer. The characteristics gained in each sphere are certainly also the leading ones of each human character. Egeus shows theoretical wisdom, and Theseus the power to act successfully. The lovers' fates are determined on the one hand by the passion which leads Palamoun to pray to Venus, on the other by the warlike courage which causes Arcite to put his faith in Mars. Emely, as the virgin follower of Diana who is converted to marriage, lends herself at last to the φυτικόν, which she at first repudiates when she prays 'noght to ben a wyf and be with childe'.

Macrobius, as a neo-Platonist influenced by Stoic ideas, does not regard the planets as in any way evil. How ideas derived from him could be combined with the idea of Saturn as an influence producing evils in the world – fraud, deceit, melancholy, for example – is shown by a writer like William of Auvergne in the thirteenth century, who argues for the fundamental goodness of the planet, as accomplishing the divine will, and places the blame for any evil results on the misuse of its gifts by mankind.[48] Another thirteenth-century writer who takes an optimistic view of the planets is Alexander Neckham. He equates them with the seven gifts of the Holy Spirit, and his description of Saturn is very close to Chaucer's:[49]

Sapientia vero quae superiorem videtur tenere locum inter dona, sicut Saturnus inter planetas, maturitatem generat ex se sicut Saturnus in cursu peragendo longum tempus sibi vendicat. Nec sine causa fingitur a philosophis quod Saturnus sit senex, maturi enim pectoris senes esse consueverunt.

(Wisdom, which occupies the highest place among the gifts, as Saturn does among the planets, is generated by maturity from itself, just as Saturn takes a long time to complete his course. And Saturn is rightly described as an old man by the philosophers, because old men are of mature judgement.)

32

The existence of such well known authorities (although we cannot say precisely which Chaucer might have read) justifies the supposition that he knew of a Saturn who, though he may be associated with disagreeable accidents, is still fundamentally beneficent, is wise with the experience of old age and, if we follow out the hint given by Macrobius, is associated with the order and stability of the universe in a way which gives him (together with the whole planetary system) something of the function which Chaucer elsewhere attributes to Nature as God's Vicaire on earth or to Love as the force which holds the warring elements together. He would certainly have found this idea reinforced by his reading of Boccaccio's *de Genealogia Deorum*, where the old etymology *sacer nus*, that is, the neo-Platonic universal spirit which made everything, is given as an explanation of the name Saturn (VIII, 1),[50] and where Saturn is a god of sowing, that is, natural increase, as well as time. His scythe is explained as denoting agriculture in this chapter, and Ceres is one of his daughters. Boccaccio, too, has the peculiar blend of Classical myth and astrological lore which is so typical of Chaucer's treatment of the gods in the *Knight's Tale*, and especially of Saturn;[51] and, through his genealogical method of organizing his material, he naturally gives Saturn the supreme place above his descendant gods (see Plate I).

It is, I think, this activity of Saturn as a composer of strife and a bringer of order out of disorder, achieved in combination with Jupiter – *vis agendi* to Saturn's *theoretikon* – which is the 'grete effect' which Chaucer announces as the subject of the poem as a whole – 'for which that I bygan' – and of the fourth part in particular. It is not, I think, likely that he would use these words merely of the tournament, which is no more spectacular as a set piece, and no more important to the unfolding of the story, than the great descriptive passages of part iii. We must rather take them as an indication of a single, overriding purpose towards which the whole narrative is tending, and this, clearly, is the final solution, not any one incident on the way towards it.

The relation of Saturn and Jupiter may seem puzzling to the modern reader. On the one hand, Saturn acts here to bring about the denouement, as he says, in the cause of peace and the restoration of order. On the other, it is Jupiter who is the supreme ruler of the gods, who corresponds to divine providence and who is invoked as the ultimate source of order in Theseus's speech. The reason for this is that in a moral-philosophical view of the gods, of the kind that

Chaucer would find indicated in the *Thebaid* and, at times, in Macrobius and other sources of the same type, it is Jupiter who rules the world and who exists on a different plane to the lesser gods, who are equated with Fortune. But in a purely astrological system, the fact that Saturn, according to ancient and medieval knowledge of the planets, is the highest planet, with the widest course, tends, at any rate for those who reflect neo-Platonic ideas about the planets, to put him in the supreme place. We can see too, from Macrobius, that if Saturn (who significantly heads his list, coming before Jupiter since it is a list of planets not of gods) is theory, while Jupiter is practice, they form a natural and, even necessary, pair and can, indeed, be regarded as different aspects of one whole. In the same way, Venus as passion and Luna as increase could be regarded, especially by a reader of the *Roman de la Rose*, as two aspects of the natural order of the propagation of the species.

On the human plane, the third part of the *Knight's Tale* continues the development of the theme of order and disorder in various ways. The orderliness of Theseus's dispositions is shown in other ways besides the architecture of the theatre. For example, in line 2190, he treats his guests to an ideal hospitality which fulfils all the requirements of social order – each man is lodged 'at his degree' (2192) and the festivities are so well organized

> That yet men wenen that no mannes wit
> Of noon estaat ne koude amenden it.
>
> (2195–6)

In contrast, the lovers remain in a state of disorder. Just as, in part i, love was said to bring physical disruption to Arcite, now Palamoun laments his state of mental confusion:

> 'Allas! I ne have no langage to telle
> Th' effectes ne the tormentz of myn helle;
> Myn herte may myne harmes nat biwreye;
> I am so confus that I kan noght seye
> But, "Mercy, lady bright, that knowest weele
> My thought, and seest what harmes that I feele!"'
>
> (2227–32)

The motif of the wild beasts, which was used of the savagery of the quarrel between the sworn brothers earlier in the poem, is used again in the description of their chief supporters, Lygurge, King of Thrace, who is compared to a griffon and accompanied by huge white hounds, and Emetreus, King of Inde, who is compared to a lion and accompanied by a tame eagle and by lions and leopards. As Curry points out, these two are probably also to be understood as easily recognizable types of the Martian and the Saturnian man,[52] and are thus a further reminder of the vulnerability of the unbridled passions to the influence of the planets in its, apparently, most capricious and dangerous form.

Part iv of the *Knight's Tale* is dedicated, as we have said, to the 'grete effect' towards which the whole work is designed. It is, of course, dominated by the ordering figure of Theseus, although it also contains the final, and fatal, development of disorder in the overthrow and death of Arcite. Since, however, this is brought about by Saturn, it is also part of his intervention to resolve the problem. As we have seen, Arcite's subjection to Saturn, although fatal to him, is a necessary part of the final solution.

This part begins with Theseus's just and merciful rules for the conduct of the tournament, intended to prevent needless slaughter. The people applaud him, crying 'God save swich a lord, that is so good' (2563). Theseus here, in fact, exercises an important function of the medieval good king, who was particularly required to protect his subjects by preventing needless warfare.[53] The lists are now put to use, and the fight itself is described with great technical relish by the Knight, of whose professional expertise we are once more reminded. There is a return to the motif of the savage beasts when the prowess of Palamoun and Arcite is in question:

> Ther nas no tygre in the vale of Galgopheye,
> Whan that hir whelp is stole whan it is lite,
> So crueel on the hunte as is Arcite
> For jelous herte upon this Palamon.
> Ne in Belmarye ther nys so fel leon,
> That hunted is, or for his hunger wood,
> Ne of his praye desireth so the blood,
> As Palamon to sleen his foo Arcite.

> (2626–33)

As in the case of the fight in the grove, described with similes of the same kind, Theseus puts a stop to this savagery and, unlike the cruel gods as they were conceived by the lovers, promises to be 'trewe juge, and no partie' (2657).

His verdict, however, leaves room for a further turn to the story. He had decreed that the lovers must experience their destiny if they both persist in the pursuit of Emely and, in the actual lists, must put their fortune to the test. Now he says:

> 'Arcite of Thebes shal have Emelie
> That by his fortune hath hire faire ywonne.'
>
> (2658–9)

Fortune, or Mars, has given Arcite the immediate victory; but destiny has not finished working itself out. Saturn, to help Venus, brings about just such a tragic accident as we hear about in his list of evil influences. He causes a fury to start out of the ground; Arcite's horse stumbles, and he receives a fatal injury and dies in a manner which is, as Curry has shown, peculiarly Saturnian.[54]

Yet the description of his death, with all its harrowing and accurate medical detail, is set within a further exposition of the theme of order. Theseus takes all proper action for the due care of Arcite and all the other wounded. He makes special provision against 'disconfytinge' (2716 f.), that is, he sees to it that no further quarrels break out as a result of the tournament. And, more important still, Arcite dies reconciled to Palamoun, with his 'manie' apparently cured. His speech in lines 2783 ff. is significant:

> 'I have heer with my cosyn Palamon
> Had strif and rancour many a day agon
> For love of yow, and for my jalousye.
> And Juppiter so wys my soule gye,
> To speken of a servaunt proprely,
> With alle circumstances trewely –
> That is to seyen, trouthe, honour, knyghthede,
> Wysdom, humblesse, estaat, and heigh kynrede,
> Fredom, and al that longeth to that art –
> So Juppiter have of my soule part,
> As in this world right now ne knowe I non
> So worthy to ben loved as Palamon,

36

> That serveth yow, and wol doon al his lyf.
> And if that evere ye shul ben a wyf,
> Foryet nat Palamon, the gentil man.'
>
> (2783–97)

For the first time he recognizes with regret that his love has broken his friendship with Palamoun, a friendship, as we have seen, of a particularly serious and important kind; and he now calls not on Mars, but on Jupiter, as he urges Emely to provide a final solution to the conflict, and places Palamoun before her, and before us, in a light which, for the first time, allows us to see a lover not as brought to the level of the wild beasts by his passion, but, as Troilus was, ennobled by it. It is, of course, essential that our view of love, and of at least one of the lovers, should undergo this shift, since the solution depends on our recognition of the other, uniting aspect of the ambivalent love which brought Arcite to dissolution. This speech is thus an important structural device, and it is important too in that it prepares the way, through the appeal to Jupiter, for Theseus's speech, in which, since the ideas it expresses are philosophical not astrological, the emphasis shifts once more from Saturn to Jove.

Arcite dies with reconciliation in his heart and a proposal for a solution. Chaucer, however, leaves him at this point:

> His spirit chaunged hous and wente ther,
> As I cam nevere, I kan nat tellen wher.
> Therfore I stynte, I nam no divinistre;
> Of soules fynde I nat in this registre,
> Ne me ne list thilke opinions to telle
> Of hem, though that they writen wher they dwelle.
> Arcite is coold, ther Mars his soule gye!
> Now wol I speken forth of Emelye.
>
> (2809–16)

The opinion which he does not wish to reproduce is that of Boccaccio in the *Teseida*, who had described the flight of Arcite's soul under the guidance of Mercury. There are practical reasons for Chaucer's omission of this. For one thing, he had used it in the *Troilus* – if we accept that this poem probably preceded the final version of the *Knight's Tale* – for another, the introduction of Mercury here would have upset the symmetry of his arrangement of gods and human

37

protagonists. It is more appropriate to leave Arcite to the care of Mars, from whom he got the warlike courage which gives him success in the lists, but not in love. A celestial flight would, also, be even more inappropriate in his case than in that of Troilus – where, as we have seen, Chaucer encounters some difficulty – since it would mean sending to the spheres and the blissful realm the soul of one who actually dies (as Troilus does not) through his indulgence of 'the blinde lust'. Such an ending, too, would have spoilt the uncompromising naturalism with which Chaucer has depicted Arcite's plight. He does not, in the *Knight's Tale*, give us a happy ending which is an easy or sentimental solution of the human problem. Arcite's death, like all individual deaths, is a part of the cycle of change which leads to true stability; but, as an individual case it loses none of its painfulness through serving as part of a process which leads to happier things. Arcite's last despairing protest is so poignant, and so convincing, that some critics have even been tempted to see in it the main theme of the poem. Such a view, however, disrupts the work and puts it out of period. When Chaucer makes Arcite ask:

'What is this world? what asketh men to have?
Now with his love, now in his colde grave
Allone, withouten any compaignye.'

(2777-9)

he is only giving us a peculiarly forceful repetition of the lovers' earlier speeches. He is also providing support for the development of the theme of the cruel gods in the temple descriptions. From the viewpoint of the philosophical ideas which inform the *Knight's Tale*, this, as we have seen, is only part of a whole which, seen whole, has a very different significance. But it is, nevertheless, one of the emotional mainsprings of the poem, not only in the sense that it accounts, naturalistically, for the part Arcite plays, but also in its inevitable effect on the reader. These passages work together to build up the tension which it is the function of the 'grete effect' to resolve.

The resolution is prepared in the second half of Arcite's speech through his concern for his soul's fate at the hands of Jupiter – a reminder of the source of providential order which he has up to now forgotten. Egeus and Theseus, in their key speeches, provide in full the theoretical basis for the solution, which is acted out in practical

terms by Palamoun and Emely at the end of the poem. This, however, is to anticipate.

The natural and violent outburst of sorrow which follows Arcite's
death is checked and brought to order by the speech of Egeus:

> No man myghte gladen Theseus,
> Savynge his olde fader Egeus,
> That knew this worldes transmutacioun,
> As he hadde seyn it chaunge bothe up and doun,
> Joye after wo, and wo after gladness,
> And shewed hem ensamples and liknesse.
>   'Right as ther dyed nevere man,' quod he
> 'That he ne lyvede in erthe in some degree,
> Right so ther lyvede never man,' he seyde,
> 'In al this world, that som tyme he ne deyde.
> This world nys but a thurghfare ful of wo,
> And we been pilgrymes, passynge to and fro.
> Deeth is an ende of every worldly soore.'
> And over al this yet seyde he muchel moore
> To this effect, ful wisely to enhorte
> The peple that they sholde hem reconforte.
>
>   (2837–52)

This speech has been criticized as trite, or even as the utterance of a
dotard; but this, I think, is to read too hastily and to be misled by two
devices which Chaucer employs seriously. One is the circular form of
statement within the speech, which is used not because Egeus is
represented as repeating himself, but because he is describing the
movement of a cyclic process; and the other is the assurance that he
said much more, which is, surely, intended to indicate the extent of
his wisdom and to emphasize that he made an important contribution, not to suggest that he was a long-winded bore. We need, rather,
to ask why Chaucer should bring Egeus forward at this important
moment as the poem moves towards its conclusion – and here only.
The reason, I think, is obvious if we pay due attention to the introduction to his speech. Arcite's tragic death has threatened to throw
everything into confusion, since its immediate effect is grief and
dismay, and it can only help towards the solution when it has been
understood and, through the proper exercise of reason, brought
within the scheme of order. Theseus is as grief-stricken as anyone

else and unable to see any way to proceed, now that his practical scheme of the tournament has, apparently, failed. We thus have the counterpart to the situation among the gods at the end of part iii, when Jupiter was unable to compose their strife, but a way was found when Saturn came forward with the theoretical wisdom to guide Jupiter's *vis agendi* into a profitable channel. Now, in part iv, Jupiter's human counterpart, Theseus, is similarly helpless until Egeus, described in terms which echo those applied to Saturn at the end of part iii, provides the necessary *logistikon* and *theoretikon*. As soon as he has done this, Theseus is able to embark on the series of practical measures, the first of which is the provision of appropriate funeral rites, which lead to the ultimate solution. We can now see why a speech which Boccaccio could give to Theseus is no longer appropriate to him, although it perfectly suits Egeus as the human counterpart of Saturn.

Egeus, like Saturn, is old. Like Saturn, too, with his 'olde experience', Egeus knows 'this worldes transmutacioun / As he hadde seyn it chaunge bothe up and doun'. If we are to judge from the opening of the *Fortune*:

> This wreched worldes transmutacioun . . .
> Governed is by Fortunes errour –

Chaucer uses the word 'transmutacioun' to mean change, not merely from one thing to another, but from one thing to its opposite (since the change of fortune is in the form of a wheel, and anything fastened to it must eventually pass opposite points). Such pairs of opposites form a totality of which the wheel is, of course, the figure. There may also be a hint of another meaning in 'transmutacioun', since it is a meaning well established in the fourteenth century,[55] that of what we should call 'chemical change', that is, change which brings into being something new. Egeus restricts his consideration of such changes – at any rate in the quotation Chaucer gives from what he tells us was a longer speech – to the cycle of life and death, a pair of opposites making up the totality of human earthly existence, whose 'transmutacioun' is a new and different state of being. This new state is suggested by the image of the pilgrim. This image is, of course, a predominantly Christian one – it is used in unequivocally Christian terms in the *Parson's Tale* – but, as we have already seen in the case of *Truth*, it lends itself to combination with a philosophical viewpoint compatible with Christian thought without necessarily being explicitly Christian, and therefore does nothing to disrupt the epic-pagan tone which the use of the figures of the gods, whether astro-logical or philosophical, helps to sustain in the *Knight's Tale*.[56]

Egeus's speech is thus an important one and occupies an important position in the scheme of parallel gods and men. It releases Theseus from his momentary inactivation, and he proceeds with the funeral rites. A proper period of mourning follows, and it is only 'By processe and by lengthe of certeyn yeres' – a state of affairs which, again, suggests both due decorum and the working out of a natural cycle[57] – that we arrive at a point at which it is proper for the development of the action to continue to its end. In this final development, Theseus is the dominant figure – Egeus-Saturn does not reappear – and Theseus acts as an ideal ruler who brings about the solution to the dilemma of the love story only as part of a wider scheme for the common profit. He acts, at last, because it becomes politically desirable

> To have with certein contrees alliaunce
> And have fully of Thebans obeisaunce.
>
> (2973–4)

The old, evil problem of Thebes is to be dealt with; high policy is to be served; and, at the same time, but not necessarily as the primary purpose, the love story is to be brought to a happy conclusion. This final scheme of order is prefaced by the long and famous speech in which Theseus is at his most kingly, and the poem at its most philosophical. Since this speech is an important part of the 'grete effect' which Chaucer tells us is the subject of part iv (and, so that there is no mistake, he repeats the phrase in line 2989), we must pause over its content.

Chaucer's problem, in writing Theseus's speech is, it is obvious, to provide something which will be worthy not only of a major char-acter who has been built up in an extremely impressive way, but also of the climax of an extremely ambitious work. To do this he needs to draw on philosophical material which would be reasonably well known to his audience and, therefore, calculable in its effect – and material, moreover, which would have its full share of what Lovejoy has aptly called 'philosophical pathos', that is, which involves ideas with the power, within a given period, to exert a strong emotional effect on the audience. It is, I think, true to say that, in his handling of philosophical matter, it is always considerations of this kind which concern Chaucer: his aim is always to make structural use within his poem of the ideas he takes from the philosophers, not to explore and develop their meaning for its own sake. The latter course, indeed, is apt to be a dangerous one for poets, as we can see from the way in which Langland's grim struggle to follow out all the implications of an idea can, on occasion, disrupt his poem. If we try to trace out the different threads which Chaucer twists together in the speech, we shall see that he achieves his purpose in a way which shows full knowledge and mastery of the various arguments involved and, incidentally, the use of considerably more than an amalgam of phrases and ideas from Boethius.[58] Much, certainly, does come from the *de Consolatione*, but combined with material from other sources and arguments.

Theseus's argument is built up in the following way:

1. He takes as his premise the idea of God as both first mover and first efficient cause, Who begins the work of creation, that is, of out-flowing love, by binding together the elements in such a way that they cannot fly apart and return created matter to its original state of chaos (2987–93). The ideas involved in the chain, or bond, of the elements and the various sources Chaucer used have already been discussed at length.[59] Here, two aspects are of importance: first, the idea of an order which is at the same time a limitation – 'In certeyn boundes, that they may nat flee' – and, secondly, the idea of a stability which is brought about by cyclic change. In the case of the elements this is the perpetual transmutation of one to another described, for example, by Cicero in the *de Natura Deorum*, II, xxxiii.[60] This second idea is present by implication in the chain-image, but only comes to the fore in the application of the argument to 'speces of thynges' in lines 3013 ff.

2. The argument now turns from the elements, matter itself, to the actual kinds of things which are produced from it in the world. All these are subject to time – 'certeyne dayes and duracioun' – and, therefore, the limitation which is part of the creative order is, in their case, primarily a temporal one – they have a limited period of existence:

42

> Over the whiche day they may nat pace,
> Al mowe they yet tho dayes wel abregge.
>
> (2998–9)

This is proved (3000 ff.) by experience, not 'auctoritee' (written evidence), because it is sufficiently obvious, and also because the unfolding of a process in time can only be comprehended by an observer who lives through it – just so in the *Wanderer*, the old English poet, who also utilizes philosophical commonplaces concerning the nature of the world's existence, remarks that a man cannot become wise until he has spent time in the world; that is, not that age is automatically wise, but that process, unlike state, in the nature of the physical world, requires time for its apprehension.[61]

3. In lines 3003 ff. Chaucer returns to the idea of order and takes the presence of order in the world as proof of the stability and eternity of God. This is because the part must resemble the whole from which it derives. The orderliness of the world implies the perfection of God, its stability within time His eternity. This is the argument for the existence of God from observation of the world which is to be found, for example, in Cicero's *de Natura Deorum*, where, after describing, as an instance of the natural order, the progression of the seasons, he concludes:[62]

Haec ita fieri omnibus inter se concinentibus mundi partibus profecto non possent nisi ea uno divino et continuato spiritu continerentur.

(These processes and this musical harmony of all the parts of the world assuredly could not go on were they not maintained in unison by a single divine and all-pervading spirit.)

(II, vii)

4. From this idea, Chaucer passes at once to another: that of the actual way in which the parts, which together make up the natural world, derive from the divine whole. Here he uses the idea of the Scale of Creatures – the Homeric chain which Macrobius describes in the *Somnium Scipionis*.[63] This scale of descent is also referred to by Boethius in the *de Consolatione*, Book III, prosa x, in a passage which Chaucer follows here:

For the nature of thinges ne took nat hir begynnynge of thinges amenused and inparfit, but it procedith of thinges that ben alle hole and absolut, and descendith so doun into uttereste thinges and into thinges empty and withouten fruyt.

(Chaucer trans.)

This corresponds to lines 3007–3010 of the *Knight's Tale*:

> For nature hath nat taken his bigynnyng
> Of no partie or cantel of a thyng
> But of a thyng that parfit is and stable,
> Descendynge so til it be corrumpable.

5. Boethius's argument in Book III, prosa x, is concerned with the contrast of the incorruptible 'one' and the degree of corruptibility which comes with multiplicity. This would not suit Chaucer's purpose, and the 'therefore' of line 3011 introduces a different conclusion. He returns to the idea of cyclic transmutation, and says that permanence in the world means

> That speces of thynges and progressiouns
> Shullen enduren by successiouns,
> And nat eterne.
>
> (3013–15)

Boethius, in Book IV, prosa vi, also has this idea:

> Thilke ordenaunce moveth the hevene and the sterres, and atemprith the elementz togidre amonges hemself, and transformeth hem by entrechaungeable mutacioun. And thilke same ordre neweth ayein alle thinges growynge and fallynge adoun, by semblable progressions of sedes and of sexes.
>
> (Chaucer trans.)

Lines 3017–33 support this argument by a series of instances drawn from the natural world. These are: (a) the growth and decay of the oak tree; (b) the wasting away of the rock; (c) the drying up of a broad river; (d) the rise and fall of a great town; (e) the inevitable progress towards death of human beings of all kinds. These are all 'preeved by experience', but, although 'Ther nedeth noon auctoritee t'allegge', it is likely that the list does, in fact, owe something to books.

Lists of natural phenomena of this kind used to illustrate duration, change and succession as the order of nature are fairly common in works which have a philosophical tendency. Boethius, for example, has one, featuring living creatures with souls (i.e., human beings), trees and stones, in the *de Consolatione*, Book III, prosa xi. Here the examples are used to prove that all created things naturally try to ensure their continued duration and eschew corruption, and only fail of this end in so far as they are separated from the one and eternal. Ovid uses the argument at length in the *Metamorphoses*, XV, 175 ff. Here he marshals time and the seasons, the alternations of sea and land, and of mountain and plain, the growth and decay of animals, the fall of cities and nations and, finally, the life of individual men, in support of the thesis:

Cuncta fluunt, omnisque vagans formatur imago.

(All things are in a state of flux, and everything is brought into being with a changing nature.)

(XV, 178)

Jean de Meun uses a similar sequence in Nature's complaint, where the mutability of the species of things is made the basis of her plea for the reproduction of the human race, which is alone in disregarding this fundamental necessity. She cites the movements of the heavens (i.e., the seasons and weather); the sea; the plants, including trees; the beasts and man; in lines 18947 ff. The argument long remained a powerful one. Spenser used it in the *Mutabilitie Cantos*,[64] and Hakewell set it out at length in his *Power and Providence of God*.[65] The ultimate source of such lists is the argument in the *Meteorologica* of Aristotle for an eternal world of continual cyclic change. In Book I, 14, this is proved by the example of the interchange of water and dry land; rivers dry up, creating more land, only to reappear elsewhere, thus restoring the balance of land and water (351a). This process is compared to the length of human life and to the life of nations and cities (351b). The basic list is, thus, the water and the dry land ('stone', 'rock', 'mountain', which, for Aristotle, are particularly concerned in the making of rivers and lakes [see 352b]), the nation or city and the short-lived human being. The addition of the tree or plant and the beasts, which are not needed in Aristotle's original argument, seems natural enough.

In the *Meteorologica* these changes are, it is emphasized, (a) cyclic

45

(see the summary in 358a) and (b) caused by the alteration of the humours, wet and dry, cold and warm. They are thus linked both to the transmutation and to the qualities of the elements and so, quite properly, belong within the sequence of ideas unfolded so far in Theseus's speech.

6. For Aristotle, the cyclic progressions of nature simply make a closed system in which the earth is eternally wasted and eternally renewed:

> 'All of these [he refers to the processes of change by
> evaporation] are in a constant state of change, but the form and
> quantity of each of them are fixed, just as they are in the case
> of a flowing river or a burning flame. The answer is clear, and
> there is no doubt that the same account holds good for all these
> things alike. They differ in that some of them change more
> rapidly or more slowly than others; and they are all involved in
> a process of perishing and becoming which yet affects them all
> in a regular course.'
>
> (357b–58a)

For Boethius, in a famous passage wholly Platonic in tone, the case is different – and it is Boethius whom Chaucer follows in drawing a conclusion from the principle of cyclic change:

> Hic est cunctis communis amor
> Repetuntque boni fine teneri,
> Quia non aliter durare queant,
> Nisi conuerso rursus amore
> Refluant causae quae dedit esse.

(This is the comune love to alle thingis, and alle thinges axen to ben holden by the fyn of good. For elles ne myghten they nat lasten yif thei ne comen nat eftsones ayein, by love retorned, to the cause that hath yeven hem beinge (*that is to seyn, to God.*)
de Consolatione, IV, m. vi, Chaucer trans.)

In the *Knight's Tale* this becomes the assertion of an ascending, as well as a descending, sequence:

> What maketh this but Juppiter, the kyng,
> That is prince and cause of alle thyng,

46

Convertynge al unto his propre welle
From which it is dirryved, sooth to telle?
And heer-agayns no creature on lyve,
Of no degree, availleth for to stryve.

(3035–40)

With the last two lines, Chaucer links the argument from a cyclic
system of change, which now includes a return to the unity and perfection of 'the Firste Moevere of the cause above', to the immediate
problem of the death of an individual creature. To strive against the
divine order is only to cling to imperfection and change and to
refuse the perfect good, which, according to Boethius in the *de
Consolatione*, III, prosa x, consists in union with the godhead.

From this point, the culmination of the philosophical argument,
Chaucer turns back to the matter in hand, that is, to Arcite's death;
and in the next few lines, he uses material typical of the *consolatio* –
the topic of condolence addressed to the survivors that was developed
so often by Seneca and by many medieval authors after him.[66] To
this topic belong such arguments as the need to make virtue of
necessity and that it is best for a man to die 'in his excellence and
flour'. But Chaucer uses this passage in a way which has little to do
with the conventional *consolatio*. In a manner which is very typical of
his treatment of philosophical argument, he turns from general,
abstract considerations to the particular and concrete and, in the
process, develops the hint in line 3040 of a return from philosophical
tranquillity to the mood of earlier passages. The suggestion in line
3040 that it will avail no creature to strive against the divine process,
inevitably bringing the idea of conflict before us, is quite out of keeping with the noble detachment of the main part of the argument – a
detachment like that of Boethius's Lady Philosophy, who speaks with
magisterial certainty and feels none of the doubts and temptations of
mortality. The idea of rebellion – that, even though death may bring
the ultimate good, we may yet be perverse enough not to want to
die – is developed in lines 3041 ff. with the idea of a forced submission
to what cannot be avoided (3043); this is further emphasized by the
repeated 'gruccheth' (3045) and 'grucchen' (3058) and in the use of
terms like 'rebel' (3046) and 'wilfulnesse' (3057). In fact, Chaucer
once more allows the painful, bewildered and fundamentally pessi-
mistic viewpoint of the earlier parts of the poem, and of Arcite on his
deathbed, to make its impact, with the result that, while in a sense

Philosophy speaks a tranquil last word, we are not allowed to forget the difficulty of applying her tenets in an actual world of contradictory and contradicting beings. In the same way the clearcut formulation of Nature's position in the *Parlement* was applied not by an ideal, submissive audience, but by a quarrelsome set of birds clinging determinedly to a variety of irreconcilable viewpoints.

Theseus's speech is thus, philosophically speaking, much more comprehensive and closely argued than has sometimes been allowed. It shows a free and flexible use of several well-known philosophical topics which range far beyond a mere rehash of disconnected passages of Boethius. But, typically with Chaucer, although it leads logically into the final solution of the poem, it is not allowed to stand as an unchallenged last word – any more, indeed, than any implied challenge to the solutions of philosophy contained in lines 3039 ff. is allowed to stand as final. Chaucer is not in the habit of speaking definitively or of giving us a final pontification.

The close of Theseus's speech, as we have said, reintroduces the specific instance of providential activity with which the poem is concerned, that is, Arcite's death. Reconciliation to the sorrow that this causes is certainly sought, but this is not the whole of the 'grete effect' which we have been promised. Something more is needed if the poem is to end with a satisfactory solution to all the problems it has raised. Theseus, in fact, has more to offer than the proposition 'after wo I rede us to be merye'. Even this means submission to, and cooperation with, the divine plan for the world; but his further proposal for the marriage of Palamoun and Emely goes beyond submission, to the enactment of something which parallels the creative union of the elements and brings the remaining characters within the links of the fair chain in a literal and practical sense. To see how this can be, we need to look closely at the way in which Chaucer uses the theme of marriage in this particular context.

What the marriage means is apparent from the terms which Chaucer causes Theseus to use of it:

> 'I rede that we make of sorwes two
> O parfit joye, lastynge everemo.'
>
> (3071–2)

It is to be a combination of two things, both sorrows, and both, therefore, painful and imperfect, and it is to produce unity and perfection ('O parfit joye') and duration ('lastynge everemo'). To achieve such a result, the two things combined must necessarily be opposites, as the two sorrows are, since they arise from love and death. Through the marriage, therefore, a true conjunction of opposites is achieved, just as it is in the reconciliation of the warring pairs of elements and in the 'marriage' of the masculine and feminine (odd and even) numbers. Moreover, love and death, which, according to Theseus's exposition, together represent the cyclic change in which the stability of the world resides, are here combined to produce an ascent towards the single, the perfect and the durable – the 'thyng that parfit is and stable' of line 3009 – which parallels the descent into the 'corrumpable' described in lines 3005 ff. Thus, all the implications of the poem's earlier references to the creative cycle and its relation to divine providence are developed and fulfilled in a conclusion which is, indeed, a 'grete effect'.

We are, it is obvious, dealing with marriage seen from a viewpoint which is, in part at least, symbolical or even archetypal. It is by no means the only possible point of view in the fourteenth century, as Chaucer himself shows us in the *Wife of Bath's Prologue* and *Tale* and elsewhere;[67] but it is, nevertheless, not an uncommon one. The idea of marriage as a state capable of showing a supreme perfection and unification of humanity is, in fact, rooted in Christian tradition, in spite of the influence of St Paul and of the monastic bias in favour of virginity.[68] This is largely due to the way in which the creation of man is described in Genesis, where the marriage of Adam and Eve and its issue is a part of man's perfection in paradise:

And God created man to his own image: to the image of God he created him. Male and female he created them. And God blessed them, saying: Increase and multiply, fill the earth and subdue it.

(1:27–8)

Thus, the *Parson's Tale* praises marriage because it was instituted by God in the Garden of Eden,[69] and Langland can even use it as a paradigm of the perfection of the Trinity:

Adam owre aller fader, Eue was of hym-selue,
And the issue that thei hadde, it was of hem bothe,
And either is otheres Ioye, in thre sondry persones,
And in heuene and here, one syngulere name;
And thus is mankynde or manhede, of matrimoigne yspronge,
And bitokneth the Trinite and trewe bileue.

(B, XVI, 205–10)

Although Langland is perhaps eccentric, it is easy to find patristic authority for an exalted view of marriage. Two citations from well-known and influential works will suffice. The first is from St Ambrose on the creation of Eve, in the *de Paradiso*:[70]

'And God cast Adam into a deep sleep, and he slept.' What does the phrase 'deep sleep' signify? Does it not mean that when we contemplate a conjugal union we seem to be turning our eyes gradually in the direction of God's kingdom? Do we not seem, as we enter into a vision of this world, to partake a little of things divine, while we find our repose in the midst of what is secular and mundane? Hence, after the statement, 'He cast Adam into a deep sleep and he slept', there follows: 'The rib which God took from Adam he built into a woman'. The word 'built' is well chosen in speaking of the creation of a woman because a household comprising man and wife seems to point towards a state of full perfection.

The second quotation is from St Augustine's treatise on *The Good of Marriage*.[71] The language is more restrained, but the basic viewpoint is the same:

The first natural tie of human society is man and wife. Even these God did not create separately and join them as if they were strangers, but he made the one from the other, indicating also the power of union in the side from which she was drawn and formed. They are joined to each other side by side who walk together and observe together where they are walking. A consequence is the union of society in the children who are the only worthy fruit, not of the joining of male and female, but of sexual intercourse.

The Parson's account of marriage, in his tale, has much in common with these authorities, although he draws on other sources as well:

> Trewe effect of mariage clenseth fornicacioun and replenysseth hooly chirche of good lynage; for that is the ende of mariage; and it chaungeth deedly synne into venial synne bitwixe hem that been ywedded, and maketh the hertes al oon of hem that been ywedded, as wel as the bodies. / This is the verray mariage, that was establissed by God, er that synne bigan, when natureel lawe was in his right poynt in paradys.
>
> (*CT* X, 919–20)

Moreover, there is a sense in which marriage belongs to those human goods which are not under the sway of fortune. Chaucer makes this point (in the context, with ironical effect) in the *Merchant's Tale*:

> A wyf is Goddes yifte verraily;
> Alle othere manere yiftes, hardily,
> As londes, rentes, pasture, or commune,
> Or moebles, alle been yiftes of Fortune.
>
> (*CT* IV, 1311–14)

His immediate source here is Albertano of Brescia, *Liber de Amore Dei*, but the ultimate authority is Biblical – Prov. 19:14; 'a prudent wife is properly from the Lord.' A similar distinction between the love which is at the mercy of fortune and that which, because it is in accordance with reason, is not, is made by Jean de Meun. This passage is included in the Chaucerian translation, 5201 ff. Here, the love that is free of fortune is *amicitia*, which, as we shall see in the next chapter, plays an important part in Chaucer's conception of married love.

To the idea of marriage as a source of unity and perfection for humanity, Chaucer adds the idea of it as a source of unity and peace in the state. This, as we have said, is the real reason why Theseus, the ideal ruler, concerns himself with it. This conception of marriage, which, of course, arises from contemporary practice in royal marriages as well as from theory, is one that recurs in Chaucer's writings. It is important in the *Clerk's Tale* and also in the *Man of Law's Tale*, while we have seen that in the *Troilus* a marriage which would have dangerous political results is not considered possible for a member of the royal house.

The *Knight's Tale* ends with a description of the blissful state brought about through the 'bond' of matrimony, when this bond is seen as a repetition of the bond or chain which brings harmony to the discordant elements through a marriage of numbers. This state is, in every way, the opposite to that of unhappiness and disorder in which the lovers were formerly tormented. Fear, jealousy and all discord are banished:

> For now is Palamon in alle wele,
> Lyvynge in blisse, in richesse and in heele,
> And Emelye hym loveth so tendrely,
> And he hire serveth al so gentilly,
> That nevere was ther no word hem bitwene
> Of jalousie or any oother teene.
> Thus endeth Palamon and Emelye,
> And God save al this faire compaignye!
>
> (3101–8)

The 'grete effect' is so complete, and the influence which brings harmony out of the discordant elements of the universe proves itself capable of harmonizing the painful and discordant elements in human life into a new and creative unity. But just as, in the case of the elements, the fundamental discord is not eliminated, but remains as the basis of their cyclic transformation, so, as far as the poem is concerned, Arcite's death and all its painful associations remain an unaltered part of the process of transformation which culminates in the union of Palamoun and Emely. Chaucer makes no attempt to soften the facts. He merely exhibits to us what happens in a world controlled by a love which, as Boethius tells us, not only 'halt togidres peples joyned with an holy boond, and knytteth sacrement of mariages of chaste loves' (II, m. viii, 21), but which is also the cause of that 'attempraunce which hideth, and bynymeth and drencheth undir the laste deth, alle thinges iborn' (IV, m. vi, 34).

2

The *Canterbury Tales*: the problem of narrative structure

Most modern critics of Chaucer have, sooner or later, raised the question of the overall structure of the *Canterbury Tales*. It is a puzzling question, partly because the work is unfinished and partly because what is left suggests a unique combination of an extremely varied selection of tales, on the one hand, and, on the other, of a much fuller and more coherent development of the frame device than is usual.[1] Many of the tales are so closely interwoven with the frame, and consequently with each other, that we seem to glimpse a method by which their very diversity is made to serve a consistent purpose. The aim of this and the next two chapters is to explore the various ways in which this purpose manifests itself, principally through the very nature of Chaucerian comedy as it appears to us in the *Canterbury Tales*, but also through the use of complexes of tales and frame to develop certain major themes. First, however, since the most obvious and the most important fact about the *Canterbury Tales* is that it employs (with the exception of two tales) the medium of narrative poetry, it is essential to ask what this kind of writing meant to Chaucer – what, in fact, did he consider to be the purpose of narrative? How did he expect it to be read? And what kind of structural principles would he expect to govern it? These are not questions that can be answered either fully or confidently. They must be asked; but to answer them adequately would require a treatise on medieval aesthetics of a kind which can probably, in the absence of contemporary critical writing, never be written.[2] At any rate, only the briefest sketch can be attempted here.

There are two ways of approaching the problem – neither will give a complete answer, but both can provide useful indications. One is through Chaucer's own rare references to his art. These have little to do with the special problem of narrative, and indeed, in the main, concern only the common topic of the relation of art to nature. The other method is to look at the kinds of narrative with which Chaucer was familiar and to examine his use of earlier examples and his choice among them.

To take the latter first: in Chaucer's day the long narrative poem existed in a number of different forms, all worthy of imitation.[3] There was, first and most distinguished, the Classical epic of Virgil and Statius. In Ovid similar material could be found, but differently organized by being broken up into smaller units within the overall scheme of the *Heroides* and *Metamorphoses*. There was, secondly, the typically medieval form of romance in its various branches and types; and, thirdly, the kind of writing broadly covered by the term allegory, including as one branch the kind of visionary journey outside normal terrestrial places (whose greatest achievement was Dante's *Divina Commedia*) and, as another important branch, allegorical satire. Jean de Meun's section of the *Roman de la Rose* could be taken as the supreme achievement of this branch. In varying degrees, Langland, in England, and de Guilleville, in France, used similar methods. Works of this kind, however, tend to display great individuality. There are, for example, points of view from which Dante's work is not allegorical or Langland's satirical; all have, however, in common a narrative method which is fundamentally unlike that of all other narrative kinds – a point to which we must return.

Chaucer's attitude towards the great Classical narrative poems is not likely to have been a simple one. Much has already been said on the subject in relation to both the *Knight's Tale* and the *Troilus*. There is, I think, no doubt that he reacted in a straightforward, uncomplicated way to the sheer achievement in poetry of these Classical authors, and that, like any Renaissance poet, it is this he hopes to equal or at least approximate in the *Troilus*, with its final plea to be measured against the work of 'Vergile, Ovide, Omer, Lucan and Stace'.[4] But there are signs that he saw something more than a successful style to admire and imitate. We have seen his insistence on purpose of the *Knight's Tale* to unfold a 'grete effect', and it is likely that the phrase has the same meaning for him when he applies it to the *Aeneid* in the *Legend of Good Women*. The whole direct reference to Virgil, with which the 'Legend of Dido' begins, is worth quoting:

> Glorye and honour, Virgil Mantoan,
> Be to thy name! and I shal, as I can,
> Folwe thy lanterne, as thow gost byforn,
> How Eneas to Dido was forsworn.
> In Naso and Eneydos wol I take
> The tenor, and the grete effectes make.
>
> (F, 924–9)

The 'tenor' is the meaning, the narrative content:[5] Chaucer under-takes, by translation (in fact, largely paraphrase), to follow the content of the story, using both Virgil and Ovid. This, indeed, implies the assumption that Classical subject-matter, as distinct from Classical narrative, has a kind of absolute existence in its own right. Thus, the story of Dido is something which exists and which finds special and particular expression in the version of Virgil or the version of Ovid. Either, or both, can be used to make a fresh version. This kind of approach to Classical story is implied, as we have seen, in the *House of Fame*, in which Dido's fame (insisted on by both Virgil and Ovid) is considered in relation to the 'facts' which give rise to it, as well as to the versions of the 'excusing' poets. Considered from this point of view, the Classical poets are repositories of material, in the form of stories, of which they give not the thing itself, but their own redactions.[6] This material can be used by later generations as they please, either to make new versions – Chaucer's usual purpose – or as repositories of useful information. That this latter was a common attitude to Classical writers during the Middle Ages is well known. It led to such later reworkings as Bersuire's *Ovide Moralisé* and to the collections and interpretations of classical material like Boccaccio's *de Genealogia Deorum* and Christine de Pisan's *Othéa*. In the last two, and in many other works, even the form of Classical poetry dis-appears, and the aim is a useful reorganization and interpretation of its basic material.

We have to distinguish here between two distinct tendencies. One is to what may roughly be called the allegorization of a Classical work, that is, the consistent reading of its situations and characters in a new sense, thought of as existing at the same time as, and parallel to, the literal one.[7] The second is the use of incidents, legends, tales, from the past for the practical information they supply about life or morals. The first method affects poetry, the second does not.

To use a story as a warning, or to extract a moral from it, has nothing to do with allegory, nor does it involve any necessary alteration of the original writer's intention. Thus, Aeneas's behaviour as a lover – left in a fascinatingly ambiguous state by Virgil – could be held up as a warning to women not to trust to men's constancy or to fear the results of irregular marriages; or the useful lesson could be drawn that love and statesmanship can seldom be reconciled. None of these applications would invalidate the story or involve any doubt about Virgil's purpose. If, however, the story were to be read with Dido standing consistently as Sensuality to Aeneas's equally consistent Reason – and this kind of interpretation was often proposed in the Middle Ages[8] – we should constantly find ourselves running counter to Virgil's obvious intention, as it is expressed in the structure of his narrative. The storm and the scene in the cave, for example, as they stand, are obvious and straightforward narrative devices, used in order to place the two main characters in the appropriate position at the appropriate moment. It is easy to see how, in a Spenserian narrative, for example, they would feature quite differently, and how the tumult and disturbance of the storm and the darkness of the cave would be brought to bear on the story in a different way, so as to emphasize what would, in such a context, be the real action in which the protagonists were involved – that of virtue against vice.

Now, Chaucer promises us not only the story – the 'tenor' – which could be used in various ways, but also that he will make the same 'grete effectes'. This means, I think, that his aim is to reproduce, as we should say, 'the spirit' of Virgil's writing – or at any rate to try to retell his story in a comparable way and with a comparable purpose. That this is the meaning of the phrase 'grete effect' (and its precise meaning was left somewhat in the air when we were considering the *Knight's Tale*) is, I think, shown by Chaucer's use of it elsewhere. In the two places in which he uses it in the *Knight's Tale*, it refers to a creative purpose. First, to Chaucer's own, in the work he is writing – 'The grete effect for which that I bygan' (*CT* I, 2482) – and, secondly, to the creative purpose of the First Mover in forming the chain of love – 'Greet was th'effect, and heigh was his entente' (2989).[9]

For Chaucer, therefore, it is characteristic of the greatness of Virgil's work (the whole tendency of the Dido introduction is towards serious praise of an important poet) that it is conditioned and controlled by a high purpose; and this could, of course, well be an allegorical one. It would, indeed, be quite possible that Chaucer misunderstood Virgil; but we are not now concerned with the correctness or otherwise of his understanding, but only with the idea of narrative to which this understanding led him. Chaucer makes ample use of Classical material for the purpose of *exempla*, that is, he is always ready to use the moral-encyclopaedic method.[10] But, in his two retellings of the story of Dido, there is, I believe, no sign that he was concerned with anything but the face-value of the narrative and the reproduction of a clear and single narrative line without allegorical significance. His very manipulations of Virgil (and they are numerous) go to prove this. We have already discussed the special function of the story of Dido within the larger frame of the *House of Fame*. In the *Legend of Good Women* version, Chaucer makes two important changes, both of which have significance as a part of the organization of his version of the narrative, *qua* narrative, but which cannot be related to any interpretation of its meaning. First, he adds a passage clearly designed to support his view of the characters as peculiarly magnificent and princely:

> To daunsynge chaumberes ful of paramentes,
> Of riche beddes, and of ornementes,
> This Eneas is led, after the mete.
> And with the quene, whan that he hadde sete,
> And spices parted, and the wyn agon,
> Unto his chambres was he led anon
> To take his ese and for to have his reste,
> With al his folk, to don what so hem leste.
> There nas courser wel ybrydeled non,
> Ne stede, for the justing wel to gon,
> Ne large palfrey, esy for the nones,
> Ne jewel, fretted ful of ryche stones,
> Ne sakkes ful of gold, of large wyghte,
> Ne ruby non, that shynede by nyghte,
> Ne gentil hawtein faucoun heroner,
> Ne hound, for hert or wilde bor or der,
> Ne coupe of gold, with floreyns newe ybete,
> That in the land of Libie may be gete,
> That Dido ne hath it Eneas ysent;
> And al is payed, what that he hath spent.
> Thus can this quene honurable hire gestes calle,
> As she that can in fredom passen alle.

(1106–27)

It is obvious that this passage is used not for any associations with Luxuria nor to strengthen the idea of the temptation of Aeneas by a Dido who has a more general application than that of the heroine of a particular story, but simply to make the narrative clearer and more easily understood. This is the nobility of a noble queen, and it helps to explain the strength of Aeneas's reaction and the proportionate strength of her despair. Both characters, however, remain parts of a straightforward action and have no resonance in a world of general ideas. That the passage also bends the Classical story in the direction of romance is another matter, to which we must presently return.

Another major change in this version is the elimination of the references to the gods and to the dubiousness of the validity of the marriage. This point had been retained in the *House of Fame* version. Now, probably with Ovid rather than Virgil in mind,[11] Chaucer places the responsibility on Aeneas alone and does not allow him the measure of excuse which the use of the figures of the gods provides. The result is, again, a strengthening of the purely narrative line. Chaucer would not, I think, have regarded himself as altering Virgil's intention. We have seen that his treatment of the Classical gods is always worked out in relation to free will and personal responsibility – so that in the *Knight's Tale*, for example, they become little more than extensions of the human actors – and that it is likely that he thought the same attitude was characteristic of the Classical poets.[12] What he has done here, therefore, is not to alter Virgil's intention, as it appeared to him, but merely to alter the pace of the story by removing a piece of machinery appropriate to a more leisurely and philosophical treatment of the narrative. In this he is only taking Ovid a little further, since Ovid eliminates most of the heavenly machinery and, accordingly, deals with the validity of the marriage in a less clearcut way than Virgil does.[13]

Chaucer's manipulation of the Classical story, therefore, in a context where it stands by itself, and is not subordinated to any wider purpose, is conditioned by purely narrative considerations, that is, his changes relate to motivation, to effective presentation of the main characters, to pace. There is no sign – even in the passage on the splendours with which Dido welcomes Aeneas, which could easily lend itself to such a purpose – of the manipulation of the material in order to extend the meaning beyond the face-value of the literal narrative. In fact, the 'grete effect' which he thinks Virgil is aiming at must be contained within the narrative, understood in the ordinary way as a sequence of events concerning the characters and consist, therefore, in a structural purpose – in the intention to shape an effective work of art, not to expound a serious moral – although we must allow that these two aims are not necessarily incompatible.

Since the 'Legend of Dido' is not, in fact, a particularly successful reworking of the Classical material,[14] we cannot use it with any confidence to show just where, in Chaucer's eyes, this structural greatness within the narrative lay. He has not, unfortunately, achieved any effects here, or carried out any purpose comparable to Virgil's. In the *Knight's Tale*, however, we have an example of Classical epic material – admittedly transmitted via Italian romantic-epic – which is superbly handled in such a way as to show us exactly what Chaucer meant. Here the 'grete effect' is carried out through the successful structuring of the narrative, a constant and deliberate patterning of incidents and characters, in such a way that everything contributes to the resolution of the conflicts which form the substance of the work. The pace is leisurely, but the narrative drive is unbroken; it does not, however, work itself out in purely naturalistic terms, as the 'Legend of Dido' does. Nevertheless, the method is the reverse of that used in the fully non-naturalistic form of allegory. All the elements of the work, the philosophical passages, the machinery of the gods, are brought to bear upon the particular problem of the pro-tagonists. This, it is true, is, in its widest sense, seen as a problem which is common to mankind; but, nevertheless, the movement is always inwards – the wider applications only deepen our compre-hension of the particular instance before our eyes. In allegory the reverse is true. We proceed from the particular of the story material outward, to its implications in ideas and concepts which are general.

It may be helpful here to pause for a moment over the question of the meaning for Chaucer, if we can establish it, of the relation of art and nature. Paradoxically, it is not likely that the conviction which he expresses in the *House of Fame* – that the great artists, among whom he certainly includes the Classical masters, imitate nature – would have led him in the direction of what we mean nowadays by naturalism in art. We tend to equate this with realism and mean by reality the external world as it actually presents itself to our percep-tions. It then has the characteristic of lack of deliberate organization. Thus, nature is opposed to art as simpler, cruder or less selective and so more inclusive, but lacking in the planning of detail to make a significant pattern. From this idea, of course, it is possible to progress to something like its reverse: that nature, owing to its vast amorphousness, is actually more significant and meaningful than the particular patternings which can be arrived at by organized selection. Chaucer would certainly not have associated any of these ideas with nature. For him, and for his age, amorphousness and lack of organization were the well-known characteristics not of nature, but of nature's enemy and raw material, chaos. Nature's function is to create significant forms out of this shapelessness and to organize and maintain purposeful processes. For this reason, it is not really correct to speak of the discussion of the relation of art to nature in the Middle Ages. It is, rather, that the *artist* is compared to nature, because both use a creative, ordering process which results in the emergence of clearly defined and demarcated things. Thus, the usual illustration of the likeness (and unlikeness) of the artist to nature is that of Pygmalion.[15] Like nature he makes a form out of the formlessness of the unshaped stone; but, unlike nature, he cannot give it the special quality of life. Art, therefore, always falls short of nature, but it is an analogous activity.

Chaucer, as we can, I think, see from the *House of Fame*, is interested in the problem of the relation of the poet's narratives to actual events. There is no reason, however, to believe that he would have related the idea of 'truth to a particular actuality' to that of 'truth to nature' in the poet's work. Truth to nature would, rather, consist in the imitation of her ordering, organizing methods so as to produce significant forms; and, in the case of narrative this would necessarily mean the shaping of a story by a clearly apprehended purpose rather than any devotion to 'realism'. This is the kind of procedure we actually find, for example, in the *Knight's Tale*. In the case of Virgil's and Ovid's treatments of the story of Dido, it is likely that Chaucer saw the same kind of thematic structure, as the story unfolds in terms of a conflict of love and duty, in which the crucial question is (as he understood it) the personal responsibility of Aeneas for his own conduct.

If we turn from Classical, or Classical-derived, narrative to pure romance, we shall find Chaucer's attitude harder to define. On the one hand, he seems reluctant to use the form, or rather forms, and never does so in their own right. On the other, we can, I think, detect a kind of pull towards a way of ordering the narrative which is more characteristic of romance than of anything else, and this tendency crops up in surprising places.

There are, in fact, a number of puzzles involved in Chaucer's apparent attitude to romance. One would like to know why he shows so little interest in the greatest achievements of the French romance writers. It is possible that he knew the romances of Chrétien de Troyes and learnt, directly, from their technique,[16] but he shows no obvious sign of having done so and never attempts to write anything of the same kind. He shows no knowledge of or no interest in – we do not know which – the cyclic Arthurian romances: he does not appear to have been inspired by the possibilities of the allegorical treatment of romance themes or by the potentialities of *entrelacement*.[17] All this is surprising when we consider the very detailed way in which he utilizes possibilities and techniques derived from the *Roman de la Rose* and from later love visions. One would like to know whether he equated the long Classical-derived poems of Boccaccio with romance, or whether he regarded them as something new and different. Among all the uncertainties, one thing is abundantly and rather surprisingly clear: what actually ring in his ears are the phrases and rhythms not of sophisticated French romance, but of much less sophisticated English ones, and it is in the direction of these that he sometimes diverts the narrative method of a more sophisticated author, by using the moment-to-moment techniques of popular romance writers in order to move his story on from point to point in a particular way.

Chaucer showed in *Sir Thopas* a detailed knowledge of a number of more or less popular English romances, as Mrs Loomis's study of the poem has proved.[18] It has sometimes been assumed that this is the only place in which he draws on the English romances, and that his only interest in them was therefore to poke fun at them.[19] This, however, is clearly not the case. It is minstrel inconsequence and verbal incompetence that Chaucer laughs at in *Sir Thopas*. Elsewhere he shows that he can prefer the techniques of romances of this popular type to more sophisticated ones, and that he considers them compatible with writing of the highest kind. We have already seen that, in the 'Legend of Dido', for example, in his list of the splendid gifts given to Aeneas by Dido, he can write in a passage which is absolutely unclassical and, at the same time, absolutely typical of romance, and we have seen how this addition is made to serve the narrative development as Chaucer handles it. It is not possible to say whether this particular list derives from English or French romance, but it is typical of romance method and pace. The narrative method of the

simple type of French romance, and the majority of English ones, is
one of enumeration or, to put it another way, of coordination rather
than subordination. In the smallest units, this appears as the list. In
the larger units of the narrative, it can be seen as the presentation of
the separate scenes or incidents as of equal value and perhaps
duration. There is no attempt at an organization which subordinates
one part of a narrative to another in such a way as to concentrate
attention on certain aspects of its development rather than others.
Even in a poem as highly organized as *Sir Gawain and the Green
Knight*, the author keeps to this method, and the hunting scenes are
laid out on exactly the same scale, with the same amount of detail, as
the indoor scenes which develop the main plot-line. We can, if we
choose, perform for ourselves the act of subordinating the hunting
scenes to the main plot by regarding them as implied comments on it,
but there is nothing in the author's actual treatment which compels
us to do so.[20] In extreme cases, for example in that of *Guy of Warwick*,
the succeeding incidents are never welded into a whole. In this
romance the first part is devoted to the noble deeds by which Guy
proves himself worthy of his love, Felice. In the second, having
married her, he decides that his future adventures shall be in honour
of God, and Felice plays little part in this section. This means that we
have to take the love story as it stands and then transfer our attention
completely from it to the quasi-religious story which follows. If we
try to link the two into a coherent scheme, we cannot account for
Guy's final lack of interest in his wife, so hard-won in the first part.
The art of such narrative lies in the selection of episodes which are, in
their own right, sufficiently interesting to engage the audience's
whole attention for their duration, so that there is no room left for any
sense of clashes and inconsistencies between them.

This episodic method of laying out the material in the romance
leads to the development of various devices for making the transition
from one self-contained unit to another. Thus, for example, the
author of *Sir Gawain and the Green Knight* links the succeeding indoor
and outdoor scenes by indicating their relative positions in time –
while one set of characters does one thing, another does another.[21]
Chaucer uses the same, somewhat sophisticated method in the
Knight's Tale to mark off and interrelate the episodes in which the
different characters offer their prayers in the temple. Palamoun goes
to the Temple of Venus 'The Sonday nyght, er day bigan to sprynge'
(2209); Emely starts for the Temple of Diana:

> The thridde houre inequal that Palamon
> Bigan to Venus temple for to gon.
>
> (2271–2)

Arcite goes to the Temple of Mars 'The nexte houre of Mars folwynge this' (2367). Here the device is useful not only as a framing one, to separate and keep distinct the three episodes involving the three characters, but also because the times are astrologically significant – the prayers are made in suitable 'hours' for appealing to the different planets.[22] Chaucer uses the same temporal device to describe the incidents which bring together the three characters – Arcite, Palamoun and Theseus – in the grove. Palamoun happens to make his escape 'of May / The thridde nyght' (1462–3). Arcite goes out because it is a fine May day 'for to doon his observaunce to May' (1500); and Theseus is also influenced by the time of year – 'That for to hunten is so desirus, / And namely at the grete hert in May' (1674–5).

A more usual framing method, common in both French and English romances, is the formula 'now we will leave A and turn to B'.[23] Chaucer uses this, in its simplest form, in the *Squire's Tale*, to end each part – indeed, he brings in the device so simply and blatantly that we cannot help wondering whether he is entirely serious. Thus, at the end of the second part, the Squire starts in the normal way 'Thus lete I Canacee hir hauk kepyng', but goes on not merely with the other half of the formula, but with a complete table of contents, combined with a description of his prospective method as a story-teller:

> I wol namoore as now speke of hir ryng,
> Til it come eft to purpos for to seyn
> How that this faucon gat hir love ageyn
> Repentant, as the storie telleth us,
> By mediacion of Cambalus,
> The kynges sone, of which that I you tolde.
> But hennesforth I wol my proces holde
> To speken of aventures and of batailles,
> That nevere yet was herd so grete mervailles.
>   First wol I telle yow of Cambyuskan
> That in his tyme many a citee wan;

And after wol I speke of Algarsif,
How that he wan Theodora to his wif,
For whom, ful ofte in greet peril he was,
Ne hadde he ben holpen by the steede of bras;
And after wol I speke of Cambalo,
That faught in lystes with the bretheren two
For Canacee er that he myghte hire wynne.
And ther I lefte I wol ayeyn bigynne.

(652–70)

This suggests a composite romance of the scope of a *Faerie Queene*, and it is hard to believe that Chaucer ever seriously considered including anything on this scale in the *Canterbury Tales*.[24] It seems more likely that the exuberance of the project is intended to match the exuberance of the Squire's youth and inexperience. Nevertheless, whether seriously or not, Chaucer lays the ambitious plan out in relation to narrative construction; he does not merely give a list of adventures to be related. Thus, Canacee's ring will come in again when 'it come eft to purpos', that is, at the appropriate point in relation to other parts of the narrative. The Squire promises 'hennesforth I wol my proces holde'. 'Proces' could mean simply 'story' and refer to the adventures and battles – that is, this section will be a straightforward, unbroken account of the deeds of Cambyuskan, Algarsif and Cambalus, whose adventures will be given one after another ('And after wol I speke . . .' 663, 667) – or it could mean 'plan', 'constructive design'.[25] In either case, it implies a preoccupation with the shape of the narrative, which is further emphasized by the promise to pick up the story once more, when it is 'to purpos' again, where it left off at the end of part ii – 'And ther I lefte I wol ayeyn bigynne'. The joke, if there is a joke, is surely against the Squire's literary ambition. It is unlikely that Chaucer regarded the careful construction of a composite narrative as in itself a bad thing; although he does not himself attempt – or, if he meant the *Squire's Tale* to be taken seriously, complete – a romance of this kind. The passage does, however, show that, just as he had a reasonably clear idea of the characteristics of Classical epic narrative, so he was fully aware of the constructional problems of the long romance narrative. That the overall problem comes into his mind in connection with the framing device is also significant. It suggests that, whether with or without the added complexity of *entrelacement*, he considered this separation of the story into comparatively independent episodes to be typical of romance structure – as, indeed, it was.

In the *Knight's Tale*, Chaucer uses the same framing formula to effect transitions from one episode, and character, to another. Here, however, we can see even more clearly what he is aiming at, because he is working from a known source, and the introduction of this narrative device is a departure from it. The main differences between Chaucer's treatment of the story and Boccaccio's have already been discussed.[26] We can summarize the result by saying that Chaucer has made the story much tauter by cutting away material which, in Boccaccio's version, is not sharply focused on the main plot. He has also used the story to develop ideas and themes which are not present in the *Teseida*. In imposing this kind of thematic development on the Italian poem, he has, I think, gone back to the methods and purpose, according to his understanding of it, of Classical epic. Yet, paradoxically, in imposing this more coherent structure on the material, he makes use, as we have seen, of a technique which properly belongs to a more loosely constructed kind of narrative, that is, to the episodic romance. There are, I believe, two main reasons behind this paradox. In the first place, it would seem that Chaucer could rely on a very considerable familiarity with, and liking for, the older type of romance, whether in French or (more probably) in English, on the part of his audience – indeed, unless this were the case, *Sir Thopas* would have fallen very flat. To adjust the unfamiliar Italian type of narrative in this direction would, therefore, be to make it more immediately acceptable and comprehensible. It is notable that Chaucer, who clearly assumes intimate knowledge of French love vision – and, I would suggest, of English romance and lyric[27] – does not appear to assume that his audience had any knowledge of Italian literature. Here, he seems to work as a popularizer and transformer of essentially foreign material into something more suited to the taste of his own audience.

The use of the framing device is not the only means by which Chaucer suggests the style and approach of earlier romances in the *Knight's Tale*. He treats the description of the tournament in a way which, by its general method and also by its actual phraseology, suggests the use of several specific English romances known to us and may have suggested more to Chaucer's audience. The use of alliteration in the lines beginning 'Ther shyveren shaftes upon sheeldes thikke' (2605 ff.) has often been remarked on. If Chaucer has a specific model in mind here, he is probably drawing on either *Ipomedan* or *Partonope of Blois*.[28] It is significant, however, that other English romances use alliteration as an appropriate part of battle description. *Ywain and Gawain*, which is, of course, based on a French source, also slips into this peculiarly English way of writing on this subject.[29] The reason for Chaucer's use of it here is, therefore, probably not so much that the sound-effects of alliteration are appropriate to the noise and confusion of battle, but that it had become an accepted part of the romance writer's technique, no doubt in the first instance because of the superiority of alliterative romances in descriptions of this kind, but becoming equally appropriate to romances using the normal, non-alliterative style based on French. But it is not only through this momentary use of the technique of alliteration that Chaucer recalls the English romance type of battle description. The Italian provides a leisurely passage, employing similes; and, after a general description of the onslaught, first singles out Palemone and Arcita, then gives a long passage describing 'Come gli altri baron tutti s'afrontarono' (VIII, st. 18 ff.). Chaucer substitutes a general description of a quite different kind and cuts out all the references to the other knights. This general description, in contrast to the Italian, is of the enumerating kind common in English romances, laid out by weapons and not by heroes – it proceeds from spears and shields to swords and helmets and on to maces.[30] Further, Chaucer uses a device which helps to organize enumerations of this kind by dividing them into sections. This is the formula 'Ther seen men' introduced in line 2604, which is found, for example, in *Guy of Warwick* and in *Havelok*.[31] The chief organizing device, however, is the general 'he': 'He feeleth', 'He rolleth', 'he foyneth', etc. The whole passage (2600–51) should be compared with *Teseida*, VIII. The contrast between the knightly setting, which forms a fitting background for the deeds of Palemone and Arcita, and the destructive and impersonal violence of the weapons, which leads up to the even more violent encounter of Palamoun and Arcite, is very striking.

If we now return to the framing device and examine some of Chaucer's transitions in relation to his source, it will, I think, be possible to understand the paradox of this use of an episodic technique to promote an essentially closely constructed narrative.[32] Chaucer uses the device three times within 150 lines, at the end of part i and the beginning of part ii of the *Knight's Tale*. First:

> Now wol I stynte of Palamon a lite,
> And lete hym in his prisoun stille dwelle,
> And of Arcita forth I wol yow telle.
> (1334–6)

Secondly:

> And in this blisse lete I now Arcite,
> And speke I wole of Palamon a lite.
> (1449–50)

And thirdly:

> Now wol I turne to Arcite ageyn,
> That litel wiste how ny that was his care,
> Til that Fortune had broght him in the snare.
> (1488–90)

Even before this, Chaucer uses repetitive introductions to the passages in which the two lovers lament and make their philosophical speeches, which have a similar framing effect:

> How greet a sorwe suffreth now Arcite!
> The deeth he feeleth thurgh his herte smyte;
> He wepeth, wayleth, crieth pitously;
> To sleen hymself he waiteth prively.
> He seyde, 'Allas . . .'
> (1219–23)

> Upon that oother syde Palamon,
> Whan that he wiste Arcite was agon,
> Swich sorwe he maketh that the grete tour
> Resouneth of his youlyng and clamour,
> The pure fettres on his shynes grete,
> Weren of his bittre, salte teeres wete.
> 'Allas', quod he . . .
> (1275–81)

All these passages help to separate the two characters whose fate is in many ways so alike. Taken together, they emphasize the fact that

their love has a disruptive effect, breaking their friendship and part-
ing them. If we turn to the other framing passages in the poem, we
shall see that they serve a similar purpose. They all work to keep
characters, or groups of figures, separate from each other. Thus
Theseus, who acts on the basis of a different view of the world and a
different set of assumptions to those of the lovers, is introduced in
this way when he comes to interrupt the fight in the grove, in lines
1661–2; a similar formula emphasizes the separate plane of action
of the planet-gods and ends part iii (2479–82); and, finally, Chaucer
uses the same device to dismiss Arcite from the action and to bring
forward Emely, now at last an effective character, in the final section
of the poem (2815–16).[33]

In all these passages, the Italian treats the material quite differently. The enmity of the two lovers, and their philosophical speeches,
are changes made by Chaucer. In the *Teseida* there is no initial
quarrel and nothing to correspond to the bitter arraignments of fate
and the gods; the lovers part with embraces (at the end of Book III).
In the case of Theseus's sudden arrival to stop the fight, Boccaccio
seems to feel a difficulty. His solution is to emphasize this one abrupt
coincidence in his otherwise smooth, consecutive narrative by
excusing it as allowable:

> Ma come noi veggiam venire in ora
> Cosa che in mill' anni non avvenne,
> Cosi avvenne veramente allora
> che Teseo. . . .
>
> (V, 77–80)

Chaucer uses these lines; but not to help to smooth over an awkward
moment in the narrative. After the framing formula:

> And in this wise I lete hem fightyng dwelle,
> And forth I wole of Theseus yow telle,
>
> (1661–2)

he gives us a passage which, in its general, philosophical content,
corresponds, as has already been noted,[34] to the speeches of Palamoun and Arcite, and he puts Boccaccio's lines on coincidence into
the middle of this, thus making them refer to the general way in
which Theseus's actions correspond to destinal forces, rather than to

the immediate succession of events. Indeed, the generalization is taken even further, by linking the coincidence on the one hand to God's 'purveiaunce' and on the other to all human appetites:

> The purveiaunce that God hath seyn biforn,
> So strong it is that, though the world had sworn
> The contrarie of a thyng by ye or nay,
> Yet somtyme it shal fallen on a day
> That falleth nat eft withinne a thousand year.
> For certeinly, oure appetites heer,
> Be it of werre, or pees, or hate, or love,
> Al is this reuled by the sighte above.
>
> (1665–72)

The total impact of the passage, which has the effect of a digression, is, of course, to reinforce the reader's feeling of the separation of the characters and the incidents, by emphasizing the difference between the basis of Theseus's actions and that of the lovers.

Just as Palemone and Arcita are not treated primarily from the point of view of the disruption of their friendship by love in the *Teseida*, so the machinery of the gods is not given the same separate existence; Boccaccio, through the conceit of the flight to heaven of the prayers, incorporates the temple descriptions and the actions of the gods much more closely into the action of the three human characters and, in fact, never devotes a separate section to them. Thus, where Chaucer has a framing passage (2479–82) to end part iii and introduce part iv, Boccaccio merely describes Emilia's reactions to the doubtful reception of her prayer and goes straight on to the events of the next morning (VIII, st. 93–4). Lastly, Chaucer does everything possible to emphasize the finality of Arcite's end and his cutting off from the rest of the story. Thus, instead of finishing off his account of this major character by describing his soul's destination, as Boccaccio does, he repudiates any further knowledge of him:

> His spirit chaunged hous and wente ther,
> As I kam nevere, I kan nat tellen wher . . .
> Arcite is coold, ther Mars his soule gye!
> Now wol I speken forth of Emelye.
>
> (2809–16)

Boccaccio, apart from allowing Arcita a more gradual exit from the story by his description of his soul's flight, eases the transition to the lamentations which follow his death ('Shrighte Emelye and howleth Palamoun', 2817) by relating them specifically to his last words:

> A la voce d'Arcita dolorosa
> quanti v'eran gli orecchi alti levaro,
> aspettando che piú alcuna cosa
> dovesse dir; ma poi che rimiraro
> l'alma partita, con voce angosciosa
> pianse ciascuno e con dolore amaro;
> ma sopra tutti Emilia e Palemone,
> la qual cosí rispose a tal sermone. . . .
>
> (XI, st. 4)

In all these passages, where Boccaccio takes pains to ensure smooth transitions in a narrative which develops in a very leisurely, but a strictly consecutive way, Chaucer takes equal pains to introduce devices which break the narrative flow and ensure the effective separation of its episodes and, at the same time, its characters. This, it is obvious, helps to develop his very different conception of the main themes of his poem and, especially, of the theme of disorder *versus* order and of the disruptive nature of love.[35] Chaucer, therefore, uses a device, which was originally developed to help to make the necessary transitions in an episodic type of narrative, for the purpose of thematic development. He has thus, I believe, achieved a poem which has, on the one hand, a greater superficial similarity to a kind of romance which would be more familiar to his audience than his source, and, on the other, a method of handling the narrative entirely new to a work of this type. Both his purpose and the way he sets about achieving it show that he was fully aware of the problems of narrative structure and had a clear idea of certain ways in which they could be solved.

Chaucer uses different types of romance in the *Man of Law's Tale*, the *Franklin's Tale* and the *Wife of Bath's Tale*. The first of these belongs to the special category of the hagiographic romance and has also a special thematic relation to the *Knight's Tale* – in fact it plays such an important part in the exposition of the major themes of the *Canterbury Tales* that discussion of it must be held over to chapter 4. The other two are both short romances; one, the *Franklin's Tale*, belongs to a special category of shorter romances, the Breton lay.[36] The narrative form in short romances presents no problems – their very briefness compels a closer structure and allows of less diversity of episodes than is the case with the long romances. It may be significant, however, that the Franklin tells his tale out of compliment to the Squire, and that it is, at the same time, something of the sort that the Squire has shown himself to like and also a marked contrast to the enormously complicated narrative on which he had embarked. It would be rash to conclude that it implies Chaucer's own preference for a more manageable type of narrative; but it is certainly one that is easier to finish. All three of these romances, as we shall see, play an important part in the development of certain themes which are of major importance in the *Canterbury Tales* as a whole. In fact, apart from the doubtful case of the *Squire's Tale*, there is every sign that Chaucer found romance particularly suitable for thematic development, in spite of his recognition of its episodic nature.

The third important type of narrative structure of which Chaucer would have known is the allegorical one. Its main characteristic, in sharp contrast to the other two we have been considering, is that it seldom aimed at a naturalistic method of developing the story, that is, the sequence of events and the behaviour of characters are not conditioned by the ordinary successions of cause and effect or of temporal development which typify ordinary experience and are therefore characteristic of realistic treatment.[37] Chaucer never attempted a complete narrative of this kind, but he does use some of its methods in his handling of certain comic characters – a tribute to the great importance in the Middle Ages of allegorical satire.[38] It seems likely that he would have understood – as we are now beginning to understand – a type of structure in a long narrative work which depended on the development of ideas and of themes, rather than on the devising of a plot with appropriate characters.[39] If so, this would have reinforced any feeling that narrative structure was dependent on a more total and intimate organization of the material than could be achieved by a construction which was based on the story line alone. This, I have suggested, seems to have been his view of epic and romance. It is possible, however, that we should include allegory not so much in the category of the individual narrative, as in that of the long work which included within its organization a number of separate narratives. The various devices of confession (Gower's *Confessio Amantis*);[40] a journey (Dante's *Divina Commedia* which, with a relation to the *Metamorphoses* probably more obvious to Dante and to Chaucer than to us, might well strike a medieval reader as a story collection within a frame); and pilgrimage or quest (*Piers Plowman* with its separate dreams and episodes; the two *Pèlerinages* of de Guilleville, and, most important of all, the *Roman de la Rose* with its diversity of material and its many stories and separable speeches) all lend themselves to the creation of works which can best be seen as large composite narrative structures. They have in common the inclusion of very diverse material within this structure, and this diversity is characteristic of the *Canterbury Tales*, in contrast to the collections of tales within a frame which are usually cited as Chaucer's models. These, no doubt, play their part, but they are not enough to account for the distance Chaucer has travelled in his conception of a tale collection.

The question of Chaucer's knowledge and use of collections of tales within a framing device is discussed at length in the contribution of R. A. Pratt and Karl Young to the *Sources and Analogues of the Canterbury Tales*.[41] Broadly speaking, these collections fall into two main groups. There are those held together by linking devices which merely provide a reason for bringing the tales together.[42] Secondly, there is the more didactic approach which makes the framing device determine the nature of the stories, by setting out a problem to be discussed or a subject to be elaborated, so that all the stories have some relation to a central theme.[43] This is the method used by Chaucer in his two unfinished series, the *Legend of Good Women* and the Monk's series of tragedies. He is, thus, well aware of the possibility of using the frame to ensure a kind of unity through the content of the tales in the series; and, if we are to judge from their unfinished state, he is also aware of the drawback, that is, of the difficulty of sustaining interest through a series of similar tales. In the *Canterbury Tales* the frame is, obviously, basically of the other kind, that is, it lends an air of probability and gives a solid background to the telling by different persons of a series of otherwise unconnected tales. The advantage of this method, of course, is that there is no reason why the tales should all be of the same kind, or why their content should relate to any one central subject. In choosing a pilgrimage, as has often been pointed out, Chaucer is able to bring together the widest possible variety of tellers and to exploit this fact to provide the widest possible variety of tales. In this, although the Italian collections of *novelle* may well have given him a hint,[44] he goes further than any other medieval user of the device. Nevertheless, with this very complete exploitation of the possibilities for variety and dissimilitude goes an obvious interest in certain major recurrent themes which are developed by means of both frame and tale. These will be discussed in detail in chapter 4. As far as the overall narrative structure of the *Canterbury Tales* is concerned, their presence suggests that Chaucer was ready to exploit the advantages of both types of story collections: the advantage of a connecting theme for unification and the achievement of coherence within the collection; and the advantage of the looser type of device, which made probable and acceptable the introduction of any type of tale, without necessary reference to the central purpose of the collection as a whole. Everything that we can tentatively conclude about Chaucer's understanding and use of narrative structure, in the long single narrative and in composite form, suggests, I believe, that he would have regarded it as something which, while it was certainly not obliged to serve the special purposes of allegory, yet owed its coherence and shape to the underlying ideas and themes which it expressed. It seems likely that, if the *Canterbury Tales* had ever been finished, it would have been possible to see some coherence of this kind within the variety of its parts, that is, a 'grete effect' carried through to the end, although it could hardly have been of the clearcut kind of the *Knight's Tale*.

It is necessary, in fact, to be very careful in defining exactly what is meant by thematic development in the *Canterbury Tales*. There is no doubt that, in his experimentation with and blending of different narrative techniques, Chaucer has achieved something that is substantially new, and a naïve attitude towards the way in which he manipulates his major themes could lead to serious misinterpretation. As we have said, for Chaucer, the successful artist imitates nature, not other works of art, and his success is measured by the degree to which his work approximates to its model. So much emerges, for example, from the *House of Fame*. The perfection of nature, as we learn from, *inter alia*, the *Parlement of Foules*, consists in the fulfilment of that infinite possibility for variety and completeness through which it expresses the infinitude and perfection of the One from which it has its source: this is 'God's plenty' as Dryden perceived it in Chaucer. If there is any work of Chaucer's which could, by any stretch of the imagination, be said to attempt to imitate this natural variety, it is, surely, the *Canterbury Tales*; and, if we try to isolate the special quality and achievement of this work, taken, as far as we can do so, in its unfinished state, as a whole, we cannot do better than to fix on the variety and inclusiveness which it achieves through its wide choice of subject-matter and kinds of writing. To look, except with extreme caution, for any more specific architectural principle is, in fact, to negate a good deal of Chaucer's achievement. If, for example, we think that he devised the series primarily to explore certain leading themes, then a number of the tales have to be dismissed as irrelevant to the main purpose or, alternatively, interpreted in a way which does violence to their author's obvious intention. Certain major themes do recur in the *Canterbury Tales*, and, as we shall see, we cannot fully appreciate the work without some understanding of them. But it is only to a very limited extent that they provide any obvious organizing principle. There is no indication that the *Canterbury Tales* would ever have become a work comparable to the *Confessio Amantis*, with its more or less clearcut exposition of love in relation to the vices and virtues; to the *Faerie Queene*, where the choice of the story material is determined by the ideas to be expressed; or even to Jean de Meun's part of the *Roman*, whose structure is conditioned by the need to work out a variety of ideas in their relation to love, rather than by any necessary, predetermined progression of the love story.

Similar difficulties arise from any such thesis as, for example, that the individual tales, and the characters who tell them, are designed as a series of *exempla* in illustration of the Christian moral system laid out in the *Parson's Tale*.[45] True, the Parson deals systematically with the deadly sins, and equally true that most of the characters of the tales, especially of the churls' tales, are busily engaged with one or other of them; but difficulties arise when we come to tales like the Knight's and the Franklin's. To fit this scheme these tales have to be shorn of a good deal of their subtlety. Tales of a more light-hearted kind, on the other hand, especially the *Nun's Priest's Tale* and *Sir Thopas*, have to be invested with so much subtlety that they become scarcely recognizable to the unprejudiced reader. Characters, too, have to be distorted – the Wife of Bath and the Prioress are obvious examples. The first has to be reduced to a schema and shorn of her humanity, the other built up so as to serve as a more serious warning against sin than Chaucer appears, at first sight, to have intended. In the same way, too earnest a concern with the souls and ultimate destinations of the *fabliau* characters introduces distortion into the churls' tales: we need to allow for a certain willing suspension of the moral faculty in this genre. Such a suspension is not total – the *fabliau* kind has a rough justice, based on the acceptable social norm, built securely into it; but to read the tales with too sensitive a moral awareness is surely to suffer an unnecessary degree of disquietude.

If, bearing all this in mind, we try to see what the completed series would have been like, we can, I think, only postulate more variety and, no doubt, more complexes of links and tales, more thematic interlacing of all kinds. But it seems clear that Chaucer would never have allowed the *Canterbury Tales* to develop the kind of schematization which is reached either by giving all the parts a uniformity which arises directly out of the nature of the frame or by a development of the frame which would render it completely independent of the tales and so allow complete freedom to introduce stories of any kind without any thematic interconnection. What he has arrived at, it seems to me, is a method by which frame and tales grow together, as the characters of the tellers reveal themselves increasingly through the frame and as the tales, in their turn, continue the revelation or arise naturally from one another, as Miller 'quites' Knight, or Clerk the Wife of Bath, or as Friar quarrels with Summoner. But with all this, there seems no reason to believe that Chaucer would have entirely given up the licence to introduce the occasional unconnected tale, as he does in the case of the Canon's Yeoman and of the saints' tales of the two Nuns. All these are linked into the frame by their appropriateness to their tellers but do not play an appreciable part in any thematic development between a group of tales. In thus extending the problem of narrative structure, solved so often and so brilliantly in so many individual tales, to that of a narrative complex, Chaucer seems, as far as we can judge his unfinished work, to have drawn on many different prototypes to produce something which would have been wholly new.

3

The *Canterbury Tales*: Chaucerian comedy

It is obvious that the inclusiveness and variety of the *Canterbury Tales* help to provide ideal conditions for the exploitation of comedy to an extent which had not been practicable in Chaucer's early works. In these, indeed, comedy only enters in as an incidental.

In the love visions – the *Parlement of Foules* and the *House of Fame* – the only characters to emerge as clearly comic are birds – those of the lower classes in the *Parlement* and the pedagogic eagle in the *House of Fame*.[1] It is notable that, in the *Parlement*, Chaucer makes no attempt to treat the assembly of birds as a whole, or its purpose, in a comic spirit. He merely introduces the comic viewpoint through some individual members. This fact may perhaps give us a clue to one of the most characteristic aspects of Chaucerian comedy: that it arises out of the breadth and inclusiveness of his view of the world. Love is a serious subject and, as we have seen, has cosmological as well as individual implications. But the very fact that it is a fundamental and inescapable part of nature as a whole makes any consideration of it incomplete which does not extend through the whole of nature – and the whole of nature includes the vulgar-minded, but essentially useful and practical, duck. In the *Troilus*, the serious and beautiful description of the lovers' bliss when they are finally physically united grows out of a scene of comic intrigue, and this sudden emergence of seriousness out of comedy gives us a sense of completeness we could not otherwise feel. Elsewhere, the bedroom scene can have the reverse effect and becomes a kind of common denominator of humanity, which brings excessive dignity of rank or splendour, or even of sainthood, into a more comprehensive picture of mankind. The resulting sense of completeness is experienced by the reader through a momentary invasion of the comic spirit into a serious passage. Thus, for example, the high-flown description of the divine lovers Venus and Mars and their extremely overwrought emotional reactions ends in one blunt line:

> Ther is no more, but unto bed thei go.
>
> (73)

And, of the saintly Constance, Chaucer relates:

> They goon to bedde, as it was skile and right;
> For thogh that wyves be ful hooly thynges,
> They moste take in pacience at nyght
> Swiche manere necessaries as been plesynges
> To folk that han ywedded hem with rynges,
> And leye a lite hir hoolynesse aside,
> As for the tyme, – it may no bet bitide.
>
> (*CT* II, 708–14)

It is notable that in one of the rare cases where exclusion, not inclusion, is his aim, in the *Clerk's Tale*,[2] he is careful to avoid this modulation. There is no description of the marriage bed of Walter and Griselda. At the two points where it would naturally come (*CT* IV, 392 and 422), Chaucer breaks off and substitutes praise of Griselda's virtue.

In the two instances just quoted, we have only a moment which we feel is in any sense comic, and the structure of the narrative as a whole is not affected. In the treatment of the two figures who act as observers of the story in the two great philosophical poems, the element of comedy affects the structure of the whole work. Without Pandarus and Theseus, handled as Chaucer handles them, the stories in which they play a part would have totally different implications – as, indeed, we can actually see if we look at the sources, in which these characters are not treated as Chaucer treats them.

In Pandarus's case, comedy arises mainly from the fact that he represents a different view of the world to that of the other characters. In a sense he is in closer touch with actuality – he can recognize a farm cart when he sees one, unlike Troilus – and, as we have seen, he helps to link the intensity and self-centredness of the love story to a wider, more diffuse context. But there is also comedy in the fact that, however accurate his vision is where facts are concerned, he is all at sea when values are involved. Troilus's assessment of the nature of his loss, and of his own tragedy, is more truthful than Pandarus's.

There is no indication that Theseus's view of the world is a false or mistaken one. On the contrary, the whole structure of the poem depends on its acceptance as true. The denouement, in fact, can only work when we realize that the divergent views on the nature and function of love of the two lovers and of Theseus have at last converged in an understanding of the function of married love as a unifying and ordering force. Like Pandarus, however, Theseus is a link with a wider, less obsessive world, and the humour arises from the discrepancy between the lovers' view of life and life as we see it in this wider world, not from their clash with Theseus. In both poems, it is obvious, the inclusion of a character which in some sense belongs to comedy results in the enlargement of the scope of the whole work and, in these two great philosophical poems, in a widening and deepening of our comprehension of the themes.

So far, humour plays a strictly subordinate part in Chaucer's work – neither Theseus nor Pandarus are wholly comic characters, and the poems to which they belong never fail to keep in strict perspective our perception of a kind of comic disproportion which is, perhaps, inherent in reality itself, but which never for a moment invalidates or hinders our sympathy with the seriousness of the central situation. In many of the *Canterbury Tales*, comedy is more complete, and we have numerous characters presented in a wholly comic spirit in tales which have no overt serious aspect.

In developing the characters in tales of this kind, or in the frame, Chaucer uses methods of which there is no sign in the earlier works – and for which there was no need. Comedy is always particular – it exploits the way in which the individual case fails to fit the norm, the discrepancies between reality and a particular, partial view of the facts. Tragedy takes a wider sweep, and its characters do not need the kind of minute particularization required by comedy. In the Prologue to the *Canterbury Tales*, for example, Chaucer presents the characters through a cumulative list of details, in which every item helps to mark this particular figure off from any other. He avoids, however, the catalogue-type of visual description and mingles details of appearance, dress, etc. with those of occupations and habits, of past history and present employment. The section on the Squire provides a good example of this method at its most straightforward. He is not, it is true, an altogether comic figure, but there is an element of comedy in his behaviour as a lover and in his youth, which gives a certain extravagance to his occupations and dress not found, for example, in the more sober portrait of the Knight:

> With hym ther was his sone, a yong SQUIER,
> A lovyere and a lusty bacheler,
> With lokkes crulle as they were leyd in presse.
> Of twenty yeer of age he was, I gesse.
> Of his stature he was of evene lengthe,
> And wonderly delyvere, and of greet strengthe.
> And he hadde been somtyme in chyvachie
> In Flaundres, in Artoys, and Pycardie,
> And born hym weel, as of so lytel space,
> In hope to stonden in his lady grace.
> Embrouded was he, as it were a meede
> Al ful of fresshe floures, whyte and reede.
> Syngynge he was, or floytynge, al the day;
> He was as fressh as is the month of May.
> Short was his gowne, with sleves longe and wyde.
> Wel koude he sitte on hors and faire ryde. . . .
>
> (I, 79–94)

The narrative method here, with its apparent lack of organization, its rapid transitions from a detail noticed in the figure before the eye to a bit of information about its history, helps to ensure that we react as to an individual seen at a specific moment of time. What Chaucer, in fact, does is to present himself, as narrator, as reporting to us on what he sees before him. He gives us a detail as it happens to catch his eye, coming back, after each digression into the history or habits of the figure, to its actual appearance at the moment of speaking. Thus, after a reference to the Squire's habitual singing or fluting, Chaucer returns to the actual figure on horseback as it rides at that moment in the pilgrimage.

With all the emphasis on individualization and particularization, we must not lose sight of the fact that, for Chaucer, the figures of the Prologue, as of many of the comic tales, also represent clearly recognizable types, with vices or virtues which are commonly attributed to persons of their order.[3] In some cases, however, this conformity to type only results in a sharper focus on the individual. The joke against lovers is, after all, that 'thise loveris al' indulge in the same antics, however different their characters may be. In the Prioress's case, conformity to the convention which equips wealthy and fashionable ladies with little dogs is, given her ecclesiastical rather than worldly status, a decidedly individualizing trait.

Simple as the description of the Squire seems, it depends for its effect almost entirely on our acceptance of the observer – in this case of the narrator who presents him to us. The observer, indeed, often used in much more complicated ways, is an essential part of the machinery of Chaucerian comedy. He is, however, an unobtrusive figure, only emerging into the foreground with a comment on rare occasions. These calculated emergences, in fact, as well as his equally calculated withdrawals, convey a great part of the comedy of the *Canterbury Tales*. His elusiveness and the method by which straight description, without the slightest indication of evaluation, is tellingly interspersed with a rare, unemphatic comment or a half concealed allusion compel us to join him and to become observers ourselves. This is characteristic of Chaucer's approach to his subject-matter in comedy. If we identify ourselves with anyone, it is with the half-glimpsed narrator. We are carefully kept at a distance from the characters: our sympathy may be from time to time engaged, but never as a participant in the action and seldom even as a partisan. It is, indeed, rather that, as Raleigh said of the best of Boccaccio's stories,[4] we react to something 'so entirely like life that the strongest of the emotions awakened in the reader is not sympathy or antipathy, not moral approval or moral indignation, but a more primitive passion than these – the passion of curiosity'.

These results are largely achieved by the exploitation of variations in style similar to those we have already seen in the earlier works and, above all, in the *House of Fame*. For comedy Chaucer uses as the basic medium the simple style, with mainly coordinate or paratactic sentence structure. This style is typical of earlier narrative poetry in English, although it is also, of course, found in French. There is no doubt that, to build up the narrator's attitude to and evaluation of his story, the more complex periodic sentence is needed; it is through the connectives – a reluctant 'although', a 'nevertheless' or an apologetic 'but yet' – that a complex attitude is most easily conveyed, and the subordination of one part of a lengthy sentence to another generally coincides with the writer's estimate of its value to the whole. In the descriptions in the Prologue, Chaucer uses simple, paratactic structure so as to allow detail to pile on detail without the slightest overt indication of their relation to each other or their relative value – we are left to supply our own assessment, guided by the narrator's hidden skill in timing and placing:

> He was nat pale as a forpyned goost.
> A fat swan loved he best of any roost.
> His palfrey was as broun as is a berye.
>
> (205–7)

Here the effect depends on the ironical reversal of positive and negative: he was *not* pale, as a monk properly devoted to asceticism should be; he *did* enjoy fat swans and good horses. The unemphatic line opening 'He was nat' is, as it were, counterbalanced and contradicted by the emphatic position before the line pause, of 'loved he'.

> His typet was ay farsed ful of knyves
> And pynnes, for to yeven faire wyves.
> And certeinly he hadde a murye note:
> Wel koude he synge and pleyen on a rote;
> Of yeddynges he baar outrely the pris.
> His nekke whit was as the flour-de-lys;
> Therto he strong was as a champioun.
>
> (233–9)

The emphatic placing of the apparently conventional epithet 'faire' in the second line, where it carries the penultimate stress, causes it to linger in our minds and so to reinforce the sensuous and virile description of the last two: such a man would certainly be likely to pick out the prettiest women as the recipients of his gifts.

> Wel koude he stelen corn and tollen thries;
> And yet he hadde a thombe of gold, pardee.
> A whit cote and a blew hood wered he.
> A baggepipe wel koude he blowe and sowne,
> And therwithal he broghte us out of towne.
>
> (562–6)

Here the effect depends upon the ambiguity of the opening 'wel'. The first impression is of a line of good humoured praise for a good point in the character, but the smoothly running first half 'wel koude he . . .' is set against the heavily regular stress of the last 'stelen corn and tellen thries'. The narrator's amiable praise turns out to be directed at skill in thievery, unambiguously described. The apparently apologetic 'and yet' with the reinforcing affirmation tagged on like an innocent afterthought at the end of the line, develops the irony further. The proverb 'an honest miller has a golden thumb' is not altogether appropriate to this one. He is, the narrator indulgently adds, after all as honest as such men usually are, and we are left to decide for ourselves whether the golden thumb benefits its owner or his customers. The apparently inconsequent piling up of the details of dress and equipment in the last three lines helps to build up the portrait, developed in the passage as a whole, of a colourful, vulgar figure. The bagpipes, of course, were not a refined instrument.

The longer, consecutive or periodic sentences, which do indicate a definite attitude to the matter in hand, stand out sharply in contrast. The passage in which the good priest is compared to the 'shiten shepherde' provides a good example:[5]

> This noble ensample to his sheep he yaf,
> That first he wroghte, and afterward he taughte.
> Out of the gospel he tho wordes caughte,
> And this figure he added eek therto,
> That, if gold ruste, what shal iren do?
> For if a preest be foul, on whom we truste,
> No wonder is a lewed man to ruste;
> And shame it is, if a prest take keep,
> A shiten shepherde and a clene sheep.
>
> (496–504)

Or again, in one of the rare passages in which the narrator actually joins in the conversation, he commends the logic with which the monk argues against confinement to the cloister in a paragraph of complex structure:

> And I seyde his opinion was good.
> What sholde he studie and make hymselven wood,

Upon a book in cloystre alwey to poure,
Or swynken with his handes and laboure,
As Austyn bit? How shal the world be served?
Lat Austyn have his swynk to hym reserved!
(183–8)

And he continues with a telling 'therefore':

Therfore he was a prikasour aright;

and justly indulges 'al his lust', sparing no expense in his pursuit
of the chase (177–92).

The technique of bare statement is not, of course, restricted to
the Prologue. It is often used in the comic tales themselves. For
example:

A theef he was for sothe, of corn and mele,
And that a sly, and usaunt for to stele.
His name was hoote deynous Symkyn.
A wyf he hadde, ycomen of noble kyn;
The person of the toun hir fader was.
(*CT* I, 3939–43)

Or:

This carpenter out of his slomber sterte,
And herde oon crien 'water' as he were wood,
And thoughte, 'Allas, now comth Nowelis flood!'
He sit hym up withouten wordes mo,
And with his ax he smoot the corde atwo,
And doun gooth al. . . .
(*CT* I, 3816–21)

Here the syntax produces the effect of speed in the narrative and
also, with its plain enumeration of detail after detail without
comment on the narrator's part, helps to build up the outrageous
climax. The same effect is produced by the relentless accumulation
of detail in the *Reeve's Tale*. Narrator and audience alike are helpless
before the ineluctable logic of events:

This John stirte up as faste as ever he myghte,
And graspeth by the walles to and fro,
To fynde a staf; and she stirte up also,
And knew the estres bet than dide this John,
And by the wal a staf she foond anon,
And saugh a litel shymeryng of a light,
For at an hole in shoon the moone bright;
And by that light she saugh hem bothe two,
But sikerly she nyste who was who,
But as she saugh a whit thyng in hir ye.
And whan she gan this white thyng espye,
She wende the clerk hadde wered a volupeer,
And with the staf she drow ay neer and neer,
And wende han hit this Aleyn at the fulle,
And smoot the millere on the pyled skulle,
That doun he gooth, and cride, 'Harrow! I dye.'

(*CT* I, 4292–307)

Such gross overworking of the conjunction 'and' with the minimum of explanatory 'buts' and 'fors' would be easy to parallel from many English narrative poems before Chaucer. But we should find no parallel to its deliberate exploitation for a comic effect which depends on the cumulative weight of the sentence structure.

This strict selectiveness in the style works together with another kind of selectiveness which is characteristic of the *fabliau*. This is the narrative selectiveness, which pares down all accompanying or background detail to the bare minimum which is actually needed for the exposition of the plot. There is no exuberance in the description of the settings; any detail that is mentioned is mentioned in explanation of the action, as Muscatine has pointed out.[6] The passage just quoted from the *Reeve's Tale* provides an excellent example of the technique. As in the passage in the *Troilus* in which Pandarus introduces Troilus into Criseyde's bedroom, each detail helps us to understand and visualize the exact progression of events, and nothing is mentioned which is outside this immediate purpose. Everything is given the most precise definition. The inadequate light is 'a litel shymeryng'. This is because although the moon, its source, is bright, it comes 'at an hole'. It is 'that light' by which the Miller's wife sees 'a whit thyng in hir ye'. This 'white thyng' looks to her like a 'volupeer' worn by one of the clerks. With care and accuracy 'the staf she drow ay neer and neer', with the result that she, of course, succeeds in placing her blow on the white thing, now only too clearly identified as the miller's 'pyled skulle'.

Passages showing a similar method could be quoted from most of the *fabliau* tales, and it is this new precision of style, with its exact selection of relevant detail and its accurate timing and placing which is the great innovation of Chaucer's comic art. The more obviously literary earlier works allowed a good deal of slacker writing – passages which, if not padding, are at least leisurely and make their mark through cumulative effect rather than immediate impact. The success of the *fabliau* style and its novelty in English were fully appreciated by Chaucer's immediate successors.[7]

The technique of the comic tales assumes, but never openly states, a standard and a norm which is shared by narrator and audience, and it is in this implicit comparison of the characters and their behaviour with something accepted as normal and desirable that the comedy largely consists. In these tales, this is where the clash of interests and standards comes, not, as in the *Knight's Tale* or the *Troilus*, in the conflicting views of reality held by different characters within the story. In the comic tales, all the characters accept the foibles on which the plot depends in the same way. Their reactions may differ – husbands of erring wives do not view their error in the same light as their lovers do – but they all inhabit the same world, a world in which fraud and cuckoldry are accepted as the norm, and the only valid motto for those possessed of money or wives is *sauve qui peut*. The reader stands with the narrator on the edge of this narrow comic vista and, it is flatteringly assumed, is capable of appreciating other views of reality and of setting the limited comic norm over against one of more universal validity. He is capable, too, of appreciating what is not necessarily apparent to the characters within the tale: the justice and satisfactory fittingness of the denouements. In a work like the *Troilus*, on the other hand, comedy consists in an internal clash of viewpoints which is inherent in the story itself, and the conclusion involves a resolution, not the restoration of a sense of order and decorum temporarily in abeyance.

To press the exclusion of the audience from the tales too far, however, would be to oversimplify. Chaucer's art as a story-teller ensures its involvement as far as continued and vivid interest is concerned, and we cannot say that our sympathies are never engaged. How far and at what point interest passes into sympathy is a delicate matter – the boundary probably comes at a slightly different point for every reader. There is always a moment at which sheer delighted appreciation of the perfection and completeness of the character and situation which develops before our eyes passes into something indistinguishable from sympathy, even though it does not necessarily carry with it acquiescence in the standards of conduct involved. This is, perhaps, most obviously true in the case of that most complex and complete of Chaucer's comic creations, the Wife of Bath. A simpler case is that of Alisoun in the *Miller's Tale*. Taken at its face value, there is certainly nothing sympathetic about her conduct towards either of her lovers. She yields easily to one and helps play a somewhat brutal joke on the other. Moreover, her story consists in nothing but the immediate satisfaction of impulse; it has no reverberations beyond the moment. In Chaucer's hands, however, this is more than enough. Alisoun, like so many of Chaucer's comic characters, absorbs us through the sharpness of the definition; she is herself to a superlative degree:

> There nys no man so wys that koude thenche
> So gay a popelote or swich a wenche.
>
> (*CT* I, 3253–4)

Judging from May's indignant, and unjustified, cry that she is 'a gentil womman and no wenche', this places Alisoun with exactitude.[8] Chaucer develops her portrait through comparisons with birds and young animals:

> But of hir song, it was a loude and yerne
> As any swalwe sittynge on a berne.
> Therto she koude skippe and make game,
> As any kyde or calf folwynge his dame.
> Hir mouth was sweete as bragot or the meeth,
> Or hoord of apples leyd in hey or heeth.
> Wynsynge she was, as is a joly colt,
> Long as a mast, and upright as a bolt.
>
> (*CT* I, 3257–64)

The birds and young animals share the same characteristic of total absorption in their own vigorous and, from the human point of view, quite incalculable life and happiness. Alisoun, by the com-

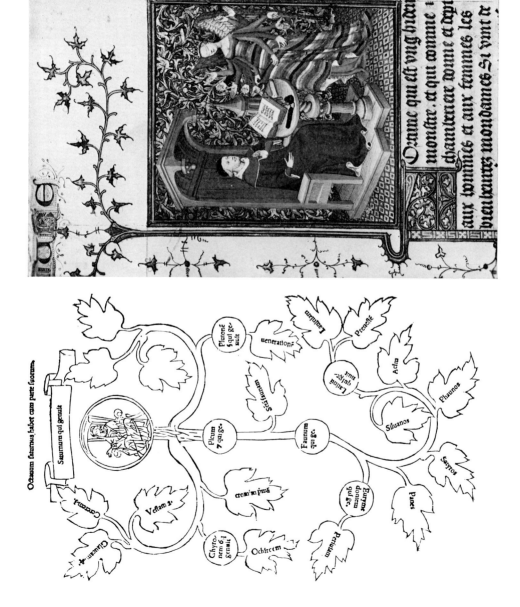

I (*left*) Saturn page of Boccaccio's *de Genealogia Deorum* (Venice, 1497). The blank leaves should contain the names of Juno, Neptune and Jove.

II (*right*) The Poet and Fortune

III   The Marriage of Adam and Eve

parison, is thus invested with a kind of liveliness and also a kind of innocence, which is certainly not centred in the specifically human virtues. This is not quite to say that she is what we should call amoral. It is rather that her conduct is made fully explicable, and in this sense fully 'right', in natural rather than moral terms. Nicholas's wooing of her takes full account of this. He shows his 'subtlety' as a clerk by paying lip-service to a more sophisticated form of love-making (although his words echo popular vernacular lyric rather than the tremulously respectful pleas of a lover like Troilus) :[9]

> And seyde, 'Ywis, but if ich have my wille,
> For deerne love of thee, lemman, I spille'
>
> (3277–8)

and:

> 'Lemman, love me al atones,
> Or I wol dyen, also God me save!'
>
> (3280–1)

But his actions are even less sophisticated:

> And prively he caughte hire by the queynte . . .
>
> (3276)

> And thakked hire aboute the lendes weel . . .
>
> (3304)

Alisoun takes no more notice of his words than the swallow would have done, but reacts predictably to his actions:

> And she sproong, as a colt dooth in the trave,
> And with hir heed she wryed faste awey,
> And seyde, 'I wol nat kisse thee, by my fey!
> Why, lat be,' quod she, 'lat be, Nicholas,
> Or I wol crie "out, harrow" and "allas"!'
>
> (3282–6)

This is, of course, only the prelude to her practical and unemotional consent to

> been at his comandement,
> Whan that she may hir leyser wel espie.
>
> (3292–3)

In the end, when she makes her final contribution –

> 'Tehee!' quod she, and clapte the wyndow to –
>
> (3740)

the intensity of our pleasure in her is in proportion to the unflawed perfection with which she acts out the nature Chaucer has given her. We can say with the narrator:

> This passeth forth; what wol ye bet than weel?
>
> (3370)

In the *Reeve's Tale* the characters are probably even less sympathetic, in any normal sense of the word, than those of the *Miller's Tale*, and the elaborate manœuvres of the communal bedroom scene would be almost too shallow if they were not for a moment brought to life by the reactions of Malkin. She is a plain girl, left unmarried by the haggling methods of her family in the conduct of marriage negotiations (she is twenty; the Wife of Bath, like the young bride of the *Clerk's Tale*, started her married career at twelve; May was eighteen when she married January). Whatever her parents suffer, she, at least, enjoys her night with the clerk and parts with him on the best of terms:[10]

> 'Fare weel, Malyne, sweete wight!
> The day is come, I may no lenger byde;
> But everemo, wher so I go or ryde,
> I is thyn awen clerk, swa have I seel!'
> 'Now, deere lemman,' quod she, 'go, far weel!'
>
> (*CT* I, 4236–40)

And she also, of course, contributes the necessary turn to the plot by gratefully telling him of the whereabouts of the stolen cake.

Even the *Summoner's Tale*, which illustrates his own vice of *ira*,[11] gives us a figure, in the maddening friar, which is made enjoyable and so far, in a sense, sympathetic by the very perfection and completeness of its self-consistency. Every tone of his voice seems to reflect his nature, and his unconscious self-betrayal in a gesture like the putting aside of the cat, which, in the nature of things, would .have been occupying the most comfortable place on the bench, completes the picture:[12]

> '*Deus hic!*' quod he, 'O Thomas, freend, good day!'
> Seyde this frere, curteisly and softe.
> 'Thomas,' quod he, 'God yelde yow! ful ofte
> Have I upon this bench faren ful weel;
> Heere have I eten many a myrie meel.'
> And fro the bench he droof awey the cat,
> And leyde adoun his potente and his hat,
> And eek his scrippe, and sette him softe adoun.
>
> (*CT* III, 1770–7)

The conclusion of this tale is interesting, because in it Chaucer shows us the reaction of an audience placed within the story to the plot enacted in it – and by so doing, suggests, I think, the way in which he intends his own audience to react. Thomas has set the outrageous and insoluble problem of the division of the fart and with it provoked a burst of anger in which the friar appears 'as dooth a wood leoun' (2152). We are then shown the reactions of the 'lord of that village', to whom the story is told. First the lady reacts with fascinated astonishment:

> 'Ey, Goddes mooder,' quod she, 'Blisful mayde!
> Is ther oght elles? telle me feithfully.'
>
> (2202–3)

Then the lord's even greater astonishment is described:

> The lord sat stille as he were in a traunce
> And in his herte he rolled up and doun,
> 'How hadde this cherl ymaginacioun
> To shewe swich a probleme to the frere?
> Nevere erst er now herde I of swich mateere,
> I trowe the devel putte it in his mynde.
> In ars-metrike shal ther no man fynde,
> Biforn this day, of swich a question.'
>
> (2216–23)

The tale, in fact, makes its point on both the internal and the external audiences by the sheer perfection in virtuosity of each of its participants. The begging friar is a prince among his kind. The churl calls forth exclamations of maddened and delighted astonishment at his brilliant improvisation, and the squire, of course, further astonishes and delights the audience by providing a solution even more outrageous than the original insult.

The reactions of an internal audience are important in other tales. In the *Merchant's Tale*, for example, the denouement is played out before the audience of fairy gods as well as the suddenly sighted January. In the *Shipman's Tale* of the young monk who cheats his friend out of his wife and his money, the internal audience is also put to subtle use. It helps to build up and to make at once credible and tolerable this rather dubious ecclesiastic, in that no opportunity is lost of describing his popularity and the effects of his charm on those he meets with. This results in a comic clash of values between what we actually see him doing, and know him to be, and the kind of man the characters in the story think he is.[13]

The *fabliau*, as we have said, depends on an in-built, if rough, sense of justice. The denouement, in which the characters who act with vice or folly are fittingly punished – or, in the case of most of the erring wives, escape punishment by a stroke of superlative wit which brings retribution on their husbands' heads instead – depends on a standard of what is at least socially acceptable being shared by narrator and audience. Thus, in the *Reeve's Tale*, the elaborate build-up concerning the false social aspirations of the miller's family, even more than his actual dishonesty, makes the ending not only poetic, but desired justice; while the pretensions of Absolon and the folly of the carpenter make their somewhat violent punishment at least tolerable. To go beyond this, however, and to apply a sensitive or puritanical scale of moral values to the tales would be as far beside the mark as to dispute the question of *meum* and *tuum* with the swallows Alisoun resembles.

It is, however, another question altogether, as to whether we can regard the tales, within the whole complex of the pilgrimage, as reflecting, or helping to reflect, a view of the world which belongs neither to the individual character who is presented as narrator nor to the individual tale, but to Chaucer himself, whose perceptions are, obviously, a good deal more comprehensive as well as a good deal more sensitive than those of his Miller or Reeve. Here, it seems to me that to press the issue too hard is to destroy the effect of the tales. In the last resort it means turning them into allegory of a curiously ill-managed and unsatisfactory kind.[14] Nevertheless, in trying to define the special nature of Chaucerian comedy, we cannot ignore the fact that in all his purely comic writing he has chosen to set the piece within a framework. He has left us no isolated or entirely self-contained comic poem. This, in fact, seems to bring us very near the heart of Chaucerian comedy. It is not only that, as we have seen, we are imperceptibly lead to play the part of external audience to, rather than participator in, the individual tales: through the organization of the tales within the framework of the *Canterbury Tales* as a whole, we get the effect of comic worlds within worlds, of layers of different perceptiveness, arising from the fact that the tales exist in and for themselves but at the same time reflect, in varying degrees, the minds and limitations (in themselves part of the stuff of comedy) of the tellers. These, in their turn are reflected – together with their tales – in the mirror of the larger audience, of the pilgrims, while we, as final audience, through all the devices of Chaucerian description and presentation, are inevitably drawn into the position of the final mirror of all.

More than this, the comic tales are an inextricable part of a series which includes the serious and 'noble' tales. They are only more closely linked to the special characteristics of their tellers because comedy, as we have seen, gains from particularization, while tragedy does not. It is for this reason, I think, rather than because of greater maturity in his art or any change in purpose in the *Canterbury Tales*, that Chaucer exploits the individual characteristics and foibles of the pilgrims more fully in the comic tales than elsewhere.[15] Here the character of Harry Bailey, the Host, is important. His reactions to the tales and tellers emphasizes their precise position within the whole. He has an unfailing appreciation of order and degree. His submission to the authority of the Knight is unquestioning, and he shows more delicacy in his approach to the Prioress than some of her modern critics. He has, also, an unfailing flair for the order of disrespect. His reaction to the Pardoner is crucial, and he strikes exactly the right note for the sub-comedy of the pilgrim Chaucer. He has an equally unfailing zest in his praise and disparise of the entertainment provided, and the very naïvety of his reactions – always to the content in the most superficial sense, never to the art of the tales – enhances the comedy, in the case of the humorous tales, by helping to pin-point the special comic involvement of the teller through his pet vice or cherished misfortune;[16] and also gives a wider perspective to some of the serious ones. His extravagant reaction to the pathos of the *Physician's Tale*:

> Oure Hooste gan to swere as he were wood;
> 'Harrow!' quod he, 'by nayles and by blood!'
>
> (*CT* VI, 287–8)

should at least give us to think before we dismiss it as a rather colour-less and characterless example of Chaucer's art. It would seem that here, as, perhaps, in the *Clerk's Tale*, Chaucer is relying on a sensi-bility which we do not altogether share with his age.[17] There is no more reason to reject the validity of the Host's reaction here than there is to reject his appreciation of the Knight. Nevertheless, the form it takes is vulgar and exaggerated, and there is no doubt that his impassioned championship of Virginia does bring her pathetic fate within the confines of the comic world. I do not think that, through this somewhat subtle manœuvre, Chaucer invalidates the pathos of the tale or calls its internal values in serious question. He merely once more demonstrates – and this is the essence of comedy – that there is more than one way of looking at a thing and, through the very fervour of the simple Host's undiscriminating agreement, suggests the possibility of a different reaction.

The Host is not, however, the only means of achieving this interweaving of the comic and serious in the *Canterbury Tales*. Nor is he the only literary critic. Just as he puts a stop to the in-tolerable din of Chaucer's own drasty rhyming, so the Knight, like Theseus in a similarly unbearable situation, calls 'Ho' and puts a stop to the Monk's depressing flood of tragedies. The effect, like that of the Host's overexuberant appreciation of the *Physician's Tale*, is again to bring the tales into juxtaposition with another viewpoint. The Knight, too, has to act as mediator between the Pardoner and the Host and is thus involved, as is the Parson, in a clash with some of the characters of comedy.[18] The Clerk, in spite of the serious nature of his tale, ends with a humorous reference to the Wife of Bath; and we are made vividly aware of the 'gentles' as part of the audience of the more outrageous tales when they all protest in chorus against the kind of tale they fear the Pardoner is about to tell, or share in the laughter produced by the Miller's 'nyce cas'. In the same way,

after the *Prioress's Tale*, which is perfectly serious and perfectly
seriously received:

> Whan seyd was al this miracle, every man
> As sobre was that wonder was to se
>
> (*CT* VII, 691–2)

the silence is broken by the Host's return to a jesting mood.

The choice of tale for teller is at times used as another means of
producing this kind of juxtaposition and interpenetration of the comic
and the serious. The Man of Law, the Physician and the Franklin
are all presented as having their share of folly, if not vice; that is, they
are typical figures of comedy. Yet they tell fundamentally serious
tales. The *Franklin's Tale* is perhaps not entirely serious: there is
incipient comedy in the exuberance with which it treats the important virtue it exemplifies. Dorigen and her husband are extravagantly
honourable: Dorigen could not normally be considered bound by
a promise whose fulfilment would involve her in the sin of adultery.
Nevertheless, it is a gracious story, graciously told, and I think that
to see it as a parody of courtliness is to underrate it grossly. In the
Man of Law's Tale, Chaucer may occasionally smile at the conflicts
with which saintliness at large in the world is inevitably faced –
whether in bed or in those situations, so common to heroines of this
kind, in which would-be ravishers are repelled with uncompromising
violence.[19] Chaucer, indeed, treats with unqualified approval
the god-sent 'vigour' of Constance, when she pushes the 'renegat'
overboard to his death. The only hint of any other point of view
lies in the elaboration of the rhetoric with which he praises it;
and I think that this is here to be taken at its face-value.[20]

In the case of the Wife of Bath, Chaucer seems first to have
planned to give her a tale (which we know as the Shipman's)
typical of the kind of marital strategy sketched out by La Vieille
in the *Roman de la Rose*. There is no doubt that it was a good second
thought by which he gave her a story which has an element of
romance as well as *fabliau* and which, while it certainly develops
the view of woman as dominating over man by her wit (which the
Wife shares with La Vieille), also has room for serious themes like
that of patient poverty and true gentility.[21] This helps to fill out
the impression we have of her through her Prologue – an impression
which is immeasurably more complex than that of Jean de Meun's
Vieille.

93

Another method of linking the comic to the serious is by the juxtaposition of the tales themselves, irrespective of the tellers. In the absence of Chaucer's final order, it is not easy to say how much use he intended to make of this method. In the groups which we can accept with most probability, we have some extreme contrasts like that between the *Shipman's* and the *Prioress's Tales*. This transition is made without emphasis by the Host:

> 'But now passe over, and lat us seke aboute,
> Who shal now telle first of al this route
> Another tale.'
>
> (*CT* VII, 442–4)

In this, as in other cases, Chaucer seems quite content to allow free play to the principle of variety and contrast, which his choice of the frame mechanism ensures. There is, however, one case in which he himself seems to direct us to read the two contrasting tales together. This is the case of the *Knight's* and the *Miller's Tales*, which are elaborately linked. The Host calls on the Monk as a proper person to provide something to 'quite with' the *Knight's Tale* but is interrupted by the drunken Miller who, echoing the praise of the Knight's 'noble storie' offers a 'noble tale' of his own 'With which I wol now quite the Knyghtes tale' (*CT* I, 3127). Since the meaning of 'quite' here is obviously 'be a return or equivalent for, to balance' (*OED* II, 11, c.), the Miller is offering his story as in some way directly comparable to the Knight's. It is obvious, as we read, that the equivalence is indeed fully worked out in the tale, as most commentators have pointed out.[22] We have the pair of lovers – perhaps with the significant reversal that, while it is the man of action who fails to win the lady in the *Knight's Tale*, in the *Miller's Tale* Nicholas, who is as 'sodeyn' as Diomede, is more successful than the gentler parish clerk Absolon. We also have the lady who, unlike Emely, is perfectly ready to cope with a love affair; and the astrological pretensions of Nicholas, which provide an important part of the plot machinery, replace the epic machinery of the planet-gods in the *Knight's Tale*. There is even the significant verbal echo of the line 'Allone, withouten any compaignye' (*CT* I, 3204) which, in the *Knight's Tale*, is movingly used of Arcite's death, but in the *Miller's Tale* is used to indicate a gap in Nicholas's life shortly to be filled by Alisoun.

Some critics have gone so far as to see in all this a straightforward parody of the *Knight's Tale*. This, I think, is to impoverish our understanding of both tales. It is, surely, rather that, having whole-heartedly, and certainly without the slightest poetic reservation, given us a poem which embodies everything that is most noble and most profound in the poetry of his day in the *Knight's Tale* – but always, we must remember, with that leavening of the heroic tone which Theseus continually introduces – Chaucer now chooses to show us how a superficially similar arrangement can be handled to totally different effect, as well as how a totally different perception of life can have its own validity. He has already indicated as much in his treatment of the different types of birds and their contrasting viewpoints in the *Parlement of Foules*. It is now as if he actually showed us the love story of the noble birds re-enacted by a troop of ducks. There is no doubt that we emerge from the experience of plunging out of the *Knight's Tale* into the *Miller's Tale* with our understanding of the themes of both much enriched, but the enrich-ment comes from the perception of difference as well as from a pleasant apprehension of sameness under differing disguises. We do not really think that the nobility of Palemoun and Arcite is debased by the comparison, though we may feel that their undoubted moments of folly are pointed up. But our chief gain, I think, is insight into the way in which Nature crams the world full of differing creatures, whose difference tends to find its most common ground at the point where Nature and Venus join hands to work out their plan for even further increase, until

> erthe, and eyr, and tre, and every lake
> So ful was that unethe was there space
> For me to stonde, so ful was al the place.
> (*Parlement*, 313–15)

It is, of course, true that human beings, even more than the birds, tend to abuse Nature's laws and that not all their manœuvres help to fulfil her plan. Nevertheless, even these deviations can be seen as an expression of her infinite variety. If there is any moral in the juxtaposition of the *Knight's* and the *Miller's Tales*, it seems to me to lie more in this direction than in that of a heavy-handed comment on the noble, but not always strictly practical, flights of heroical love. The latter, we must also remember, do yet culminate in a

95

marriage in strict accordance with Nature's mandates, while, ironically, the uncomplicated lovers of the *Miller's Tale* never get beyond an adulterous union which is, from Nature's point of view, disruptive and useless.

So far, in considering Chaucerian comedy, we have seen characterization handled in various ways and on various levels, but always subordinated to plot. In three cases Chaucer does something different and shifts the emphasis from the telling of the tale to the presentation of the character. In each case this results in a new synthesis of prologue, or links, and tale. These three cases are those of the Pardoner, the Wife of Bath and the Mal Marié, January, in the *Merchant's Tale*, which has its own internal prologue. Each of these is differently developed, but they have this in common: they are all derived from stock figures of earlier satirical or comic genres. The Wife of Bath, as, again, has often been pointed out, follows closely in the steps of La Vieille, in the *Roman de la Rose*, who is herself a stock figure of anti-feminist writing.[23] January has affinities with *fabliau*, but he is also closely modelled on another figure of the anti-feminist tradition, Jean de Meun's Le Jaloux.[24] The Pardoner stands alone, in that his development as a character is not connected with any wider thematic development. The figures of the Wife of Bath and of January are so inextricably involved in the marriage theme that their discussion in full must be held over to chapter 4.

The Pardoner, as has often been pointed out, has clear affinities with the kind of self-revealing and self-describing vice figures common in allegorical writing.[25] In particular, Chaucer has borrowed much from the confessions of Faux Semblant in the *Roman de la Rose*.[26] Characters of this kind are often made into ecclesiastical hangers-on. Langland, for example, gives his Fals and Favel, figures belonging to the same tradition, an ecclesiastical-legal retinue.[27]

In the nature of things, figures of this kind are neither sensitively nor naturalistically treated in the kinds of writing to which, traditionally, they belong. The allegorical vice figure, indeed, needs no sympathy. It is a self-contained, self-conditioned entity, operating according to the laws of its nature with perfect self-satisfaction.[28] Any mitigating circumstances or softening traits would merely destroy the allegorical meaning. Falsehood can be conquered or replaced by Truth, but it cannot become less false and still remain a convincing part of the allegory. The convention by which such figures describe their own characteristics is firmly entrenched as a normal part of the machinery of allegorical satire. Such confessions do not need either motivation or excuse. They are merely a part of the exposition. Thus Langland, for example, may give some air of probability to his self-characterizing vices by using the general framework of the confessional; but he has no hesitation in departing from this frame whenever it suits him – giving, for example, actions as well as words to Glutton, or allowing the confessions to become cheerful descriptions of activities quite satisfactory to the confessing figures, as in the case of Avarice, who evades all Conscience's efforts to bring him to a state of contrition. There is little or no satire involved in the presentation of figures of this kind, and comedy only arises through their grotesqueness and through their obvious deviation from what is normally acceptable.

Anyone who reads through fragment C of the Chaucerian translation of the *Roman de la Rose*,[29] which contains most of the confession of Faux Semblant, will see that, although there is an obvious relationship between this hypocrite who prefers ecclesiastical disguise, and whose only devotion is to money, and the Pardoner who interprets the dictum 'Radix malorum est cupiditas' in an original way, to imply that vice exists only to be exploited for his own profit, there are also important differences. In the *Roman*, the figure of Faux Semblant is manipulated so as to serve two main purposes. There is a pleasing irony in the fact that the love story, on whose thread Jean de Meun keeps a firm hold in spite of all his digressions, is advanced by the strangling of Slander by Hypocrisy and False (i.e., pretended) Abstinence. The God of Love, like Venus in the *Parlement of Foules*, employs some dubious servants – in this case, one whose character is so sinister that, Jean seems to imply, his acceptance by Love amounts to an act of self-destruction, as the following exchange shows:

'Wolt thou wel holden my forwardis?'
'Ye, sir, from hennes forwardis;
Hadde never youre fadir heere-biforn
Servaunt so trewe, sith he was born.'
'That is ayenes all nature.'
'Sir, putte you in that aventure.
For though ye borowes take of me,
The sikerer shal ye never be

> For ostages, ne sikirnesse,
> Or chartres, for to bere witnesse.
> I take youresilf to recorde heere,
> That men ne may in no manere
> Teren the wolf out of his hide,
> Til he be flayn, bak and side,
> Though men hym bete and al defile.
> What! wene ye that I nil begile
> For I am clothed mekely?
> Ther-undir is all my trechery;
> Myn herte chaungith never the mo
> For noon abit in which I go.'
>
> (C, 7301–20)

This speech gives us a very exact definition of the allegorical vice figure. Such a figure is, obviously, an important part of Jean de Meun's satirical technique. Faux Semblant exists not merely to advance the story by his actions and reactions, but to help lay out a body of material which, branching out from the problems of the particular kind of love involved in the story of L'Amant and the Rose, includes the topical question of new and dangerous beliefs and movements among the co-called Béguins and Joachimite Friars,[30] as well as much general criticism of hypocrisy, with special, though not exclusive, reference to the clergy.

Chaucer has little to do with either purpose. The *Pardoner's Prologue* and *Tale* have nothing to do with love, and the topic of popular religious movements is not one that touches him. Langland is still concerned over the debate about religious poverty, but for Chaucer the tag phrase 'patient poverty' means something different.[31] He is not interested, either, in Jean de Meun's manning of the university barricades.[32] What does interest him is the figure itself, and the way in which it enthusiastically exposes its own nature so as to both shock and titillate the audience. The reaction of Love and his barons to Faux Semblant's revelations is reasonably polite:

> The god lough at the wondir tho,
> And every wight gan laugh also,
> And seide, 'Lo, heere a man aright
> For to be trusty to every wight!'
>
> (C, 7293–6)

They show, however, something of the same mixture of outrage and amusement with which the Host and the Knight, between them, finally silence the Pardoner, in the course of which the Host at least is far from polite:

> 'Now,' quod oure Hoost, 'I wol no lenger pleye
> With thee, ne with noon oother angry man.'
> But right anon the worthy Knyght bigan,
> Whan that he saugh that al the peple lough,
> 'Namoore of this, for it is right ynough!
> Sire Pardoner, be glad and myrie of cheere;
> And ye, sire Hoost, that been to me so deere,
> I prey yow that ye kisse the Pardoner.
> And Pardoner, I prey thee, drawe thee neer,
> And, as we diden, lat us laughe and pleye.'
> Anon they kiste, and ryden forth hir weye.
>
> (*CT* VI, 958–68)

The difference is that, where the reactions of Love and his barons underlines the idea which the allegory expresses – that is, of the inevitable relation of evil things to love of this kind – the Host and Knight react in an individual way to a particular situation which has arisen through the behaviour of another individual. In fact, much as he owes to a method developed for allegorical exposition, Chaucer's approach is fundamentally a naturalistic one. How far he has succeeded in reconciling these two opposing techniques in the Pardoner's case, has always been a matter for debate among critics.

Faux Semblant and the Pardoner have in common an enthusiasm in self-exposure which, as we have said, is an accepted convention in the case of the vice figure and which passes smoothly enough for motivation in the case of the more realistically conceived character. Faux Semblant, commanded by Love to describe his way of life, says:

> 'I shal don youre comaundement,
> For therto have I gret talent.'
>
> (C, 6133–4)

The Pardoner's enthusiasm is more subtly indicated, but we are left in no doubt that he shares the pleasure he confidently expects his audience to feel, as he describes how:

> 'Myne handes and my tonge goon so yerne
> That it is joye to se my bisyness, . . .'
>
> (*CT* VI, 398–9)

and he asserts that no reasonable man could fail to be pleased with his performance:

> 'By God, I hope I shal yow telle a thyng
> That shal by reson been at youre likyng.'
>
> (457–8)

There is a difference, however, between the Pardoner's claim to success and popularity and Faux Semblant's pleasure in fulfilling his allegorical destiny. The fact that both figures are, according to the kind to which they belong, treated with subtlety, only points up the difference. Faux Semblant is not mechanically handled. He is shown approaching Love with fear and shame-facedness:

> 'But Fals-Semblant dar not, for drede
> Of you, sir, medle hym of this dede,
> For he seith that ye ben his foo;
> He not if ye wole worche hym woo.'
>
> (C, 6049–52)

It is only when he is sure of a place at Love's court, as 'kyng of harlotes', that he is able to give expression to his true nature. This is convincing both in terms of the personification, which is given added liveliness by its doubts and hesitations, and of the allegorical argument. In allegorical terms, it is only when it has been established that the dubious practices to be described are an essential part of the kind of love story on which L'Amant is embarked, that they can fall into place within the structure of the exposition. Love's doubtful behaviour then runs parallel to, and in some sort reflects, the behaviour of the world at large, and the satire widens out to include issues which have little to do with love. In the case of the religious deviants, however, there is, no doubt, a particularly savage irony in the fact that the most common accusations against them were of sexual licence of a kind which throws a lurid light on the apparently gentle love story of the *Roman*. Much of the savage mood of Chaucer's *Merchant's Tale* is to be found in the *Roman*, not only in the more obviously satirical digressions, but also as an ineradicable element in the main plot – the story of Love pursued in defiance of Reason and in doubtful accord with Nature.[33]

But naturalism is not the method by which this very complex ordering of the material can be achieved, and Faux Semblant, for all his liveliness, remains a purely allegorical figure. At times he seems to split up, and we hear of a whole troop of deceivers, referred to as 'we', who carry out activities obviously too extensive for a single one – for example:

> 'Another custome use we:
> Of hem that wole ayens us be,
> We hate hem deedly everichon,
> And we wole werrey hem, as oon.'
>
> (C, 6923–6)

He shifts his dress, occupation, and even sex:

> 'For Protheus, that cowde hym chaunge
> In every shap, homly and straunge,
> Cowde nevere sich gile ne tresoun
> As I; for I com never in toun
> There as I myghte knowen be,
> Though men me bothe myght here and see.
> Full wel I can my clothis chaunge,
> Take oon, and make another straunge.
> Now am I knyght, now chasteleyn,
> Now prelat and now chapeleyn. . . .
> Somtyme a wommans cloth take I;
> Now am I a mayde, now lady.'
>
> (C, 6319–46)

The description of his dwelling is significant. It is a purely allegorical palace, not meant to be visualized in the ordinary way, but not without iconographical significance:

'My paleis and myn hous make I
There men may renne ynne openly,
And sey that I the world forsake,
But al amydde I bilde and make
My hous, and swimme and pley therynne,
Bet than a fish doth with his fynne.'
(C, 7003–8)

We are inevitably reminded of the common depiction of Luxuria swimming in the sea.[34]

The end of the passage brings us back, in a particularly skilful way, to the bones of the allegory. We are always aware that we are not watching an autonomous character in a story, but are learning, through the brilliant series of images, something about love. The more 'digressive' parts of Faux Semblant's confession shows us that Love is only part of a tangled web of human behaviour, operating through every aspect of life. The conclusion then returns to love in the narrower sense of L'Amant's pursuit of the Rose and shows it voluntarily, if blindly, involving itself with a dangerously destructive force. Or, to put it another way, 'the blinde lust', although it is potentially allied to Nature and can have its creative aspects, is all too likely to prove a destructive power. After all the ironies and ambiguities, Jean de Meun's conclusion leaves no room for doubt:

And Love answerde, 'I truste thee
Withoute borowe, for I wole noon.'
And Fals-Semblant, the theef, anoon,
Ryght in that ilke same place,
That hadde of tresoun al his face
Ryght blak withynne and whit withoute,
Thankyng hym, gan on his knees loute.
(C, 7328–34)

It is obvious that Chaucer approaches the figure of the Pardoner in a totally different way, although he uses many of the same devices to lay out his self-revelation. The initial reluctance of Faux Semblant, which serves as a warning of what is to come, is transferred to the more respectable part of the Pardoner's audience. He himself shows no reluctance to come forward. The gentils express it for him:

> But right anon thise gentils gonne to crye,
> 'Nay, lat hym telle us of no ribaudye!
> Telle us som moral thyng, that we may leere
> Som wit, and thanne wol we gladly heere.'
>
> (*CT* VI, 323–6)

This is a deliberate reminder of the figure presented to us in the General Prologue, certainly one of the most disreputable among the pilgrims and, moreover, set apart from them by his physical characteristics:

> A voys he hadde as smal as hath a goot.
> No berd hadde he, ne nevere sholde have;
> As smothe it was as it were late shave.
> I trowe he were a geldyng or a mare.
>
> (*CT* I, 688–91)

Chaucer does not re-emphasize this disability in any way which might be unacceptable to the gentle part of the audience until the end of the Pardoner's self-exposure, when he returns to it in no uncertain terms by pitting the Pardoner against Harry Bailey, the Host. The Host, as we have seen, acts, in many ways, as the norm for his section of the community, just as the Knight does for his and the Parson for the third, clerical, estate, Harry Bailey, the plain man, has his disadvantages as well as his advantages and can certainly not be taken as expressing standards which are Chaucer's own. As a literary critic, as we have seen, he knows what he likes and has a flair for the inept comment. His reaction to his fellow men is also a simple one, in so far as it is not restrained by the politeness due to the orders definitely above him. Confronted by a male, his mind runs on masculinity of an obvious kind. His remarks on the appearance of the Monk (and perhaps of the Nun's Priest)[35] are to the point:

> 'Thou woldest han been a tredefowel aright.
> Haddestow as greet a leeve, as thou hast myght,
> To parfourne al thy lust in engendrure,
> Thou haddest bigeten many a creature.
> Allas, why werestow so wyd a cope?'
>
> (*CT* VII, 1945–9)

He would certainly have approved of L'Amant's attitude to Nature's endowments in the *Roman*. The Pardoner, unfortunately, is not in a position to share L'Amant's enthusiasm, and the Host harps mercilessly on this theme in his angry rejection of the Pardoner's invitation to be the first to kiss his relics. The whole ending, by which the Pardoner's discourse merges into the link by being interrupted, rather than concluded, by the heated comments of the Host[36] and the hasty peacemaking of the Knight, is brilliantly contrived to expose the Pardoner, not as he sees himself – he has already done this – but as he really is. It leaves him as a personality which, for all his dubious friendship with the Summoner, cannot win popularity from the Harry Baileys of his world (the world of the gentles is, of course, utterly closed to him). Chaucer builds up this section on the basis of the Pardoner's attempt to conquer this difficult part of his audience through a personal attack on the Host, aimed either at his subjugation or at the turning of the rest decisively against him by making him a laughing stock:

> 'Looke which a seuretee is it to yow alle
> That I am in youre felaweshipe yfalle,
> That may assoille yow, bothe moore and lasse,
> Whan that the soule shal fro the body passe.
> I rede that oure Hoost heere shal bigynne,
> For he is moost envoluped in synne.
> Com forth, sire Hoost, and offre first anon,
> And thou shalt kisse the relikes everychon,
> Ye, for a grote! Unbokele anon thy purs.'
>
> (*CT* VI, 937–45)

Then comes the Host's ruthless and accurate counterattack, followed by the almost disproportionate intensity of the Pardoner's reaction, after the supreme self-confidence of his confessions:

> This Pardoner answerde nat a word;
> So wrooth he was, no word ne wolde he seye.
>
> (956–7)

This sudden reversal of his euphoric mood brings home to us the reality of his problem of gaining appreciation and recognition. Finally, the Host's contemptuous dismissal:

'I wol no lenger pleye
With thee, ne with noon oother angry man.'

(958–9)

confirms the total failure of his attempt. Far from winning over his
audience to laugh with him, they are now united against him:
'al the peple lough'. The Knight's intervention to resolve a situation
which has become a serious threat to the good order of the pilgrimage further emphasizes the explosive quality of this strange
eruption of feeling. The whole episode clearly points up the difference
between the Pardoner and Faux Semblant. Faux Semblant is
only describing the nature of those things which he symbolizes.
His confessions cannot arouse personal feeling. An occasional
expression of outraged amusement from his audience is the most
that can be allowed; and this is only a device to break up his
speeches and enliven the discourse by giving it the semblance of
dialogue. In the case of the Pardoner, we are shown, by the final
clash with the Host, the fundamental cleavage between his view of
the world and that of his audience, as well as a subtle distinction
between his view of his own evil-doing – frank as it is – and that of
an unsympathetic on-looker.

To overemphasize the Pardoner's lack of normal masculinity
and its social consequences would be misleading. We must not
introduce twentieth-century perceptiveness or twentieth-century
tolerance into a comic situation which, in the main, depends on
the assumption of medieval ideas about the *eunuchus ex nativitate*.[37]
We cannot, however, ignore Chaucer's own deliberate confrontation
of the two characters whom he has caused to stand for an almost
aggressively normal masculinity and its equally obvious lack.
To see the whole nature and problem of the Pardoner, and his
special needs and reactions, as the carefully worked out result of
his deviation from the physical norm would be to saddle Chaucer
with preoccupations which he almost certainly does not have.
Besides the *eunuchus ex nativitate*, he shows us a go-getter, a successful
huckster, a man dominated by a vanity which makes it impossible
for him to believe that others do not, at bottom, share his view of life.
All these characteristics help to provide a naturalistic motivation
for the extravagance of his frankness about himself. This kind of
motivation is, of course, never needed for the confessions of personifications like Faux Semblant, but the way in which the character

of the Pardoner is worked up suggests that Chaucer was well aware that, in borrowing the self-revelatory device proper to the allegorical vice for a figure conceived in naturalistic terms, much care was needed in providing a measure of probability for the confession. Like the corresponding vice figure, the Pardoner is aware of the virtue which, as it were, stands opposite to him; but, unlike the vice figure, he sees this as a part of the justification of his own cleverness. His acknowledgement of the falseness of his own pardons, and his brazen admission of his understanding of where truth really lies, comes as the crowning stroke to the whole confidence trick:

> 'I yow assoille, by myn heigh power,
> Yow that wol offre, as clene and eek as cleer
> As ye were born. – And lo, sires, thus I preche.
> And Jhesu Crist, that is oure soules leche,
> So graunte yow his pardoun to receyve,
> For that is best; I wol yow nat deceyve.'
>
> (913–18)

This is, too, the justification of the violence of the Host's reaction. Like Faux Semblant, the Pardoner has no redeeming features – unless, seeing him as a figure of comedy rather than of satire, we take into account his supremacy in life and vigour. But, while the fact that Love, the personification, admits Faux Semblant to his retinue, in spite of the knowledge that he is 'Right blak withinne and whit withoute', gives us information about love as an idea, the fact that the pilgrims do not accept the Pardoner on such easy terms, and do not share his view either of himself or of the world, gives us information about him, and them, as individuals. That they see in him cause for laughter, extends his impotence from the physical to the moral sphere – a sphere in which Faux Semblant is, of course, effective.

Faux Semblant shares with the Pardoner knowledge of the good whose rejection is a condition of his own existence. It is an essential part of the method of the satire that he should refer to the 'cursedness' and 'orribilite' of the Joachimite work which the good clerks of Paris expose, even while he still refers to it as 'our book', and remarks sadly:

> 'But hadde that ilke book endured,
> Of better estat I were ensured.'
>
> (C, 7209–10)

In the same way he speaks frankly about the good Christian's opposition to him and to his works:

> 'But he in Cristis wrath hym ledith,
> That more than Crist my britheren dredith.
> He nys no full good champioun,
> That dredith such simulacioun,
> Nor that for peyne wole refusen
> Us to correcte and accusen
> He wole not entremete by right,
> Ne have God in his eye-sight,
> And therfore God shal hym punyshe.'
>
> (C, 7225–33)

This kind of double vision is a fundamental part of Jean de Meun's satiric method and is, indeed, common to most vice figures. They tend to inhabit a world in which they automatically call into being their opposites and exist as the half of a kind of double image. Thus, most self-exposés contain warnings against the vice involved and reminders of the fate which will result from indulgence in it.[38] For medieval allegorical satirists, in fact, the idea that evil is the absence of good is ever present. To present vice without showing that it is only the attendant shadow of the corresponding virtue is unacceptable. In the Pardoner's case, however, the success of his trickery depends on his own appreciation of the reality for which he offers a shoddy substitute. If pardon for sin were not a reality for which mankind craved, it would not be possible for him to batten on their need. The result is something much more shocking than is the portrait of a Faux Semblant which teaches intellectual understanding of truth by the method of opposites.

Much of our understanding of the Pardoner and of his situation comes from his contacts with his fellow pilgrims at the beginning and end of his 'sermon'. But, by a skilful stroke, Chaucer extends the revelation through the discourse. All that the Pardoner says, in the introductory section on swearing and gluttony, and in the tale of the search for death (one of the most effectively constructed in the whole series), adds up to 'an honest thyng'. It is thus not only that the Pardoner condemns himself through his direct version of the way in which, like the wicked who ask Fame to grant that they be known as wicked, he would like to be regarded. He also, inexorably and at length, gives full expression to values which are the reverse of those he himself holds and which, if he were an allegorical vice personification, would belong to his better half. The whole complex – prologue, introduction, tale and end-link – is designed as a whole, rounded and complete, and Chaucer achieves this result by taking over and adapting in an extremely subtle way the methods of allegorical satire. The result, although the tendency is certainly towards a naturalistic conception of character, is still, perhaps, not wholly naturalistic. Chaucer has not quite bridged the gap between the kind of presentation in which the confession can be accepted as a necessary and inevitable part of the exposition and that in which it needs a motivation in keeping with the laws of probability. In his treatment of the other two figures which are derived from the stock types of allegorical satire – the Wife of Bath and January – he is able to solve the problem more completely, largely because the figures can take their *raison d'être* from their close involvement with the marriage theme. This gives them both a convincing environment and good reason for all they say and do.[39]

Chaucerian comedy has, typically, little in common with romantic comedy, if we can take the latter as characteristically involving the audience sympathetically with the characters and action. His method is, rather, to present us with typical individuals – that is, with figures which are not so particularized as to stand quite apart from the class or sub-section of society to which they belong, but which are also far from standing only for a type or class – who, through folly, eccentricity, out-and-out vice or even (in the Pardoner's case) physical abnormality, are at odds with an accepted and socially desirable norm. These he develops by all possible methods: detailed description; self-revelation within and without the tales; reaction to and from other individuals. At the same time he establishes the norm partly through characters who are not foolish, wicked or in any other way obviously abnormal (we have noticed that he gives us, significantly, one for each order of society – the Knight and Parson, who may be taken as providing absolute standards; and the Host, who has the cruder and more limited, but still sound, approach of his part of the social order) – and partly by oblique reference or even significant absence of reference, which helps to establish the importance of the observer, in whose function the reader is made to share and whose view of the world is always a wider one than that of the comic characters.

We cannot, I think, say of the spirit of Chaucerian comedy that it is especially kindly. This is hardly the epithet for the rough justice of broken arms and heads or 'scalding in the tout'. The illusion of a wide tolerance, too, surely arises mainly from the obliqueness of the narrator's comments and in part from a connoisseur's delight in the surpassing excellence of the specimens under the microscope. Chaucer's praise of the steed of brass in the *Squire's Tale*, that it 'was so horsly', could, *mutatis mutandis*, be applied to most of the pilgrims. There are, it is true, the moments of understanding of the most unpromising characters – Malkin's pleasure in her clerk; the Wife of Bath's momentary loss of confidence when she remembers her age; the appreciation of May's predicament in bed with January – but, by and large, Chaucer treats his characters with an open-eyed consistency in which justice is the ruling principle. In the case of the Pardoner, his eyes are perhaps even too widely open for modern taste. Yet Chaucer's comedy, with all this, is never inhuman; there is never any suggestion of a mere mechanical casting up of accounts in which everyone gets their true deserts. Probably the best summing up on the characters of his comic world is that of a poet writing near his own time:[40]

> It seemith vnto mannys heerynge
> Not only the word but verely the thing.

4

The *Canterbury Tales*: major themes

To show in detail how all the recurring themes, major and minor, are worked out in the *Canterbury Tales* would require a line-by-line reading and cross-referencing; and, in the process, there would be some danger that the integrity and effectiveness of the tales themselves would be lost sight of. This, after all, is the great achievement of the *Canterbury Tales*: that while it is true, as T. W. Craik puts it, 'that the story itself, *as* story, has a personality of its own',[1] yet it is still essential, if we are to appreciate the full force and the many dimensions of Chaucerian poetry, to read the series as a whole. There is danger if we are too forcible in disengaging ideas and themes from their context within a tale; but, on the other hand, the tales lose in depth of meaning if we fail to realize that they are often involved in a thematic development which extends beyond their individual context.

The method here will, therefore, be to take only a few major themes – those of Fortune and free will; of marriage in relation to Nature, and to order and disorder; of the nobleness of man – and to try to show their place both in the achievement of the individual tales in which they are important and in the development of the series as a whole. All these themes have already been discussed in relation to poems outside the Canterbury group and, within it, to the *Knight's Tale*. They form a closely related nexus, or, rather, they are part of a philosophically consistent way of looking at the world. There is, first, the fundamental theme of order *versus* disorder, which we have already seen as the leading one of the *Knight's Tale*. Order partakes of the nature of the One, perfect, stable, eternal, and is therefore directly ruled over by God. Disorder, on the other hand, partakes of the nature of multiplicity, instability and impermanence – all characteristics of the created world below the moon, which becomes more and more imperfect the further it is removed from the One from which it takes its being. The world below the moon is subject to Fortune and, in close association with Fortune, to the planets. These have power delegated to them from the One, as does Nature. Nature symbolizes the divine purpose of achieving a modicum of order out of the disorder of the world, so far removed from the perfection from which it originally sprang. But it is the very perfection of the originating One which ensures the infinite variety of Nature. Nature, therefore, while she works for order, also works with Venus, natural sexual passion, to bring about the continued propagation of the whole gamut of creatures. In the case of mankind, however, Venus all too often goes astray, divorces herself from Nature and nullifies her plan by making passion barren. Man, in fact, occupies a key position in the world of change. On the one hand, he can spoil the order which the divine plan is always working to introduce into its multiplicity. On the other, because, unlike any other creature, he is made in the image of the One, he has a potential for order far beyond any other of Nature's charges. If man is considered from the point of view of this key position in the natural world, marriage becomes the point at which he is able to exert the greatest force in either direction – for order or disorder. This is because it is through marriage that mankind achieves its fullest expression and perfection in the natural order – as Langland puts it, mankind is incomplete unless it develops into a trinity of man–wife–child.[2] Through the negation of marriage – the refusal to allow this trinity to come into being – mankind can bring about the maximum disruption in the natural order. It must, of course, be emphasized (although Langland goes pretty far in his parallelism of the human and divine trinities) that this is not the only possible way of looking at man. Yet to see man as the turning point in the natural order, by means of his direct link with the originating One, bypassing, as it were, all the descending hierarchies and so becoming the means of a fulfilment in perfection otherwise denied to Nature, is certainly to give him no insignificant position in the universe.

As far as individuals are concerned, this means that, for good, the emphasis is on the 'noble' man or woman, created in God's image and behaving 'gentilly'. In the case of women, the ideal is the good wife, 'womanly' and not 'mannish wood', who acts as an influence for order both in her husband's affairs and in the affairs of nations. On the opposite side, motivated not by love but by 'the blinde lust', we have mankind in pursuit of all the deadly sins, but especially of the violation of marriage either through direct adultery or through the barren and fleeting love outside marriage which brings with it strife and jealousy, sickness of mind and body, and every sort of disorder. This is the picture we are shown, above all, in the *Knight's Tale* and which underlies the *Canterbury Tales* as a whole.

In the *Knight's Tale* the major themes are formally presented, through the deliberate patterning of the story and through passages which are explicitly philosophical. This method of presentation is balanced by the equally formal methods, in another mode, of the *Parson's Tale*. But in between, the method is often quite different, and it is here, in tales like the Miller's and the Reeve's, the Pardoner's and the Nun's Priest's, that, if we try to see the total meaning of the *Canterbury Tales* as equally present in every part, we shall seriously distort the nature of Chaucer's art. In fact, instead of giving us the comparatively systematic exposition of ideas and themes of, for example, Langland or Jean de Meun, Chaucer places us within a world where such ideas are ruling principles, whose presence or absence is an important factor in the lives of the people who inhabit it. Unlike the allegorists, Chaucer handles his themes naturalistically, as Shakespeare was to do in drama and Henry James in the novel. Langland utilizes the basically non-naturalistic convention of allegory, which always follows a logic of its own and which can, at any given moment, cut straight across the logic of naturalism. In this sense allegory is always analytic rather than descriptive: that is, the whole selection and ordering of the material is conditioned by the structure of the ideas to be expressed, and it is no concern of the poet if clarity of exposition is obtained at the expense of natural probability. There is, thus, no reason within allegory why a character called *Activa Vita* should not be presented with a concomitant which, to begin with, seems meant to be visualized – a dirty cloak – but which turns out to be a purely explanatory device for introducing a structurally essential résumé of the material of an earlier part of the poem. Chaucer, as we have seen, deliberately rejects this method in the case of Nature in the *Parlement*, when he refuses to describe just such a garment as *Activa Vita* was wearing and places its ornaments, as living creatures in a real woodland, at their lady's feet.[3] Any exercise of critical ingenuity designed to get the goose, cuckoo and duck back on the fabric is inevitably perverse; and, in the same way, the characters of the churls' tales cannot, by more than the most distant implication, be pinned down within the strict schema of either the *Knight's* or the *Parson's Tales*.

It is important to emphasize the difference between the two methods. If we regard Chaucer as hiding under the variety of his tales the expository, schematic method, we shall find that we are introducing clearcut dividing lines where he has placed none. We shall, in fact, begin to regard all the characters who are not wholly good as wholly bad – with the result that the spirit of comedy will be lost. In fact, Chaucer presents us with a much more complex world, in which important contributions to the themes of *gentilesse* and patience – essential parts of true nobility – are made by the far from ideal Wife of Bath and in which the Pardoner, a character on whose behalf very little can be said, reaffirms the theme of the stable Lord of unstable Fortune and indicates the boundary between permanence and impermanence in no uncertain terms. We are never presented with anything approaching a *psychomachia* in the *Canterbury Tales* – or, indeed, anywhere in Chaucer's poetry. Far from externalizing the inevitable conflicts in the human soul, Chaucer does more to internalize them than any medieval writer before him and has, as a result, an approach to characterization which is both complex and essentially naturalistic. We need only compare the characters of an old-fashioned religious romance, the *Man of Law's Tale*, where the types do to some extent stand out clearcut, like vices and virtues in conflict, with even those of the *Clerk's Tale*, where the treatment is still not entirely naturalistic, to see clearly the direction in which Chaucer is moving. If we go on from there to his presentation of the Wife of Bath or of the Pardoner, we can form some estimate of the distance he actually travelled.

It is not only in his approach to characterization that Chaucer favours complexity. His view of the natural world, as I have tried to show in the case of the *Knight's Tale*, is not that it is simply divided between order and disorder. Nature, ruler of the creatures which inhabit the delusive world of change, is God's vicaire and works to bring about His plan of ordered change. Venus can work with her, as well as against her. Fortune, even though men abuse her, is also part of the divine plan and acknowledges God as her ord. Even the apparent conflict between submission to Fortune and the exertion of human free will is not a true confrontation. It consists rather in putting Fortune in the right place in the scheme of things than in setting her aside.[4] Most of the characters of the *Canterbury Tales* abuse their freedom of will and willingly bind themselves to Fortune's wheel, just as most of the plaintiffs in the *House of Fame* willingly submit to Fame's rather similar vagaries. But there are a number who do not, and who show us the reverse side of the picture.

Fortune and free will

The most clearcut discussion of the problem of Fortune and free will is provided by the *Man of Law's Tale*. The *Knight's Tale* had stated the problem and had examined it and provided a solution in philosophical terms. The *Man of Law's Tale* uses the hagiographic romance to present the explicitly Christian solution. This operates in two ways. In the first place, although Constance is shown as being peculiarly the victim of Fortune and of adverse planetary influences, she is also shown as exercising an unswerving freedom of will towards Christian virtue. Secondly, in support of Constance's will to virtue, we are shown direct divine intervention in the world, running, apparently, counter to the machinations of Fortune. As these two things – the heroic sovereignty of the human will and the possibility of direct divine intervention in the world – were precisely what the saint's legend was developed to demonstrate, Chaucer's choice of a story of this kind is particularly apt.[5] Nevertheless, I think that the importance of the tale to him, as far as its inclusion in the Canterbury series is concerned, was as a further comment on the theme of Fortune and free will; it is not developed as a religious poem in its own right. Here again, the hybrid form – this is not a saint's legend pure and simple, but a saintly romance (an equally well established, but different, genre)[6] – lends itself well to Chaucer's purpose. The tale of Constance, moreover, is particularly well adapted to this purpose. Her very name reminds us of the most essential Christian virtue with which Fortune must be opposed, and her sea voyages (although Chaucer does not stress the point) cannot fail to suggest one of the most usual figures for the Christian life on earth.

From the beginning of the tale, the astrological indications, which are bad, are carefully set against prayers for God's intervention. The fate of the pagan Sowdan is treated summarily. In his case the decree of the heavens cannot be circumvented:

> Paraventure in thilke large book
> Which that men clepe the hevene ywriten was
> With sterres, whan that he his birthe took,
> That he for love sholde han his deeth, allas!
> For in the sterres, clerer than is glas,
> Is writen, God woot! whoso koude it rede,
> The deeth of every man, withouten drede
>
> (*CT* II, 190–6)

Apart from the adverse state of the stars at his nativity, the moment chosen for the marriage is a bad one:

> O firste moevyng! crueel firmament,
> With thy diurnal sweigh that crowdest ay
> And hurlest al from est til occident
> That naturelly wolde holde another way,
> Thy crowdyng set the hevene in swich array
> At the bigynnyng of this fiers viage,
> That crueel Mars hath slayn this mariage.
>
> Infortunat ascendent tortuous,
> Of which the lord is helplees falle, allas,
> Out of his angle into the derkeste hous!
> O Mars, o atazir, as in this cas!
> O fieble moone, unhappy been thy paas!
> Thou knyttest thee ther thou art nat receyved;
> Ther thou were weel, fro thennes artow weyved.
>
> (295–308)

To set against this dark picture[7] we have first the narrator's appeal:

> Now, faire Custance, almyghty God thee gyde!
>
> (245)

then the prayers of the people for a marriage which is planned 'in encrees of Cristes lawe deere' (237):

> And notified is thurghout the toun
> That every wight with greet devocioun
> Sholde preyen Crist that he this mariage
> Receyve in gree, and spede this viage;
>
> (256–9)

and, lastly, Constance's own prayer:

> 'But Crist, that starf for our redempcioun
> So yeve me grace his heestes to fulfille,
> I, wrecche womman, no fors though I spille!'
>
> (283–5)

All this helps to build up two ideas: that God might yet intervene to nullify the portents of the stars, as far as Constance is concerned; and, secondly, that the stars, in any case, rule over a world whose values are not necessarily those of the Christian. Constance is prepared to accept the evil fate the stars indicate, but suggests that Christ may yet bring good out of it.

It is not only the stars which are in opposition to Constance. She is also assailed, like the Stoic good man, by the inevitable alternations of Fortune. The marriage feast ends in the slaughter of the Sowdan and all the Christians except Constance:

> O sodeyn wo, that evere art successour
> To worldly blisse, spreynd with bitternesse!
> The ende of the joye of oure worldly labour!
> We occupieth the fyn of oure gladnesse.
> Herke this conseil for thy sikernesse:
> Upon thy glade day have in thy mynde
> The unwar wo or harm that comth bihynde.
>
> (421–7)

The same pattern manifests itself at the end of Constance's story:

> This kyng Alla, whan he his tyme say,
> With his Custance, his hooly wif so sweete,
> To Engelond been they come the righte way,
> Wher as they lyve in joye and in quiete.
> But litel while it lasteth, I yow heete,
> Joye of this world, for tyme wol nat abyde;
> Fro day to nyght it changeth as the tyde.

Who lyved euere in swich delit o day
That hym ne moeved outher conscience,
Or ire, or talent, or som kynnes affray,
Envye, or pride, or passion, or offence?
I ne seye but for this ende this sentence,
That litel while in joye or in plesance,
Lasteth the blisse of Alla with Custance.

(1128–41)

In neither passage, it is true, is Fortune actually mentioned. That
it is meant is shown, I think, partly by the familiar Boethian pattern
of alternations, partly by the phrase 'Lord of Fortune' used, at
line 448, of Christ.[8] In lines 1128–41 Chaucer joins the Stoic idea of
enslavement by the passions to the idea (also Stoic) of involvement
in the inevitable chances and changes of the world. The best result
of such involvement is only 'joye of this world' which, throughout the
tale, by implication or direct statement, is carefully contrasted with
'the joye that lasteth everemo' (1076). He uses much the same phrase
for the couple's time of bliss – 'in joye and in quiete' – as he does
for that of Troilus and Criseyde which also proved brief and decep-
tive.[9] Indulgence of the passions, of course, lays a man peculiarly
open to the adverse influences of the stars as well as to the blows of
Fortune. Thus, at the beginning, Chaucer is careful to state that
the Sowdan actually encounters the fate written for him in the stars
because he succumbs to his passion for Constance:

al his lust and al his bisy cure
Was for to love hire while his lyf may dure.

(188–9)

'Lust' can mean 'pleasure' without any pejorative overtones; but
with the intensifying 'al' and with the sense Chaucer elsewhere
gives to 'business', of an entangling preoccupation with worldly
affairs,[10] it seems likely that this is the 'blinde lust' which, in a cruder
form, in the case of the wicked Steward, also terminates in death.
The good king Alla, on the other hand, disclaims any 'lust' which is
not in accord with Christ's pleasure:

'Welcome the sonde of Crist for everemoore
To me that am now lerned in his loore!
Lord, welcome be thy lust and thy plesaunce;
My lust I putte al in thyn ordinaunce.'

(760–3)

Here 'lust' includes Alla's love (a natural and virtuous one) of his wife and child; and, while the Sowdan was in the expectation of the joyful fulfilment of his 'lust', Alla speaks at a moment of great sorrow:

> Wo was this kyng whan he this lettre had sayn, –
>
> (757)

The incident in the plot which brings about this situation is not in itself very convincing. Chaucer takes no special trouble to give an air of probability to the unlikely news of the monstrous nature of the child born to Constance. He is not, indeed, concerned in this tale with realistic plot construction, but he *is* concerned with the exposition of certain themes and ideas, and for this purpose the old folk-tale motifs are well adapted. The tale is a suitable vehicle to show the good Christian undeservedly opposed to those alternations of joy and sorrow which are characteristic of the movement of Fortune. These alternations pose the same problem which troubled the lovers, and especially Arcite, in the *Knight's Tale*. In the *Man of Law's Tale* the same question is asked by the messenger, but in a tone of not irreverent wonder, rather than with the passionate sense of injustice of Palamoun:[11]

> 'O myghty God, if that it be thy wille,
> Sith thou art rightful juge, how may it be
> That thou wolt suffren innocentz to spille,
> And wikked folk regne in prosperitee?'
>
> (813–16)

Constance meets this problem with unquestioning steadfastness:

> But nathalees she taketh in good entente
> The wyl of Crist, and knelynge on the stronde,
> She seyde, 'Lord, ay welcome be thy sonde!'
>
> (824–6)

The end of the poem, especially, is built round the idea of the inevitable alternations of joy and woe which make up earthly experience, contrasted with the permanent joy of heaven. Sorrow and joy are formally juxtaposed in the matching pair of stanzas which describe the recognition scene; and, again, the exposition of the theme becomes more important than probability. There is nothing in the situation which really justifies such lengthy lamentations, but there is good thematic reason for an excursus on woe to balance one on joy:

> Long was the sobbyng and the bitter peyne,
> Er that hir woful hertes myghte cesse;
> Greet was the pitee for to heere hem pleyne,
> Thurgh whiche pleintes gan hir wo encresse.
> I pray yow alle my labour to relesse;
> I may nat telle hir wo until to-morwe,
> I am so wery for to speke of sorwe.
>
> But finally, whan that the sothe is wist
> That Alla giltelees was of hir wo,
> I trowe an hundred tymes been they kist,
> And swich a blisse is ther bitwixt hem two
> That, save the joye that lasteth everemo,
> Ther is noon lyk that any creature
> Hath seyn or shal, whil that the world may dure.
>
> (1065–78)

This joy culminates in the couple's happy life together, 'wheras they live in joye and in quiete'; but the warning contained in the proviso 'save the joye that lasteth everemo' proves necessary. This, for Alla and Constance, is not the everlasting joy any more than it was for Troilus and Criseyde. It is the joy which belongs to the world, and, like the world, it does not 'dure'. It is, in fact, brought to an end by the death of Alla. Constance suffers this vicissitude as she does all others:

> Wepynge for tendrenesse in herte blithe,
> She heryeth God an hundred thousand sithe.
>
> (1154–5)

The narrator gives a final emphasis to the theme in the prayer with which such romances customarily end:

> Now Jhesu Crist, that of his myght may sende
> Joye after wo, governe us in his grace,
> And kepe us alle that been in this place!
>
> (1160–2)

Here the joy that Christ sends after sorrow is, no doubt, the everlasting joy of heaven; but the prayer is also an assertion of a faith, like that which Constance shows, in God as the origin of all the events, woeful or joyful, which can befall us. In fact, the substitution of Christ for Fortune, as the source of alternating joy and sorrow in the world, is complete.

This is a process which begins much earlier in the poem and which is, indeed, its main contribution to the development of the theme of Fortune and free will. After the *exclamatio* 'O sodeyn wo, that evere art successour / To worldly blisse . . .' (421 ff.), Chaucer gives us a brief description of the calamity which ends with the placing of Constance 'in a ship al steerelees'. The narrator then intervenes with a plea for her safety:

> O my Custance, ful of benignytee,
> O Emperoures yonge doghter deere,
> He that is lord of Fortune be thy steere!
> (446–8)

This is immediately followed by Constance's own prayer to the Cross, not for safety but

> 'Me fro the feend and fro his clawes kepe,
> The day that I shal drenchen in the depe.'
> (454–5)

Constance sails on the sea 'yeres and dayes', and the narrator again pauses to comment, and to answer any possible objections:

> Men myghten asken why she was nat slayn
> Eek at the feeste? who myghte hir body save?
> (470–1)

The answer concerns, first, the general purpose of miracles:

> God liste to shewe his wonderful myracle
> In hire, for we sholde seen his myghty werkis;
> (477–8)

and, secondly, affirms the goodness of God's providence, that is, answers in advance the question of why he suffers harm to come to innocents:

> Crist, which that is to every harm triacle,
> By certeine meenes ofte, as knowen clerkis,
> Dooth thyng for certein ende that ful derk is
> To mannes wit, that for oure ignorance
> Ne konne noght knowe his prudent purveiance.
>
> (479–83)

The examples of divine intervention are all well-known instances of God's direct action to alter the natural order of things, taken from the Old Testament. They are: the preservation of Daniel in the lion's den, Jonah and the whale, and the Israelite's crossing of the Red Sea. Then, in answer to the question 'Where myghte this womman mete and drynke have?' (498), the examples of the feeding of 'the Egipcien Marie in the cave' and of the feeding of the five thousand with the loaves and fishes are given. The point, in fact, is made at length, and with emphasis, that God alters the natural order of things in Constance's case, as he had done in other cases recorded in the Bible and in the Lives of the Saints. Since the natural order includes the manifestations of Fortune, which belongs, because of its changeable nature, to the world below the moon, it is obvious that 'he that is lord of Fortune' may also alter the fate which is prepared for Constance by the alternations of Fortune's wheel or by the stars. This, indeed, God does by preserving her miraculously from what appears to be a certain death by drowning; but Constance's true victory over Fortune and the stars is to come through the freedom of her will. The pattern of woe after joy, therefore, continues to work itself out in her life to the end. Her freedom consists not in God's removal of her troubles, but in her persistence in carrying out the injunction Chaucer gives us in *Truth*:

> Know thy contree, look up, thank God of al.

To preserve the heroine to the end, it is true, 'open myracle' is more than once needed, as each temporary period of ease is predictably followed by a new woe; but this does not alter her essential function, which is to stand as a type and example of the constant Christian assailed by Fortune. After she is falsely accused before Alla and her terror is described:

> Have ye nat seyn somtyme a pale face,
> Among a prees, of hym that hath be lad
> Toward his deeth, wher as hym gat no grace?
>
> (645–7)

Chaucer pauses to address 'queenes, lyvynge in prosperitee' and to contrast her fate with theirs. It would be familiar and normal to follow the opening lines of this stanza with a reference to the inevitable reversal in the lot of the queens – such prosperity, according to the way of the world, must be followed by its reverse. Instead, Chaucer makes Constance herself stand for the expected reversal of fortune and thus emphasizes her function in the poem:[12]

> O queenes, lyvynge in prosperitee,
> Duchesses, and ye ladyes everichone,
> Haveth som routhe on hire adversitee!
> An Emperoures doghter stant allone;
> She hath no wight to whom to make hire mone.
> O blood roial, that stondest in this drede,
> Fer been thy freendes at thy grete nede!
>
> (652–8)

This, like many other stanzas containing what is technically an *exclamatio*, or *invocatio*, is not really a sign of Chaucer's addiction to formal rhetoric in this poem, but rather of the way in which he chooses to step aside from his narrative and to emphasize its thematic material. We may feel that he shows greater art in poems in which the plot and the thematic development are more intimately related; but in the special case of the hagiographical narrative, this intimate relation is very difficult to achieve. The hagiographical plot is apt to be inherently improbable and to lack the specifically human values which make a more naturalistic treatment rewarding. It is essential that each stage of the action is placed not within the ordinary scheme of cause and effect which conditions ordinary human life, but within the particular manifestation of a divine purpose which the story is intended to describe. Chaucer shows a clear grasp of both the potentialities and the limitations of the saint's legend, both here and in the *Second Nun's Tale*; and, to judge from the *Retractions*, where he mentions with pride 'bookes of legendes of seyntes', he considered this an important part of his work. We can only judge his achievement in it with due consideration to the nature of the kind he is attempting, although in the case of the *Man of Law's Tale*, we can also admire the success with which he has used the genre to further the development of the theme of Fortune and free will and to provide the Christian answer to the problem as a complement to the philosophical solution of the *Knight's Tale*.

The heroine of the *Clerk's Tale*, like the heroine of the *Man of Law's Tale*, could stand as a type of the good Christian who resists the assaults of Fortune – this time by patience, the Christian virtue closely related to constancy.[13] A recent analysis of the tale by Barbara Bartholomew (*Fortuna and Natura: A Reading of Three Chaucer Narratives*) shows how far Chaucer has gone in relating the alternations of her affairs to the idea of chance and Fortune. The husband who, in her case, acts as the immediate cause of her misfortunes, is linked to Fortune from the moment when he is first introduced:

> A markys whilom lord was of that lond,
> As were his worthy eldres hym bifore;
> And obeisant, ay redy to his hond,
> Were alle his liges, bothe lasse and moore,
> Thus in delit he lyveth and hath doon yoore,
> Biloved and drad, thurgh favour of Fortune,
> Bothe of his lordes and of his commune.
>
> (64–70)

He is represented not only as 'the child of Good Fortune', but also as having the kind of impulsive nature which, as it causes him to indulge his passions freely, would place him peculiarly at Fortune's mercy. He thinks of marriage without any care for the future: 'on his lust present was al his thoght' (79). When he begins to try Griselda, the wish to do so is an overmastering, emotional one not a reasoned purpose:

> This markys in his herte longeth so
> To tempte his wyf, hir sadnesse for to knowe,
> That he ne myghte out of his herte throwe
> This merveillous desir his wyf t'assaye.
>
> (451–4)

Just so is Troilus unable to put his desire for Criseyde out of his mind or to see where it is leading him. In the event, because Griselda remains immovable and never for a moment abnegates her function as a true wife, Walter suffers no ill effects from his self-indulgence and, finally overcome, accepts marriage in its true function as a perfecting and unifying force. Marriage in the *Clerk's Tale*, in fact, has the same high significance which it had in the *Knight's Tale*. The closing stanzas emphasize this with a triple repetition:

> Ful many a yeer in heigh prosperitee
> Lyven thise two in *concord and in reste*,
> And richely his doghter maryed he
> Unto a lord, oon of the worthieste
> Of al Ytaille; and thanne in *pees and reste*
> His wyves fader in his court he kepeth,
> Til that the soule out of his body crepeth.
>
> His sone succedeth in his heritage
> In *reste and pees*, after his fader day,
> And fortunat was eek in mariage . . .
>
> (1128–37)

The reconciliation of Walter and Griselda in a perfect marriage brings a similar reconciliation to the other characters, and the peace and unity which is produced extends even to a later generation. To lead up to this satisfactory conclusion is certainly one of the main purposes of the tale – and if it were the only purpose, we should be in no difficulty over it. The Clerk's final comment, however, suggests another, additional purpose:

> This storie is seyd, nat for that wyves sholde
> Folwen Grisilde as in humylitee,
> For it were inportable, though they wolde,
> But for that every wight, in his degree,
> Sholde be constant in adversitee
> As was Grisilde; therfore Petrak writeth
> This storie, which with heigh stile he enditeth.
>
> (1142–8)

This suggests that we are to take the sufferings and triumph of Griselda as in some sense an allegory of the ways of God with the soul – and this too, would enable us to take a straightforward view of the story. Chaucer, however, hastens to disabuse us of this idea, in any simple sense:

> For, sith *a womman* was so pacient
> *Unto a mortal man*, wel moore us oghte
> Receyven al in gree that God us sent.
>
> (1149–51)

We are not, in fact, to think of Walter as anything but a mortal man or of Griselda as anything but a real wife. Indeed, after the careful build-up of Walter as the man of impulse – Will opposed to Griselda's Wit, or Sensuality to her Reason – we could hardly with propriety see him as standing for divine providence itself, although he is certainly its unconscious instrument.

The narrator is not the only one to reprove Walter for his conduct. Griselda herself shows a perfectly clearsighted appreciation of it; and, at the one point in the story where the utterance of a rebuke is possible without detriment to her wifely obedience, she does not hesitate:

> 'O thyng biseke I yow, and warne also,
> That ye ne prikke with no tormentynge
> This tendre mayden, as ye han doon mo:
> For she is fostred in hire norissynge
> Moore tendrely, and, to my supposynge,
> She koude nat adversitee endure
> As koude a povre fostred creature.'
>
> (1037–43)

This is the only point at which Griselda clearly tells Walter that his conduct is open to criticism. There is, however, one other point in the story which shows her as a living, reacting recipient of his torments, not merely as suffering them in passive endurance. This passage is important in establishing that Griselda, like Constance, opposes a free will to the onslaughts of Fortune. This is the moment when Walter dismisses her from his house, and she contrasts her own faithfulness:

> 'God shilde swich a lordes wyf to take
> Another man to housbonde or to make!'
>
> (839–40)

with his changeableness:

> 'But sooth is seyd – algate I fynde it trewe,
> For in effect it preeved is on me –
> Love is noght oold as whan that it is newe.'
>
> (855–7)

At this moment in the story, and at this moment only, Griselda is allowed an outburst of feeling which makes both touching and credible her final plea to Walter, as much for his sake as hers, when he attempts to send her naked away:

> 'O goode God! how gentil and how kynde
> Ye semed by youre speche and youre visage
> The day that maked was oure mariage! . . .
> Ye koude nat doon so dishonest a thyng,
> That thilke wombe in which youre children leye
> Sholde biforn the peple, in my walkyng,
> Be seyn al bare.'
>
> (852–79)

Yet it is in this very passage, in which both Walter and Griselda appear as most human, that there are the strongest overtones of something more than particular and individual humanity. Griselda's expression of her faithfulness, for one thing, is cast in the form of a resolution to live well in the life of widowhood just as she had done in that of virginity and marriage:

> 'Ther I was fostred of a child ful smal,
> Til I be deed, my lyf ther wol I lede,
> A wydwe clene in body, herte, and al.
> For sith I yaf to yow my maydenhede,
> And am youre trewe wyf. . . .'
>
> (834–8)

This reference to the three states of human life, in all of which Griselda lives in perfection, places her as an ideal type of humanity rather than as Walter's individual wife.[14] Again, in:

> 'Naked out of my fadres hous', quod she,
> 'I cam, and naked moot I turne agayn',
> (871–2)

the reminiscence of the burial service suggests that her plight is generalized into that of all mankind. Even more significant is the line:

'Lat me nat lyk a worm go by the weye'
(880)

which is hardly, as Robinson suggests, 'a stock comparison',[15] but a reference to Psalm 21:7: 'But I am a worm and no man; the reproach of men and the outcast of the people.' Since this verse was commonly applied to Christ,[16] the reference makes of Griselda's departure a *via dolorosa* in imitation of Christ. The suggestion that she lives out her life as an *imitatio Christi* is supported by other Biblical echoes. Her humble upbringing is described in terms which recall the Nativity:

> But hye God somtyme senden kan
> His grace into a litel oxes stalle
>
> (206–7)

and:

> And she set doun hir water pot anon,
> Biside the thressh-fold, in an oxes stalle.
>
> (290–1)

We might even see a similarity to the Blessed Virgin's reception of the Annunciation in Luke 1:38 – 'And Mary said: Behold the handmaid of the Lord; be it done to me according to thy word' – and Griselda's reply to Walter:

> She seyde, 'Lord, undigne and unworthy
> Am I to thilke honour that ye me beede,
> But as ye wole youreself, right so wol I.'
>
> (359–61)

Her silence and submission in her time of trial certainly recall that of Christ, and the comparison to the lamb points up the similarity:[17]

> And as a lamb she sitteth meke and stille,
> And leet this crueel sergeant doon his wille.
>
> (538–9)

The cumulative effect of this treatment is to give to the figure of Griselda a depth of significance with which – and this is the crux of the matter – her wilful husband seems to have little to do. The poem fails – if it does fail – because the two main characters seem to operate on different planes of meaning. It is not, we feel, really quite fair to expose Walter to a quintessence of virtue more appropriate to the problems which humanity encounters in the religious life than to marriage. Griselda tames her husband, but an 'arche-wyve', 'strong as is a greet camaille', would have done it quicker and, perhaps, in a way more satisfactory to our sense of justice. So much, indeed, Chaucer seems to hint in his somewhat frivolous envoy. The story, in fact, suffers in part from an excess of meaning, in part from the very urbanity which makes it impossible for Chaucer to come down emphatically on one side or the other, and which ensures his success in so many other works. The themes of Fortune and free will, of marriage as a force for order and unity, of the soul in its *imitatio Christi* and also as the bride of a divinely incalculable bridegroom,[18] and of a conflict of Wit and Will – in which the normal order is amusingly inverted and Will, usually 'te fulitohe wif',[19] becomes the husband – are altogether too much for both the old folk-tale and the Chaucerian method of dealing unemphatically and sophisticatedly with the world of ideas. In his religious poetry, and even in the Man of Law's religious romance, Chaucer shows no such sophistication, but gives us a simple, single-hearted approach. In contrast, in its mingling of apparently secular elements with religious significances, the *Clerk's Tale* is like one of the religious artifacts of the fourteenth to fifteenth centuries which, increasingly, include the secular in their design – the richly bordered pages of missals, for example, which seem to aim as much at entertainment as piety, or the reliquaries in which the setting has little to do with the object of devotion.[20] Such works represent an aspect of late medieval sensibility with which it is, perhaps, difficult for us to come to terms. The secular and religious content seem to pull in different directions; and in a poem, which necessarily lacks the unifying factor of visible form and design, the difficulty is even greater than in a work of visual art. We must, however, accept it as a historical fact that works of this kind were popular and, presumably, capable of making an effective statement in the late fourteenth and early fifteenth centuries.

The characterization, too, which is partly in keeping with the older method, by which a character only exists in accordance with the requirements of a particular scene, or a given moment in the narrative, and is not required to show a consistency which extends through the story as a whole, involves a conflict with the newer, more naturalistic type which Chaucer usually prefers. Walter, like Emely, is called on by the narrative to stand at one moment in opposition to marriage through his apparent lack of love for his wife, and his separation of first mother and child and then even of the partners to the union, and at the next to take his place within a perfect married state – 'in concorde and in reste' – and unless he does so without reservation the story will not work. Yet in between he is consistently represented as a dominating, wilful character. In the same way, Griselda's lapses into naturalism tend to give the lie to behaviour which seems, in other places, to show her to us as a figure of symbolical depth and resonance. This poem, I believe, is Chaucer's one attempt to exploit that density of Christian significance and reference which is utilized with such virtuosity by Langland and by the *Pearl*-Poet. Although, in the process, he undoubtedly adds much to the development of his major themes in the *Canterbury Tales*, the method does not seem to have suited him. It needs a firmer choice between naturalism and the special formalism of allegory and its related kinds, and it needs, too, a stronger didacticism than Chaucer's urbanity ever makes possible to him.

The theme of Fortune is inevitably linked to that of free will, as far as Chaucer is concerned. This arises both from the Stoic conception of the inner self-sufficiency which stands unharmed in the face of all that Fortune can do, and from the Boethian conception of the freeing of the will as consisting in the clearing away of the clouds and mists of ignorance. For Boethius, and for Chaucer after him, a free choice is, inevitably, a choice of the good.[21] This means that it is not a theme which can play much part in the comic tales, where the wills of the characters are hardly free in this sense; they are certainly subject to the reversals of Fortune, but they contribute to their fate by their bad choices. The Miller gets his skull cracked, Absolon is scalded in the tout, old John the carpenter breaks his arm, and the begging Friar is humiliated through the ineluctable logic of events which they themselves help to set in motion, through their own folly or vice. In this sense we can say that even the lowest of the churls inhabit the same world as that in which their betters debate with high seriousness about Providence, destiny and free will; but unless we share some of their unawareness of such debates, we shall, as I have suggested, miss most of the comedy. An appreciation of the fundamental rightness of the rough justice of the tales and its ultimate compatibility with the world of the *Knight's Tale* is a part of our appreciation of Chaucerian comedy. But more than this has not been built into the tales, and any further reflections are ours, not Chaucer's.

Nevertheless, there are points at which the theme of Fortune and free will is allowed to penetrate the world of comedy. The *Monk's Tale* consists simply of a series of *exempla* of reversals of Fortune from good to bad, in illustration of the maxim:

> For certein, whan that Fortune list to flee,
> Ther may no man the cours of hire with-holde.
> Lat no man truste on blynd prosperitee,
> Be war by thise ensamples trewe and olde.
>
> (*CT* VII, 1995–8)

This is material which Chaucer uses perfectly seriously elsewhere – and, indeed, there is no reason to suppose that the *Monk's Tale* is not serious, as far as it goes. There is, however, an unusual flatness, a complacent, pounding beat in the verse which matches the flat superficiality of the conclusion. Certainly, the Monk does not go on to suggest any solution to the problem of Fortune's ravages, and the Knight is quick to point out the one-sidedness of his handling of the subject:

> 'Hoo!' quod the Knyght, 'good sire, namoore of this!
> That ye han seyd is right ynough, ywis. . . .
> I seye for me, it is a greet disese,
> Whereas men han been in greet welthe and ese,
> To heeren of hire sodeyn fal, allas!
> And the contrarie is joye and greet solas,
> As whan a man hath been in povre estaat,
> And clymbeth up and wexeth fortunat,
> And there abideth in prosperitee.
> Swich thyng is gladsom, as it thynketh me.'
>
> (*CT* VII, 2767–78)

This is the same criticism of incompleteness, delivered in much the same tone of voice, as that of the Eagle, when he points out that Chaucer the poet has so far had nothing to say about 'Loves folk yf they be glade'. The Host, in full agreement with the Knight, then gives his plain man's opinion. He has not understood a word, but he knows what he likes:

> 'Ye,' quod oure Hooste, 'by seint Poules belle!
> Ye seye right sooth; this Monk he clappeth lowde.
> He spak how Fortune covered with a clowde
> I noot nevere what; and als of a tragedie
> Right now ye herde, and, pardee no remedie
> It is for to biwaille ne compleyne
> That that is doon, and als it is a peyne,
> As ye han seyd, to heere of hevynesse.'
>
> (2780–7)

The *Nun's Priest's Tale* is closely linked to these reactions to the Monk's anecdotes of ill fortune, since it is to the Nun's Priest that the Host turns 'with rude speche and boold' to provide the desired contrast. It is not therefore surprising that the themes of Fortune and free will are woven into the burlesque tale of the cock and the fox, along with other solemnities.

From the beginning the actual farm-yard, described in plain terms, is set against the sophisticated accomplishments of its inhabitants:

> A yeerd she hadde, enclosed al aboute
> With stikkes, and a drye dych withoute,
> In which she hadde a cok, hight Chauntecleer.
> In al the land, of crowyng nas his peer.
> His voys was murier than the murie orgon
> On messe-dayes that in the chirche gon.
>
> (*CT* VII, 2847–52)

As the words lengthen and become more learned, so the cock's capabilities become more impressive:

> Wel sikerer was his crowyng in his logge
> Than is a clokke or an abbey orlogge.

By nature he knew ech ascencioun
Of the equynoxial in thilke toun;
For whan degrees fiftene weren ascended,
Thanne crew he, that it myghte nat been amended.

(2855–8)

His wife, Dame Pertelote, shows an equally profound knowledge, this time of medicine, nicely adjusted to the hen-run:

'Now sire,' quod she, 'whan we flee fro the bemes,
For Goddes love, as taak som laxatyf.
Up peril of my soule and of my lyf,
I conseille yow the beste, I wol nat lye,
That bothe of colere and of malencolye
Ye purge yow; and for ye shal nat tarie,
Though in this toun is noon apothecarie,
I shal myself to herbes techen yow
That shul been for youre hele and for youre prow;
And in oure yeerd tho herbes shal I fynde
The whiche han of hire propretee by kynde
To purge yow bynethe and eek above.'

(2942–53)

Both are learned in the matter of dreams, which, Chauntecleer explains, may be prophetic and relate to the alternations of Fortune:

'. . . dremes been significaciouns
As wel of joye as of tribulaciouns
That folk enduren in this lif present,'

(2979–81)

He gives examples of dreams which warn a man of

'. . . his aventure or his fortune,
That us governeth alle as in commune; . . .'

(2999—3000)

or of the disaster that comes about

'Noot I nat why, ne what *myschaunce* it eyled.'

(3100)

His conclusion is 'That I shal han of this avisioun / Adversitee,' (3152-3), and he proceeds immediately to demonstrate that he is in full possession of the joy that comes before such inevitable woe:

> 'For whan I feele a-nyght your softe syde,
> Al be it that I may nat on yow ryde,
> For that oure perche is maad so narwe, allas!
> I am so ful of joye and of solas,
> That I diffye bothe sweven and dreem.'
> And with that word he fley doun from the beem,
> For it was day, and eke his hennes alle,
> And with a chuk he gan hem for to calle,
> For he hadde founde a corn, lay in the yerd.
> Real he was, he was namoore aferd.
>
> (3167-76)

Chauntecleer is at the top of Fortune's wheel, both as king of his farm-yard – 'as a prince is in his halle' – and as successful lover:

> He fethered Pertelote twenty tyme,
> And trad hir eke as ofte, er it was pryme.
>
> (3177-8)

His fall is inevitable:

> For evere the latter ende of joye is wo.
> God woot that worldly joye is soone ago,
>
> (3205-6)

and the sad contrast provokes a long passage of learned lamentation from the Nun's Priest, in the course of which he insinuates part of the answer to the problem which had been lacking in the *Monk's Tale*. This consists, of course, in the discussion of necessity and free will – as to which the Nun's Priest refuses to adjudicate since 'My tale is of a cok, as ye may heere':

> O Chauntecleer, acursed be that morwe
> That thou into that yerd flaugh from the bemes!
> Thou were ful wel ywarned by thy dremes
> That thilke day was perilous to thee;
> But what that God forwoot moot nedes bee,

133

After the opinioun of certein clerkis,
Witnesse on hym that any parfit clerk is,
That in scole is greet altercacioun
In this mateere, and greet disputisoun,
And hath been of an hundred thousand men.
But I ne kan nat bulte it to the bren
As kan the hooly doctour Augustyn,
Or Boece, or the Bisshop Bradwardyn,
Wheither that Goddes worthy forwityng
Streyneth me nedely for to doon a thyng, –
'Nedely' clepe I symple necessitee;
Or elles, if free choys be graunted me
To do that same thyng, or do it noght,
Though God forwoot it er that it was wroght;
Or if his wityng streyneth never a deel
But by necessitee condicioneel.
I wol nat han to do of swich mateere;
My tale is of a cok, as ye may heere.

(3230–52)

The passage is a nice instance of the manner in which Chaucer suggests ideas clearly known to him, and, it is assumed, to his reader, through the modest confusion of a less percipient character. In the same way, though to sadder effect, Troilus gives a confused and partial rendering of the argument.

When Chauntecleer has finally encountered the inevitable reversal of Fortune, Chaucer breaks into a further lengthy passage of mock-heroic ejaculation, whose opening lines, the appeal to destiny and to Venus, make it perfectly clear on which side he stands in the argument of destiny and free will. Why, he asks, did Chauntecleer and Pertelote not use their freedom of choice to better effect and so avoid the unavoidable:

O destinee, that mayst nat been eschewed!
Allas, that Chauntecleer fleigh fro the bemes!
Allas, his wyf ne roghte nat of dremes!

(3338–40)

Moreover, it happened on a Friday, the day dedicated to Venus:

O Venus, that art goddesse of plesaunce,
Syn that thy servant was this Chauntecleer,
And in thy servyce dide al his poweer,
Moore for delit than world to multiplye,
Why woldestow suffre hym on thy day to dye?

(3342–6)

Chauntecleer, it would seem, has been indulging his passions in a manner contrary to Nature's purpose – the Venus invoked is the fallen one. He has thus placed himself peculiarly at the mercy of Fortune – and, as the *moralitas* points out, has got exactly what he asked for:

Lo, swich it is for to be recchelees,
And necligent, and truste on flaterye.

(3436–7)

Unlike the ostensible attitude of the rhetorically magnificent passages of lamentation over the cock's fate, the *moralitas* comes down bluntly on the side of personal responsibility. Fortunately for Chauntecleer, however, the fox is equally 'recchelees', and the story, as required by the host, ends happily – a double joy, not, as in Troilus's case, a double sorrow. The fox in his turn experiences a reversal of Fortune:

Lo, how Fortune turneth sodeynly
The hope and pryde eek of hir enemy!

(3403–4)

The whole story thus depends on the theme of Fortune, which had been dealt with by the Monk without the complementary one of free will and is now restored to its proper proportions. But there is much more to the tale than this. The very fact of the humorous, mock-heroic treatment adds a new dimension to the whole discussion of Fortune. It is salutary to watch the silly cock, with ideas above his station, tripping up through precisely the same kind of obtuseness and self-deception as the characters of the serious, philosophic poems. 'My tale is of a cok, as ye may heer', and the Nun's Priest does not force us to translate the behaviour of the birds into human terms, any more than Chaucer himself enforces the comparison between

Chauntecleer's sensuous delight in Pertelote, 'whan I feele a-nyght your softe syde', with that of Troilus in Criseyde, when 'Hire sydes longe, flesshly, smothe, and white / He gan to stroke'. This is not parody nor the debasement of a noble passage, but a reminder that Nature deals with all her creatures in ways which are basically the same. Chaucer's strength is that he never shows an inclination to deny dissimilitude through the assertion of similarity. His mood is as far as possible from Lear's in his sickness of mind, or even from the more light-heartedly sardonic insinuations of the Middle English Lyric:[22]

> Wormes woweþ vnder cloude;
> Wymmen waxeþ wounder proude.

Chaucerian comedy does not thrive through the debasing of the subtle and the beautiful. It has a place for the cock, whose sensuous satisfaction is somewhat diminished by the exigencies of the perch, and also for the man, who has other problems. If it compares, it is to differentiate as much as to draw together.

Another element in the tale arises through the Monk's attitude to Fortune. He had failed to distinguish between cases of bad luck and cases of bad judgement in his opening examples – the fall of the angels, for which he apologizes himself, and the fall of Adam, which were due to the abuse of free will.[23] The fall of Adam is also a type of the failure of marriage and the disruption in the order of things which it causes, since the marriage of Adam and Eve in Paradise, in which they are joined by God himself, is the type of all good marriages. Within the limitations of the humorous, mock-heroic tale, the Nun's Priest picks up the idea of the failure of Adam and Eve to use their free will rightly and also glances at the rôle of Eve as the wife who did her husband no good. Appropriately to the new setting, the story is stood on its head – it is poor Pertelote's housewifely medical advice and sound common sense which has to bear the blame for Chauntecleer's downfall.

As the catastrophe draws near, the first, oblique, comparison of Chauntecleer's state to that of Adam is made:

> Whan that the month in which the world bigan,
> That highte March, whan God first maked man,
> Was compleet, and passed were also,
> Syn March bigan, thritty dayes and two,

> Bifel that Chauntecleer in al his pryde,
> His sevene wyves walkynge by his syde,
> Caste up his eyen to the brighte sonne. . . .
>
> (3187–93)

Chauntecleer inhabits the yard which is his paradisial garden in a state of pride and outdoes Adam in the ownership of seven wives, all, alas, utilized 'Moore for delit than world to multiplye!' His experience is, however, so much like Adam's that even one of the seven is enough for his undoing:

> Wommennes conseils been ful ofte colde;
> Wommannes conseil broghte us first to wo,
> And made Adam fro Paradys to go,
> Ther as he was ful myrie and wel at ese.
>
> (3256–9)

Adam's happiness in paradise is made to sound very like Chauntecleer's – 'I am so ful of joye and of solas'. Just as Adam came to grief by paying attention to his wife's bad advice, so the foolish cock falls into the fox's jaws through attending not so much to his wife's common sense, as to her charms – 'Ye been so scarlet reed aboute youre yen' – which lull him into false security. The comedy of folly and conceit, solemnly examined in terms of destiny and free will, is enhanced by the oblique comparison with the Fall. But comedy is eliminated if we press the comparison too hard. The splendid bathos of the final human intervention in the story after the high flight, in which the woeful hens are compared to Priam's mourning wives and to Nero's senators when Rome was burned, would hardly make its point if the tale were to be taken as a moral allegory:[24]

> Ran Colle oure dogge, and Talbot and Gerland,
> And Malkyn, with a dystaf in hir hand;
> Ran cow and calf, and eek the verray hogges,
> So fered for the berkyng of the dogges
> And shoutyng of the men and wommen eeke,
> They ronne so hem thoughte hir herte breeke.
> They yolleden as feendes doon in helle;
> The dokes cryden as men wolde hem quelle;
> The gees for feere flowen over the trees;
> Out of the hyve cam the swarm of bees . . . .

> Of bras they broghten bemes, and of box,
> Of horn, of boon, in whiche they blewe and powped,
> And therwithal they skriked and they howped.
> It seemed as that hevene sholde falle.
>
> (3383–401)

With this final crescendo of noise and confusion, Chaucer makes
an abrupt transition back to the quiet, even tone of the fable narrative and the deluded world of the animals:

> Now, goode men, I prey yow herkneth alle:
> Lo, how Fortune turneth sodeynly
> The hope and pryde eek of hir enemy!
>
> (3402–4)

and so on to the final trickery which saves the cock.

The juxtaposition of the human and animal world is an essential
part of the comic method in this tale. Chauntecleer, his seven wives
and his kingdom of the farm-yard do not form an autonomous world,
as is sometimes the case in fable. They are the possessions of a good
widow, quite seriously and fully described in the opening as living
the life of patient poverty in widowhood – the kind of life Griselda
proposed going back to after her rejection by her husband:

> This wydwe, of which I telle yow my tale
> Syn thilke day that she was last a wyf,
> In pacience ladde a ful symple lyf.
>
> (2824–6)

Her life is described in the manner of the General Prologue:

> No deyntee morsel passed thurgh hir throte;
> Hir diete was accordant to hir cote.
> Repleccioun ne made hire nevere sik;
> Attempree diete was al hir phisik,
> And exercise and hertes suffisaunce.
>
> (2835–9)

It is out of this good widow's spare and sober way of life that all
the exuberance and all the delusions of the world of Chauntecleer

and Pertelote grow, until at last the human world erupts into the animal one, in an energetic and breathless attempt to rescue a valuable piece of property. This treatment of the human and the animal on two different levels, each blissfully unaware of the other's mode of experiencing life and each pursuing its ends with equal vigour and determination, is responsible for much of the comic effect of the tale.

Marriage

The *Knight's Tale*, as we have seen, depends for its denouement on a philosophical conception of marriage, both as a symbol of perfection and completeness and as an actual means of producing creative order in the natural world. The *Man of Law's Tale* and the *Clerk's Tale* develop the idea of marriage on a similarly philosophical basis. In the *Man of Law's Tale* philosophy is given a specifically Christian orientation, and marriage, like everything else below the moon, is seen primarily as part of the pattern of change which characterizes the world and contrasts with heaven. This viewpoint is not denied in the *Knight's Tale*. It is rather that the end of this tale shows us the pattern which marriage imposes on events, as it were, for a moment outside time, with the emphasis on achievement rather than on the continuity of the process. In the *Man of Law's Tale* all the emphasis is on temporal process, since life is always seen from the explicitly Christian viewpoint, *sub specie aeternitatis*. Constance achieves happiness through marriage and respite from change, but, since her eyes are fixed on the eternal stability, this moment of rest in the cyclic alternations of the world is not abstracted. It remains a part of the never-ending pattern of change, and her happiness in marriage, like everything else in nature, is brought to an end by death.

Although Constance's marriages thus certainly tend towards the achievement of some degree of stabilization in her own life and in the proper conduct of political affairs,[25] the achievement of stability within the temporal process is not the main theme. In the *Clerk's Tale*, on the other hand, as in the Knight's the degree to which marriage can bring about stability in the life of the individual and the state is one of the main interests.[26] Chaucer does not explicitly look beyond this within the framework of the tale, although other values are suggested by the Clerk's epilogue and are implicit in the way in which the figure of Griselda is treated.

These three tales – the Knight's, the Man of Law's and the Clerk's – all give us more or less abstract treatments of marriage as an archetype of order and stability in the natural world. The *Nun's Priest's Tale* provides a comic reversal of the picture in which the married life of the cock and his hens contributes to his downfall and leads to disorder instead of order. But this is by no means Chaucer's only interest in the theme of marriage. The ideal pattern, seen as a part of the mechanics and, indeed, of the very stuff of which the natural world is made, is important to him. But he shows, in numerous tales, that he also appreciates that the pattern is worked out as much through the interaction of human personalities as in the marriage of numbers which subdues the war of opposites and holds together the fabric of matter. This more personal aspect of marriage is important in all the tales of the so-called marriage group.[27] This consists of the *Wife of Bath's Prologue* and *Tale*; the *Clerk's Tale* and *Envoy*, with its references to the Wife of Bath and all her sect; the *Merchant's Tale*, which is linked to the Envoy to the *Clerk's Tale*; and the *Franklin's Tale*, included because of its subject-matter, although it is planned to stand after the *Squire's Tale*. Marriage is discussed, in all these tales, in terms of the dominance of one partner over another. This approach, apart from its sound basis in experience, would be natural to Chaucer from both his theological and secular reading. On the one hand, there is the ideal Christian marriage, as St Augustine, for example, described it and as Chaucer's Parson was to do after him.[28] This is based on mutual love and equal companionship, although the husband has a certain dominance, arising from a natural difference between the sexes, in that he must lead and protect the wife. On the other hand, there was the fashionable idea of sophisticated love-making, consisting in abject service of the lady while she is still to be won. This is described in many French and Italian sources. It was apt to involve a view of marriage not nearly so enlightened as the patristic one, either excluding it, on the assumption that it implied a masculine dominance incompatible with love, or abruptly reversing the rôles of the sexes so that the woman's brief period of importance ends with the lover's achievement of his purely sensual aim. This is the viewpoint, implied by Pandarus's bewilderment at Troilus's tragic refusal to 'unlove' Criseyde once he has had his will, when we are shown the artificiality of that faithfulness which it is the courtly lover's part to swear and to which Pandarus himself pays lip-service. Chaucer, indeed, had a *locus classicus* for the exposure of the shallowness of the sophisticated idea of love in the *Roman*, in a passage in which L'Ami pauses in his account of the trials of the jealous husband to set out the basic problem of the marriage relationship in terms which Chaucer clearly echoes in the *Franklin's Tale*:

> E se fait seigneur de sa fame,
> Qui ne redeit pas estre dame,
> Mais sa pareille e sa compaigne,
> Si con la lei les acompaigne,
> E il redeit ses compainz estre,
> Senz sei faire seigneur ne maistre. . . .
> Ja de sa fame n'iert amez
> Qui sires veaut estre clamez;
> Car il couvient amour mourir
> Quant amant veulent seignourir.
> Amour ne peut durer ne vivre
> S'el n'est en cueur franc e delivre.
>   Pour ce reveit l'en ensement
> De touz ceus qui prumierement
> Par amour amer s'entreseulent,
> Quant puis espouser s'entreveulent,
> Enviz peut entr'aus avenir
> Que ja s'i puisse amours tenir,
> Car cil, quant par amour amait,
> Sergent a cele clamait
> Qui sa maistresse soulait estre,
> Or se claime seigneur e maistre
> Seur li, que sa dame ot clamee
> Quant ele iert par amour amee.
>
>   (9425–54)

(And he sets himself up as lord over his wife, she who ought to be, not lady over him, but his equal and companion – this is the relationship in which they are joined together by law. And, in his turn, he ought to be her companion, not her lord and master. . . . The man who wants to be called master will never be loved by his wife; love dies when the lover wants to rule as lord. Love can only live and last in hearts which are generous and free. Therefore it happens to all those who begin as lovers that, when they embark on marriage, love is at an end. For the man who, while he was her lover, swore to be the servant of his lady, whom he desired to have as his mistress, now claims to be lord and master over one whom he called lady when he was her lover).

The point, of course, is not the praise of love outside marriage, but the need for a true relationship within it.[29]

In the tales of the marriage group, Chaucer deals systematically with the problem of the relationship of the partners to marriage. In the *Wife of Bath's Prologue* and *Tale*, he examines the woman's attempt to be the dominant partner. In the *Clerk's Tale* and the *Merchant's Tale*, the man dominates. All these attempts to establish an imbalance either end in disaster or need to be corrected. The *Franklin's Tale* describes a marriage in which the partners 'walk together and observe where they are walking'. The three most generalized and philosophical considerations of the marriage theme – the *Knight's*, *Clerk's* and *Man of Law's Tales* – have little to do with any courtly or sophisticated ideas concerning love.[30] Neither has the *Wife of Bath's Prologue*; but her tale has courtly leanings. And, in their different ways, both the *Franklin's* and the *Merchant's Tales* use ideas of this kind as a point of reference.

The *Franklin's Tale*, whenever it was actually written, is the conclusion to any 'marriage debate' which Chaucer may have planned for the *Canterbury Tales*, but it will be best to consider it first, since it gives us the norm – the marriage in which a proper balance between the partners has been achieved and which is therefore established on a sound basis. It also gives us a more detailed view of the somewhat rarefied unions of the more philosophical poems, set out in more naturalistic and more light-hearted terms.

Chaucer is at some pains, as he describes the culmination of Arveragus's courtship of Dorigen, to answer Jean de Meun's criticisms and to reconcile the courtly conception of a long and arduous pursuit in which the woman, through her power of refusal, is the dominating figure, while the man suffers every degree of frustration, with that of a continued relationship after the lady has

succumbed within the partnership of marriage. Arveragus is a lover
after the usual pattern:

> In Armorik, that called is Britayne,
> Ther was a knyght that loved and dide his payne
> To serve a lady in his beste wise;
> And many a labour, many a greet emprise
> He for this lady wroghte, er she were wonne.
> For she was oon the faireste under sonne,
> And eek therto comen of so heigh kynrede
> That wel unnethes dorste this knyght, for drede,
> Telle hire his wo, his peyne, and his distresse.
>
> (*CT* V, 729-37)

The conclusion is not an illicit love, but marriage, and the keyword
'lady' is replaced by 'lord', 'lordshipe':

> . . . she fil of his accord
> To take hym for hir housbonde and hir lord,
> Of swich lordshipe as men han over hir wyves.
>
> (741-3)

But, having established the themes of service and lordship, Chaucer's
conclusion is not the same as that of L'Ami in the *Roman*. Marriage
does not mean the end of love, because each partner offers submission
to the other, and the resulting balance is described in Chaucer's
favourite formula for the achievement of stability, temporary or
permanent, in love: 'Thus been they bothe in quiete and in reste'
(760):

> Of his free wyl he swoor hire as a knyght
> That nevere in al his lyf he, day ne nyght,
> Ne sholde upon hym take no maistrie
> Agayn hir wyl, ne kithe hire jalousie,
> But hire obeye, and folwe hir wyl in al,
> As any lovere to his lady shal,
> Save that the name of soveraynetee,
> That wolde he have for shame of his degree.
>   She thanked hym, and with ful greet humblesse,
> She seyde, 'Sire, sith of youre gentillesse

Ye profre me to have so large a reyne,
Ne wolde nevere God bitwixe us tweyne,
As in my gilt, were outher werre or stryf.
Sire, I wol be youre humble trewe wyf;
Have heer my trouthe, til that myn herte brest.'
Thus been they bothe in quiete and in reste.

(745–60)

The narrator now adds a long passage of comment, in which the problem is further analysed, not within the sophisticated limitations proper to the love vision, but in terms of the actual difficulties likely to be encountered in the establishment of a permanent relationship between two people. The discussion starts from a conventional tag:[31]

Love wol nat been constreyned by maistrye.
Whan maistrie comth, the God of Love anon
Beteth his wynges, and farewel, he is gon!

(764–6)

But the tag is invoked not in support of love outside marriage, but of friendship:

For o thyng, sires, saufly dar I seye,
That freendes everych oother moot obeye,
If they wol longe holden compaignye.

(761–3)

In equating the lasting love and companionship of marriage with *amicitia* rather than *amor*, Chaucer is in agreement with Reason in the *Roman* when she distinguishes between the transitory, contradictory love which is contrary to Nature and the love which is not subject to Fortune.[32] In Andreas Capellanus's *Art of Love*, the lady in one of the dialogues takes up the same position when she shrewdly defines *amor*: 'Love seems to be nothing but a great desire to enjoy carnal pleasure with someone'.[33] This, of course, as the dialogue goes on to say, can be as much a sin within marriage as outside it.[34] Chaucer, therefore, has nothing to say concerning *amor* in his discussion of the relationship of Arveragus and Dorigen. It is not rejected; but, in the limited sense in which the term is used

of sophisticated lovers, it is only one element in that permanency
of relationship which is established through *amicitia*. The Franklin
places the difficulty of establishing such a relationship firmly in the
day to day annoyances and inconveniences of life, and the solution
in mutual trust and forbearance:

> Looke who that is moost pacient in love,
> He is at his avantage al above.
> Pacience is an heigh vertu, certeyn,
> For it venquysseth, as thise clerkes seyn,
> Thynges that rigour sholde nevere atteyne.
> For every word men may nat chide or pleyne.
> Lerneth to suffre, or elles, so moot I goon,
> Ye shul it lerne, wher so ye wole or noon;
> For in this world, certein, ther no wight is
> That he ne dooth or seith somtyme amys.
> Ire, siknesse, or constellacioun,
> Wyn, wo or chaungynge of complexioun
> Causeth ful ofte to doon amys or speken.
> On every wrong a man may nat be wreken.
> After the tyme moste be temperaunce
> To every wight that kan on governaunce.
> And therfore hath this wise, worthy knyght,
> To lyve in ese, suffraunce hire bihight,
> And she to hym ful wisly gan to swere
> That nevere sholde ther be defaute in here.
>
> (771–90)

The Wife of Bath's contention 'Wommen, of kynde, desiren
libertee' (768) is given a new meaning by this definition of a life
of freedom; and, moreover, it is completed so as to become an
observation about humanity in general: 'And so doon men, if I
sooth seyen shal' (770). The conclusion makes formal, rhetorical
play with the key terms, 'service' and 'lordship', of L'Ami's speech
in the *Roman* and brings them into accord with each other and with
'the law of love':[35]

> Heere may men seen an humble, wys accord;
> Thus hath she take hir servant and hir lord, –
> Servant in love, and lord in mariage.
> Thanne was he bothe in lordshipe and servage.

Servage? nay, but in lordshipe above,
Sith he hath bothe his lady and his love;
His lady, certes, and his wyf also,
The which the lawe of love acordeth to.
(791–8)

The point of the story, as it develops after this preamble, is that this ideal marriage is nevertheless challenged in a way which affects its very basis. Dorigen engages her honour by her foolish promise. If she keeps it, she will have to deal her husband, and her marriage, the worst possible blow through her – albeit enforced – adultery. If she does not keep it, her very identity and value as a separate person will be injured, since 'Trouthe is the hyeste thyng that man may kepe' (1479). In this predicament, Arveragus is steadfast in keeping the vows he made to his wife on their marriage. He approaches the problem as it affects her as an individual, not as a wife whose identity is not separate from his own or who is thought of as his possession. This is the generosity in which his 'gentilesse' consists, and it is so remarkable that it triggers off all the subsequent acts of *gentilesse* which ensure the happy ending.

Arveragus is motivated solely by his love for Dorigen, but this love is the lasting *amicitia* which Reason urges on L'Amant in the *Roman*, not the momentary *amor* which is restricted to 'carnal pleasure':

This housbonde, with glad chiere, in freendly wyse
Answerde and seyde as I shal yow devyse:
'Is ther oght elles, Dorigen, but this?'
'Nay, nay,' quod she, 'God helpe me so as wys!
This is to muche, and it were Goddes wille.'
        'Ye, wyf,' quod he, 'lat slepen that is stille.
It may be wel, paraventure, yet to day.
Ye shul youre trouthe holden, by my fay!
For God so wisly have mercy upon me,
I hadde wel levere ystiked for to be
For verray love which that I to yow have,
But if ye sholde youre trouthe kepe and save.
Trouthe is the hyeste thyng that man may kepe' –
But with that word he brast anon to wepe
(1467–80)

This gives us, in naturalistic terms, a realization of Jean de Meun's humane conception of the lasting love in which reason has a share, which results in a marriage of true companionship. I do not think that we can doubt that in developing such ideas Chaucer is perfectly serious, or that we can detect either irony or sentimentality in his approach to the main theme of the tale. The story itself is certainly fantastical, and Dorigen is made to play out a comedy of errors, but it is a comedy which involves the characters in serious issues. Dorigen's troubles arise from her efforts to improve the reasonableness of God's world. This seems to her to be, in the matter of the Breton rocks, very imperfect:

> 'Eterne God, that thurgh thy purveiaunce
> Ledest the world by certein governaunce,
> In ydel, as men seyn, ye no thyng make.
> But, Lord, thise grisly feendly rokkes blake,
> That semen rather a foul confusion
> Of werk than any fair creacion
> Of swich a parfit wys God and a stable,
> Why han ye wroght this werk unresonable? . . .
>
> (865–72)

Her speech contains the same doubts and arguments which are put forward, with varying degrees of defiance, by many of Chaucer's characters – with the difference that here every cadence and turn of phrase develops the comedy by echoing the speaking voice. The only true solution, of course, is the exercise of free will in the face of Fortune, to whose realm such accidents as the rocks may cause obviously belong, and a patient endurance of what is sent by God's 'purveiaunce' – the solution, in fact, put into practice by Constance. Dorigen's obsession with the rocks and her lack of patience (ironically, the very virtue which ensures the success of her marriage) lead to her rash promise which, in turn, induces the subtle Breton clerk to put in motion the machinery of 'magyk natureel' in order to achieve her desire. This interference with the natural order of things – unlike the 'open myrakle' of Constance's story – is, Chaucer is careful to point out, only illusion:

> But thurgh his magik, for a wyke or tweye,
> It semed that alle the rokkes were aweye.
>
> (1295–6)

147

Dorigen herself analyses her plight with accuracy. She has been trapped and subjected to the influence of Fortune by her wish to eliminate Fortune's power in the case of the rocks:

'Allas,' quod she, 'on thee, Fortune, I pleyne,
That unwar wrapped hast me in thy cheyne,
Fro which t'escape woot I no socour,
Save oonly deeth or elles dishonour.'

(1355–8)

The elaboration of the magical marvels by which her immediate dilemma has been brought about adds to the irony of the situation. Chaucer is careful to point out that such practices are 'supersticious cursednesse' (1272) and only what 'hethen folk useden in thilke dayes' (1293). Nevertheless, they help to create a serious moral dilemma which challenges the whole basis, sound as it is, of the marriage. Appropriately, the trap is sprung, and Fortune defeated, by the very qualities of generosity and forbearance on which the marriage is built. It is in ironies of this gentle kind that the comedy of the tale depends, not on the view of marriage, of *amor* and *amicitia*, which it sets forth.

The *Clerk's Tale*, among other things, displays a marriage, in contrast to that of Arveragus and Dorigen, in which the dominance is all on the husband's side and in which the husband shows so little respect for his wife's separate identity as to call forth a final rebuke even from her patience. The Wife of Bath, on the other hand, develops the theme of feminine dominance. She describes her ideal husband bluntly:

An housbonde I wol have, I wol nat lette,
Which shal be bothe my dettour and my thral,
And have his tribulacion withal
Upon his flessh, whil that I am his wyf.
I have the power durynge al my lyf
Upon his propre body, and noght he.
Right thus the Apostel tolde it unto me;
And bad oure housbondes for to love us weel.
Al this sentence me liketh every deel.

(*CT* III, 154–62)

The Wife of Bath has nothing to say concerning *amicitia*, but she develops the idea of *amor* as 'a great desire to enjoy carnal pleasure with someone', within the frame of marriage, in a way which is frequently outrageous and always extremely funny.

The first three of her five husbands fall short of her ideal, although, in compensation, they endow her richly with this world's goods. Dame Alisoun is not, like Jean de Meun's Vieille, reduced to poverty and disgrace through her dealings with the male sex, but remains in the end a prosperous widow. The fourth husband was more suited to her tastes:

> My fourthe housbonde was a revelour;
> This is to seyn, he hadde a paramour;
> And I was yong, and full of ragerye,
> Stibourn and strong, and joly as a pye!
>
> (453–6)

But the fifth, although he gave her more trouble than all the rest, was her real love:

> Now of my fifthe housbonde wol I telle,
> God lete his soule nevere come in helle!
> And yet was he to me the mooste shrewe;
> That feele I on my ribbes al by rewe,
> And evere shal unto myn endyng day.
> But in oure bed he was so fressh and gay,
> And therwithal so wel koude he me glose,
> Whan that he wolde han my *bele chose*,
> That thogh he hadde me bete on every bon,
> He koude wynne agayn my love anon.
> I trowe I loved hym best, for that he
> Was of his love daungerous to me.
>
> (503–14)

For La Vieille, indulgence in love, rather than self-interest, proved disastrous;[36] but Alisoun does not come too badly out of her troubles with her fifth husband. He is a clerk, and his attacks on her, when they are not physical, are made through a book – 'He cleped it Valerie and Theofraste' (674) – not through disreputable conduct. In the end, the couple fight it out fairly, and Alisoun wins the victory.

After dealing her a blow which knocks her senseless, her husband is alarmed:

> And neer he cam, and kneled faire adoun,
> And seyde, 'Deere suster Alisoun,
> As help me God! I shal thee nevere smyte
> That I have doon, it is thyself to wyte,
> Foryeve it me, and that I thee biseke!'
> And yet eftsoones I hitte hym on the cheke,
> And seyde, 'Theef, thus muchel am I wreke;
> Now wol I dye, I may no lenger speke.'
> But atte laste, with muchel care and wo,
> We fille acorded by us selven two.
> He yaf me al the bridel in myn hond,
> To han the governance of hous and lond,
> And of his tonge, and of his hond also. . . .
> After that day we hadden never debaat.
> God helpe me so, I was to hym as kynde
> As any wyf from Denmark unto Ynde,
> And also trewe, and so was he to me.
>
> (803–25)

Dame Alisoun thus achieves stability and peace in marriage through a truth which is rather different from that exemplified in the marriage of Arveragus and Dorigen, but which, nevertheless, has a certain validity in terms of her own vigorous nature. In her honest satisfaction with the degree of good she has been able to achieve, there is comedy which contrasts sharply with the satire of Jean de Meun's presentation of La Vieille. The difference between the two figures, and the two methods, can be clearly seen if we compare the original lines with Chaucer's version. In the *Roman*, La Vieille attempts to cheer herself by her memories:

> Par Deu! si me plaist il encores
> Quant je m'i sui bien pourpensee;
> Mout me delite en ma pensee
> Et me resbaudissent li membre
> Quant de mon bon tens me remembre
> E de la joliete vie
> Don me cueurs a si grant envie;

Tout me rejovenist le cors
Quant j'i pens e quant jou recors;
Touz les bien dou monde me fait
Quant me souvient de tout le fait,
Qu'au meins ai je ma joie eüe
Combien qu'il m'aeint deceüe.
Jenne dame n'est pas oiseuse
Quant el meine vie joieuse,
Meïsmement cele qui pense
D'aquerre a faire sa despense.

(12932–48)

Apart from the cynicism of the last two lines, these words of the 'fausse vieille e serve' (12988) are to be read within the context of her numerous and bitter lamentations for what she has irretrievably lost.[37] Chaucer renders the passage thus, omitting lines 12945–8 entirely:

But, Lord Crist! whan that it remembreth me
Upon my yowthe, and on my jolitee,
It tikleth me aboute myn herte roote,
Unto this day it dooth myn herte boote
That I have had my world as in my tyme.
But age, allas! that al wole envenyme,
Hath me biraft my beautee and my pith.
Lat go, farewel! the devel go therwith!
The flour is goon, ther is namoore to telle;
The bren, as I best kan, now moste I selle;
But yet to be right myrie wol I fonde.

(469–79)

Dame Alisoun's momentary recognition of the power of age to poison a life such as hers is at once checked by the resilience and vital enthusiasm which has by no means left her. She is still 'stibourn and strong', and she deals with her own doubts with the same good-humoured determination which she brings to the quarrelsome interruptions to her tale – 'Al redy, sire,' quod she, 'right as yow lest' (854) – and even to her own deficiencies in the art of sustained discourse:

'But now, sire, lat me se, what shal I seyn?
A ha! by God, I have my tale ageyn.'

(585–6)

She does not solve her problems, great or small, through any depth of character or by any virtue, but by her sheer inability to loose her hold on life as she understands it.

Her tale gives a slightly romanticized version of the theme of her prologue. The heroine undergoes a transformation from age to perfect youth and beauty – thus solving the only problem which causes Alisoun any real disquiet. The hero escapes punishment for rape – a crime which, if it does not satisfy the requirements of either a romantic hero or a virtuous husband, at least shows vigour in the direction most favoured by Alisoun – by agreeing to marry the hideous old woman who supplies him with the answer to the riddle on which his life depends. In his despair he gives his wife that total sovereignty which Alisoun finally achieved in her fifth marriage:

This knyght avyseth hym and sore siketh,
But atte laste he seyde in this manere;
'My lady and my love, and wyf so deere,
I put me in youre wise governance;
Cheseth youreself which may be moost plesance
And moost honour to yow and me also.
I do no fors the wheither of the two;
For as yow liketh, it suffiseth me.'

(1228–35)

There is irony in the use of such terms by a husband whose feelings are thus described:

Greet was the wo the knyght hadde in his thoght,
Whan he was with his wyf abedde ybroght;
He walweth and he turneth to and fro.

(1083–5)

And there is added irony in the teller of the tale's easy assumption that such lip-service to courtesy – with a dash of magic to make everything comfortable – will ensure a perfect marriage. This is described in a phrase which echoes the conclusion of the *Knight's Tale*:

> And thus they lyve unto hir lyves ende
> In parfit joye –

but, incorrigibly, the Wife of Bath adds her definition of such joy, which is very unlike Theseus's:

> . . . and Jhesu Crist us sende
> Housbondes meeke, yonge, and fressh abedde,
> And grace t'overbyde hem that we wedde.
>
> (1257–60)

The fairy-tale couple have no life outside the marriage bed, and the teller of the story does not envisage any. Whether or not we are willing to go quite so far as Huppé, in his conclusion – '*Prologue* and *Tale* are a single, dramatic entity in which Chaucer searches with humour and with sympathy the mind of a worldly woman whose vivacity and laughter hide the soul of a lost and wandering pilgrim' – his final words cannot be bettered: 'It is a profound study of the highest comic seriousness.'[38]

As was the case with the Pardoner, the shift from satire to comedy is achieved in part, at any rate, through the change from the method of allegory to that of naturalism. The Wife of Bath is even more closely modelled on La Vieille than the Pardoner on Faux Semblant, but she is given a much clearer definition as a 'real' character through her function of furthering the development of the marriage theme. We have seen how the very wide field of reference of Faux Semblant, the shape-shifter, makes real individualization impossible, and how, although the field is greatly reduced, even the Pardoner does not achieve completely convincing individuality. In the case of the Wife of Bath, the wide field of the satire against women, and against sensuality in general, is narrowed to the problems and pre-occupations of her own particular marriages. Since there are five of them – 'withouten other compaignie in youthe' – the range is still wide, but the focus on her single figure is constant. La Vieille is, like Faux Semblant, involved in an improbable variety of affairs; she is at one moment bitterly vengeful, at another, triumphant in her 'joliete'. She is now in the gutter, betrayed by the male sex in general and her last husband in particular, now the trusted and prosperous guardian of Bel Aceuil. In all these metamorphoses she unswervingly serves the purposes of the allegory and allows the poet to develop the satire on a much wider front than would be possible with a character conceived in more consistently naturalistic terms.

Jean de Meun's method is comparatively straightforward. La Vieille is bluntly offered us as a detestable character – 'fausse' and 'serve'. We have fair warning that her doctrines are not likely to be true, and the satire, for the most part, consists in her description of her own practices, which are, clearly, bad ones. In spite of her dependence on Nature in her defence of promiscuity:

> 'Mais prenez bien garde a Nature
> Car, pour plus clerement voeir
> Come ele a merveilleus poeir,
> Mainz essemples vous en puis metre,'
>
> (13936–9)

('But pay due attention to Nature, for so that you may see more clearly how great her power is, I can give you innumerable examples,')

she is at odds with the son of Venus and does not, in fact, recommend love in any but the most limited sense:

> 'Qui veaut qu'amanz ait le cueur large,
> E qu'en un seul leu le deit metre:
> C'est faus textes, c'est fausse letre.
> Ci ment Amours li fiz Venus,
> De ce ne le deit creire nus.
> Qui l'en creit chier le comparra,
> Si come en la fin i parra.'
>
> (13030–6)

('If anyone teaches that a lover should have a generous heart and ought to bestow it in one place only, it is a false text and a a false doctrine. Love, the son of Venus, lies in this and ought not to be believed. If anyone does believe him, he will pay dearly for it, as I shall make plain.')

Worse than this, in at least two passages Jean de Meun allows something of the joy of love to come through La Vieille's discourse, but uses it only to give a sharper edge to the satire by the immediacy of her cynical disavowal. This is the case in the passage in which she recalls the pleasures of her youth, which Chaucer uses touchingly, but which is negated in the *Roman* by the conclusion 'a young girl can't be accused of idleness while she leads a life of joy – and especially if she keeps her eye on the profits'. Elsewhere (*Roman*, 14293–304), La Vieille gives a description of the mutual bliss of lovers which would not be entirely inappropriate to the consummation scene of the *Troilus*. But here, too, the *volte face* is immediate: 'and if the woman doesn't feel like this, she'd better take care to pretend she does!' We are reminded that love is not La Vieille's real subject – the more sharply for our brief reorientation towards a world in which other values prevail.

La Vieille's purpose is to achieve vengeance on the male sex, for the troubles it has brought upon her, by teaching Bel Aceuil how to avoid a similar fate by concentrating on rich men and a sound investment policy:

> Car aquerre, s'il n'i a garde,
> Ne vaut pas un grain de moustarde.
>
> (14455–6)

(Having without holding is not worth much.)

This device allows the satire to be as inclusive as its author cares to make it – any trick that the woman can play is relevant. The Wife of Bath, on the other hand, is shown grappling with life as she finds it, from her first marriage at the age of twelve to the moment in which she rides on the pilgrimage. Whereas La Vieille is made to present each point against women simply as a part of her own activity and experience, whose values the reader must reverse, the Wife of Bath argues out the case, with the same combative zest with which she tames her husbands. Her repeated 'thou seyst . . . seydest', 'thou liknest' (256 ff.), indeed, make the argument a part of the taming process, since they form the framework of the type of speech she was accustomed to address to her husbands. She may reciprocate a blow on the ear, but she is not motivated by any general desire for vengeance, and rides her waves as they reach her. Her love of her fifth husband is not seen as a disastrous backsliding, but as a fulfilment of her general hopefulness towards matrimony – in which she nevertheless shows no surprise when the rough comes with the smooth. There is, indeed, no room in her mind for *arrières pensées*. The singleness of vision which shows her nothing but the immense

desirability of Jankin's handsome legs as she follows her fourth
husband's bier, rules her life and even gives her a kind of innocence –
or at least shows her in that analogous state of genuine inability to
appreciate even the existence of any other point of view – and also
a degree of positive achievement. She lives out her life wholeheartedly
according to her lights. That they are not everyone's lights is obvious
– her own career is sufficiently checkered to show them as somewhat
unreliable. Comedy lies in her own almost complete self-satisfaction
– and the very thin crack which Chaucer allows us to glimpse
in this satisfaction only enhances the comedy. That her values
are not accepted by all her audience is shown by the Clerk's reaction
and by the amused comment of the Friar. The remarks of the
Pardoner and Summoner show no comprehension of the issues
involved and merely offer a clamorous insistence on their own
experience of the world, in its way as limited as hers.[39] Her tale,
like that of the Pardoner, has built into it an implicit criticism of her
point of view, through its references to true 'gentilesse' and patience
and to the truth on which marriage ought to be founded. Ironically,
however, none of these virtues are required. In the make-believe
world of the tale, the happy ending is achieved without them.
Chaucer, characteristically, guides his reader's reactions through
the total context, but not by any straightforward directives of the
kind which Jean de Meun employs when he openly tells us that
characters are good or bad. Neither, in the comic world to which
the Wife of Bath belongs, do we necessarily make our decisions in
the clearcut terms which satire demands.

The interest of the three most complex figures of the *Canterbury Tales* –
the Pardoner, the Wife of Bath and January (to whom we must
now turn) – as far as technique is concerned, is not only that, in
their creation and presentation, Chaucer shows a unique interest
in naturalism. He uses naturalism elsewhere within the series, as
well as outside it – notably in the *Troilus*. Nor is it the case, as we
have seen in connection with the Pardoner, that his methods with
these three are, on analysis, exclusively naturalistic. It is rather that
in their case he explores and exploits more fully than had ever been
done before all the opportunities for the development of character
afforded by the device of the series of tales within a frame. No other
way of laying out a work could give the poet quite the same oppor-

tunities for self-revelation, oblique or direct, on the part of the characters or could place them in quite the same complexity of relationships
with other figures. Chaucer is able to have the best of two worlds.
He can, if he chooses, exploit the isolated tale – amuse his audience
by a 'nice cas', a dilemma which is particular and has little reference
beyond itself – or he can, as is the case with the marriage theme,
gain something of the width of generality which belongs to allegorical
satire – but gain it without the sacrifice of personality which is
necessary for the proper development of this genre. Jean de Meun's
Jaloux is dissolved, as far as individuality is concerned, in a flood
of generalizations about jealousy. January is defined and delimited
with the accuracy and particularly of all the figures of the *Canterbury
Tales*, although, as he wrestles with his own special problems,
he casts a flood of light on the general topic of good and bad
marriages.

The *Clerk's Tale* and the *Wife of Bath's Tale* form a pair, in that
they show marriages in which the domination is, respectively, on
the male and on the female sides. The *Merchant's Tale* also shows us
an attempt at male dominance, but it is really the converse of the
true marriage of the *Franklin's Tale*. Its marriage is everything
which Chaucer and Jean de Meun tell us that marriage should not
be. In it, the wife is a chattel, bought by the marriage settlements.
The husband is exacting and jealous. No confidence exists between
the two. The husband's only thought is to use his wife for his own
enjoyment, the wife's is to escape in any way she can. This is the
kind of situation which Jean de Meun develops through the speeches
of Le Jaloux; but, once again, Chaucer treats the same subject in
a way which is both more particular and less extreme. Jean de
Meun sets out to give an exhaustive study of the effect of jealousy
on marriage and examines every possible permutation of events to
which it can give rise. Le Jaloux and his wife are every jealous
husband and abused wife. January and May are a particular
couple, although their predicament is described in such a way as
to give it reference beyond their individual case. They contribute
to the marriage discussion, but, as in the case of the Wife of Bath,
their contribution cannot be entirely disengaged from Chaucer's
handling of them as naturalistically conceived characters.

As far as marriage is concerned, January demonstrates what
happens when the husband approaches it for the sake of selfish
lechery and of nothing else. His sole aim in marrying is to legitimize

pleasures to which he has long been habituated, and which age affects only in so far as some fear for the ultimate destination of his soul is now forcing itself on his consciousness. This complexity of motivation is, in itself, enough to mark him off from the allegorical or type figure which is, necessarily, dominated by a driving force as single as it is strong, since in such figures we see the quintessence of what they stand for. January is not a quintessential figure. He is an ingenious old man who plans to have his cake and eat it:

> Whilom ther was dwellynge in Lumbardye
> A worthy knyght, that born was in Pavye,
> In which he lyved in greet prosperitee;
> And sixty year a wyflees man was hee,
> And folwed ay his bodily delyt
> On wommen, ther as was his appetyt,
> As doon thise fooles that been seculeer.
> And whan that he was passed sixty yeer,
> Were it for hoolynesse or for dotage,
> I kan nat seye, but swich a greet corage
> Hadde this knyght to been a wedded man
> That day and nyght he dooth al that he kan
> T'espien where he myghte wedded be . . .
>
> (*CT* IV, 1245–57)

The long series of speeches in which the theme is developed serves as a kind of internal prologue to the *Tale*. Like the Wife of Bath, January uses material which in fact proves the opposite of what he wants to prove, since, like her, his aim is to show that marriage legitimizes lust. Even the logicians of Andreas Capellanus's dialogues know better than this.

January is the traditional figure of the *Senex Amans* only in so far as age makes him repulsive. His boast:

> For, God be thanked! I dar make avaunt,
> I feel my lymes stark and suffisaunt
> To do al that a man bilongeth to,
>
> (1457–9)

is so far justified that he does get May with child – and so gives her an excuse for an urgent longing for small green pears, to his ultimate undoing. Chaucer dwells on the lechery of January in line after relentless line descriptive of his enjoyment of May, writing with a savagery and remorselessness of unpleasant detail which is unparalleled elsewhere in his work. The ultimate triumph of sensuality for two well-matched lovers in the *Troilus* is firmly, but delicately, drawn. There is no delicacy and no restraint in the *Merchant's Tale*, where sexuality is deliberately used as the chief weapon of the satire against both marriage partners, in a comedy of a kind which we do not encounter anywhere else in Chaucer's work. It is a double comedy: both the main characters are equally self-deluded in their attempts to delude each other – in contrast to the *Roman*, where Le Jaloux's wife is merely the victim (not an altogether unresisting one) of his persecution. May marries for money, as Chaucer shows by his emphasis on the marriage settlements and the luxury of the feast:

> I trowe it were to longe yow to tarie,
> If I yow tolde of every scrit and bond
> By which that she was feffed in his lond.
> (1696–8)

She shows no dissatisfaction with her bargain. She is described at the feast as:

> Mayus, that sit with so benyngne a chiere,
> Hire to beholde it semed fayerye,
> (1742–3)

and her acquiescence to all January's demands continues to the end. Chaucer questions her thoughts, but not her words or actions, when he describes her in bed with January:

> He was al coltissh, ful of ragerye,
> And ful of jargon as a flekked pye.
> The slakke skyn aboute his nekke shaketh,
> Whil that he sang, so chaunteth he and craketh.
> But God woot what that May thoughte in hir herte,
> Whan she hym saugh up sittynge in his sherte,
> In his nyght-cappe, and with his nekke lene.
> (1847–53)

In a similar situation, the knight of the *Wife of Bath's Tale* expresses his feelings freely. There is no 'rape of May', but rather a willing prostitution, in which the silence with which she receives all January's advances acts like a savage parody of Griselda's silence in the face of her husband's persecution.

January thus has no reason to complain, as has Le Jaloux, that his wife does everything she can to hinder his enjoyment.[40] In fact, Chaucer borrows a detail from Le Jaloux's speech and turns it to an opposite effect. Le Jaloux complains at length of his wife's extravagance. The splendour of her clothes, he says, is nothing but useless ostentation:

> Que me fait ele de profit?
> Combien qu'ele aus autres profit,
> A mei ne fait ele fors nuire;
> Car, quant me vueil a vous deduire,
> Je la treuve si encombreuse,
> Si grevaine e si enuieuse
> Que je n'en puis a chief venir.

(What good is it to me? However much you may please other people, it's nothing but a nuisance to me. For, when I want some pleasure from you, I find them so much in the way, such an encumbrance and such an inconvenience, that I never manage to get anywhere.)

(8851–7)

This play on the various meanings of 'profit' is witty. Chaucer, however, does not borrow the passage for the purpose of wit. January indulges his lust at all times of the day or night and

> Anon he preyde hire strepen hire al naked;
> He wolde of hire, he seyde, han som plesaunce,
> And seyde hir clothes dide hym encombraunce.
> And she obeyeth, be hire lief or looth.

(1958–61)

There is no wit here; but the casually demanding, near querulous note which Chaucer contrives to put into January's reported speech is one of the most telling strokes in the attack on him.

May is bought, and gives value for the money – a fact which

mitigates the sympathy aroused by the reference to her inevitable thoughts. Sympathy is further dispelled by the fact that she is soon shown to be as lustful as January. Her courtship by Damyen is as swift and easily successful as that of Alisoun by Nicholas – but it lacks the freshness and the charm. May is, she insists, 'a gentil womman and no wenche' (2202), and Chaucer accordingly deals with her rapid surrender with all the trappings proper to the sophisticated ploys of *fin' amour* – the joke, of course, is not at the expense of *gentilesse* in love, but at May's assumption of it. Damyen languishes in bed like Troilus and achieves May's acceptance of a letter; but the ready wit by which she immediately understands Damyen, and finds at once the privacy to read his letter and a good way of disposing of the evidence, has little to do with Criseyde:

> She feyned hire as that she moste gon
> Ther as ye woot that every wight moot neede;
> And whan she of this bille hath taken heede,
> She rente it al to cloutes atte laste,
> And in the pryvee softely it caste.
>
> (1950–4)

In pursuance of the joke, Chaucer sets her careless speech of acceptance:

> 'Certeyn', thoghte she, 'whom that this thyng displese,
> I rekke noght, for heere I hym assure
> To love hym best of any creature,
> Though he namoore hadde than his sherte'
>
> (1982–5)

between two passages in the grand style on destiny and chance, and on the pity that belongs to *gentilesse*, both topics which he uses with serious force in the philosophical love poems. The line, indeed, in which he sums up May's soliloquy – 'Lo pitee renneth soone in gentil herte' (1986) is a key one, which he uses in all sincerity of his noble heroines, and which he here turns against May with terrible effect.[41]

Chaucer uses, too, another theme which is familiar from his more philosophical treatments of love. January, he laments, suffers a reversal, common to mankind, from the joy in which he is living with a wife, as we know, already determined to betray him:

> And in this wyse, many a murye day,
> Lyved this Januarie and fresshe May.
> But worldly joye may nat alwey dure
> To Januarie, ne to no creature.
>
> (2053–6)

January becomes blind, and for a time the state of May and Damyen is worse than before, since he adds jealousy to his other advantages as a husband. Our sympathy even veers a little towards May. 'This noble Januarie free' – Chaucer gives him a formula implying the highest virtue, to correspond to May's gentle pity[42] – becomes so exacting in his jealousy

> That neither in halle, n'yn noon oother hous,
> Ne in noon oother place, neverthemo,
> He nolde suffre hire for to ryde or go,
> But if that he had hond on hire alway;
> For which ful ofte wepeth fresshe May,
> That loveth Damyan so benyngnly. . . .
>
> (2088–93)

Chaucer, however, is quick to unsettle any feelings of this kind by beginning to build up a little sympathy for January. After the outrageous speech in which he addresses May in a paraphrase of the Song of Songs – 'swich olde lewed wordes', as they indeed become in his mouth – Chaucer makes him express a love for his wife which we may, if we choose, take as having a meaning that is a little deeper than his prevailing characteristic of lust:

> 'Now wyf,' quod he, 'heere nys but thou and I,
> That art the creature that I best love.
> For by that Lord that sit in hevene above,
> Levere ich hadde to dyen on a knyf,
> Than thee offende, trewe deere wyf!
> For Goddes sake, thenk how I thee chees,
> Noght for no coveitise, doutelees,
> But oonly for the love I had to thee.
> And though that I be oold, and may nat see,

Beth to me trewe, and I wol telle yow why.
Thre thynges, certes, shal ye wynne therby:
First, love of Crist, and to youreself honour,
And al myn heritage, toun and tour;
I yeve it yow, maketh chartres as yow leste;
This shal be doon to-morwe, er sonne reste. . . .'

(2160–74)

The ambiguities and ironies are nicely balanced. True, January did not marry for 'coveitise'; but May did, as we know. Equally true, he was dominated in his choice by 'love'; but a love which, as we have had ample opportunity to judge, was lust pure and simple. It may be that he now values 'truth' in a wife, but hardly with any real understanding of a concept which is, of course, a central one to Chaucer's view of marriage. He is, in fact, addressing a wife who, far from being true, has already betrayed him in intention and is about to do so in fact, and the only persuasion he can offer with any hope that it will prove effective is to buy her once again — to add new 'chartres' to the deeds of the marriage settlement. The fact that both he and May discuss the matter with perfunctory reference to Christian virtue enhances the irony. January promises her 'love of Crist', before he hurries on to detail the endowment he proposes to make, and May remarks, with some indignation:

'I have', quod she, 'a soule for to kepe
As wel as ye.'

(2188–9)

The whole tale develops an ironical interchange of the idea of *gentilesse* and its reverse as applied to May. The narrator comments admiringly on her 'gentil' pitifulness. She makes her claim to be a 'gentil womman and no wenche'. January hopes to buy truth from her – 'the hyeste thyng that man may kepe', in Arveragus's words – and, finally, the whole elaborate irony is brought to a point in January's outraged bewilderment when his wife is revealed to him as she really is:

'Out! help! allas! harrow!' he gan to crye.
'O stronge lady stoore, what dostow?'

(2366–7)

He roars out a confusion of epithets, appropriate and the reverse, among which, by a cunning positioning in the line, the one word, 'lady', which May claimed for herself, and to which she now has no claim whatsoever, bears witness to a lingering obstinacy in self-deception which paves the way for January's final, total subjugation by his ingenious wife. If we need a further comment on May, we can find it in the *Manciple's Tale*, where the teller, commenting on women who 'werke . . . amys', remarks:

> . . . the gentile, in estaat above,
> She shal be cleped his lady, as in love;
> And for that oother is a povre womman,
> She shal be cleped his wenche, or his lemman.
> (*CT* IX, 217–20)

The conclusion of the Manciple, who apologizes for himself as 'a boystous man', is unkindly appropriate to May:

> And, God it woot, myn owene deere brother,
> Men leyn that oon as lowe as lith that oother.
> (*CT* IX, 221–2)

It is the continual interplay in delusion between the two main characters – to which only a line-for-line analysis could do full justice – each equally duped and duping, in which the savage comedy of the *Merchant's Tale* consists. It is in this interplay, too, that we can see the fundamental difference between Chaucer's and Jean de Meun's approach to the subject of the *Mal Marié*. January is a comic figure because he is placed in the common human predicament of longing for something only dimly understood. In satisfying an apparently clear and limited desire, he finds himself with other desires still unsatisfied. He has some distant inkling of the worth of a true wife and of the true joys of marriage, but without any real understanding of what is involved and without the slightest idea of how to get them. These complexities are necessarily absent from Le Jaloux, who serves the satire as the quintessence of jealousy and unreasonableness in marriage and has no shades or half-tones about him. Both poets develop the theme with consummate skill, but they develop it differently.

The nobleness of man

In the epilogue to the *Troilus*, it is the 'grete worthyness' and the 'noblesse' of the hero that is mourned, and we have seen that the words 'noble' and 'nobleness' are key ones, which always have important connotations for Chaucer. As far as the *Troilus* is concerned, the nobleness of man consists above all in his freedom of will, which makes him independent of the tyranny of Fortune and of passion. From other passages, notably that in the *Second Nun's Prologue*, we have seen that, for the Christian, this involves, in an intimate way, the relationship of Man and God, since man's nobility comes to him from God, both by formation and reformation – through creation and redemption. Moreover, for the Christian, the term is applicable not just to the soul, as the highest part of man, but to human nature and human substance as a whole.[43] We have, further, seen how, within the *Canterbury Tales*, in the Knight's noble story, the concept of marriage, considered both metaphysically and actually, plays an important part in the development of the idea of man's 'worthiness', of his position as part of the creation, and his relation to God.

It remains to ask whether ideas of this kind extend from the *Knight's Tale*, with its strong philosophical bias, through the *Canterbury Tales* as a whole. There is no doubt that, with or without a philosophical bias, Chaucer's subject, throughout the series, is man, whether considered as worthy or, through the abuse of the nature with which God has endowed him, the reverse. Marriage, as we have seen, remains a constantly recurring theme, and so does sexuality. This is, after all, both the basis of the human union within marriage, which repeats a pattern divinely imposed on the whole natural creation, and also, when it is practised in contradiction to Nature's laws, the chief cause of the disruption of the pattern. The tales, too, obviously provide excellent opportunities to explore the more diffuse definition of human nobility supplied by Macrobius, which makes it primarily dependent on the cultivation of the virtues.[44] The *Parson's Tale*, moreover, actually contains a systematic exposition of the type of vices and virtues material which was ultimately derived from Macrobius.[45] There are, as we shall see, other signs besides the inclusion of the *Parson's Tale* that

Chaucer found this kind of approach suitable to an exploration of the idea of human nobleness. Nevertheless, it is obvious that he could never have intended to write a Book of Vices and Virtues in the *Canterbury Tales*. There is no systematic following out of any series of major virtues and corresponding vices. As has already been said, even allowing for the unfinished state of the work, it would be hard to imagine a way in which the existing tales could be fitted into such a scheme. The best way, therefore, of examining the question of how far the *Canterbury Tales* as a whole develops the theme of the nobleness of man will be to consider first, how far the ubiquitous subject of sexuality contributes to it and secondly, how far it is developed in Macrobian terms, through the vices and virtues material.

The question of whether or not sexuality played any part in an exalted and philosophical conception of love in the Middle Ages is an extremely complex one, which goes far beyond the scope of this book. It necessarily involves the whole problem of *amour courtois* – a problem which in its own right is both a delicate one and in urgent need of careful redefinition. The idea, for example, that this love was in any sense 'platonic', that is that it excluded sexual fulfilment, clearly needs modification; but so does the idea that it was inevitably and crudely adulterous. The first leads to such obviously untenable positions as that indicated by A. J. Denomy: 'Love must remain a desire in order that the end may be fulfilled. Once consummated desire weakens, and, consequently, growth in virtue and worth lessen.'[46] It is precisely such a weakening of desire after consummation which both Pandarus and Jean de Meun expect – and its failure is a large part of Troilus's tragedy. The second leads to the excessive emphasis on adultery of, for example, C. S. Lewis, who makes it one of the four 'marks' of courtly love.[47] As we have seen, to insist on this would be to place an impassable barrier between *amicitia* and *amor*, by a failure to distinguish between *amor* as 'love of kind' and as 'blind lust'. Such a barrier is not to be found in Chaucer's poetry.

Even more difficult is the question of whether the concept of natural, physical sexuality, granted that it played a part in any idea of *amour courtois*, was merged in that of a love with spiritual or even divine implications. This problem has recently been explored in relation to Dante by Colin Hardie in a paper 'Dante and the Tradition of Courtly Love',[48] and by Peter Dronke in relation to the medieval European love lyric, especially that written in Latin.[49] As far as

Dante is concerned, we can only say that Chaucer makes no reference in his own works to anything in the *Divina Commedia* which directly concerns Beatrice, so that we have no means of knowing how he would have reacted to this aspect of Dante's thought or how he would have understood it. Nor do we know, of course, which, if any, of the numerous and very diverse Latin love lyrics he might have been familiar with. Dronke, in his treatment of these poems, is in reaction against Lewis's findings that there was no place for passionate love in medieval religious thought and that the gap was, therefore, filled by the literature of *amour courtois*.[50] Both writers document their case fully, and, in a sense, both prove it, since they are drawing on two different traditions of religious writing. Lewis quotes from scholastic analysts, whose rather rigid and simplified system of human psychology leaves little room for the emotions, as we understand them, to play an important rôle. The case is otherwise with writers more closely allied to the mystical tradition, who use, above all, the terminology and the situations of the Song of Songs. These are the writers on whom Dronke draws, and from whom he is able to quote numerous passages which describe the passion of love. The difficulty, however, is to bridge the gap between sacred and profane love; we cannot always take erotic terminology, however startling to the modern reader, at its face value. There is much to be said for Étienne Gilson's vigorous warning:[51]

À quels excès d'érudition ne s'est-on pas livré, dont un peu
de réflexion aurait dispensé! Pourquoi comparer 'l'oeil du
coeur' des poètes courtois à celui des mystiques? Le premier
n'est que de l'imagination, et parfois la plus sensuelle, au
lieu que le deuxième est défini par l'exclusion de toute image
sensible, de celles que c'est précisément la fonction du
premier de nous fournir en l'absence de leurs objets. Quel
rapport entre l'oeil mystique, qui ne s'ouvre que toutes images
éteintes, et l'oeil du coeur, qui garde ces images présentes à
un amour charnel, qu'elles nourissent?

Nevertheless, there is, I think, a case to be made, if not for the full unity of human and divine love for which Dronke argues,[52] still for a view of human sexuality – the love of kind – by which it takes its place in a serious system of natural philosophy through which, since all nature derives from God, it is not wholly separated from the divine.

C. S. Lewis defined the problem, as far as Jean de Meun was concerned, in the following terms:[53]

> The doctrine that human sexuality is the μίμησις of which divine love is the παράδειγμα is not incompatible with the doctrine that human sexuality, in its place, is a glorious energy of nature; and neither of these is incompatible with scathing satire of human abuse of sexuality.

He argues that, in Jean de Meun's case, the effective linking of these ideas was never achieved. It seems to me, however, unlikely that Jean de Meun ever contemplated such an achievement as the result of the infinite complexity of irony and seriousness with which he approaches the subject of love. In fact, his position, as it is set out by Reason (who argues reasonably from given premises and, so far, presents a valid view of the world, but who does not necessarily have the ultimate word), is not an extreme one. Sexuality, Reason explains, is neither good nor bad in itself. It is a bodily function which man shares with the animals and which, like everything else about him, comes to him from his Creator. He has no reason to be ashamed of it, but also no great reason to exalt it.[54] In this exposition, *amor* takes its place in the world of Nature which is, necessarily, under God; but it would not appear to qualify for translation to heaven.

Reason's words concerning the organs of generation (which, ironically, greatly upset L'Amant's sense of propriety) are typical of her approach – and, moreover, have an interesting echo in fourteenth-century English poetry. She speaks soberly and straightforwardly:

> 'N'encor ne faz je pas pechié
> Se je nome les nobles choses
> Par plain texte, senz metre gloses,
> Que mes peres en paradis
> Fist de ses propres mains jadis,
> E touz les autres estrumenz
> Qui sont pilers e argumenz
> A soutenir nature humaine!'

('I shall commit no sin if I name the noble things, in plain words, without prevarication, which my Father made formerly with his own hands in Paradise and all the other instruments which are the props and stays of the continuance of the human race.')

(6956–63)

For Reason, human sexuality has its nobility; but this relates not so much to the passion of love, as to the way in which it takes its place as a part of the great natural cycle of change which, through birth and death, assures the continuance of the world. It is part of God's 'merveilleuse entencion':

'Pour l'espiece aveir toujourz vive
Par renouvelance naïve.'

('So that the species should live for ever through natural renewal.')
(6969–70)

In the English fourteenth-century poem *Purity*, probably by the poet of *Pearl* and *Sir Gawain and the Green Knight*,[55] the poet makes not Reason, but God himself speak in defence of natural sexuality, in contrast to the sin of Sodom and Gomorrah:

I compast hem a kynde crafte and kende hit hem derne,
And amed hit in myn ordenaunce oddely dere,
And dyȝt drwry þerinne, doole alþerswettest,
And þe play of paramorez I portrayed myselven:
And made þerto a maner myriest of oþer,
When two true togeder had tyȝed hemselven,
Bytwene a male and his make such merþe schelde co[m]e,
Wel nyȝe pure paradys moȝt preve no better,
Ellez þay moȝt honestly ayþer oþer welde;
At a stylle stollen steven, unstered wyth syȝt,
Luf-lowe hem bytwene lasched so hote,
Þat alle þe meschefez on mold moȝt hit not sleke.
(697–708)

The author knew Jean de Meun's poem – 'his clene Rose,' as he admiringly called it. The theme of his poem is 'cleanness' – purity in the sense of putting things to their right uses, that is, not defiling them through abuse. This is the meaning of sexual purity here, just as purity in the case of the temple vessels later on means using them for their proper purpose in the divinely ordained services.[56] In this sense purity becomes that bodily worship of God of which the marriage service speaks. It is clear that the English poet considered that this was what Jean de Meun's part of the *Roman* was about – otherwise he would hardly have characterized it by his own theme word 'clene'; and he may well have had Reason's defence of divinely ordained sexuality in mind when he wrote the passage just quoted. In his version of the argument, however, the poetic temperature rises considerably; and, in contrast to Reason's careful generalization, the emphasis falls not on the continuation of the species (although the poet doubtless envisages this), but on the pair of lovers lost and merged in the flame which flashes out between them, bringing them a bliss hardly to be equalled in Paradise. This comparison, together with the comment that love of this kind was 'portrayed' by God himself, might, indeed, suggest that the linking of $μίμησις$ to $παράδειγμα$, which is certainly not present in the *Roman*, is achieved in *Purity*. It seems much more likely, however, if we take due account of the whole tendency of this poem, that the poet merely means by 'portrayed' 'devised', 'made the prototype of', that is, that in the creation of man and the union of Adam and Eve in Paradise all good sexuality takes its beginning – but begins, and ends, as part of created nature.

Chaucer certainly knew the *Roman*. We do not know whether or not he knew *Purity*, or even at what precise stage of his own career the latter poem was written.[57] It may, however, be significant that ideas of this kind could find such effective and outspoken expression in serious poetry written in English during his life-time. The fundamental issue, it is evident, is that of a valuation of man which includes his natural, physical aspects and also his relation to the natural, physical world around him. We have already seen that the whole nature of man is involved in Chaucer's understanding of human 'nobility'; but, more than this, it is a question of including as a potentially valuable part of man's physical nature his ability to love physically and naturally. It is obvious that such a view would run counter to that Christian one which placed supreme emphasis on virginity, and also to the neo-Platonic idea of the physical body as a degraded and degrading prison of the soul and of physical objects as the dregs of creation, separated almost too far from the divine to take on any value at all. In such a view, natural love can only be justified as a first halting step in an ascending scale which progresses from these ultimate limits of value back to the divine and supremely valuable. This idea of love was, in fact, put forward some time after Chaucer's death by the Florentine Platonists of the Renaissance, but it was not a medieval conception.

Another view of things which makes it difficult to place any value on natural love is the Christian one which, following the neo-Platonists, emphasizes the location of the divine likeness in man in the highest part of the soul. In accordance with this emphasis, the doctrine of *nosce te ipsum* involves a turning inward and upward. The object of exploration is the capability of the human soul for comprehending and realizing its relationship with spiritual things, and the process necessarily involves a total turning away from physical phenomena. This process is described in the anonymous fourteenth-century English treatise *The Cloud of Unknowing*.[58] There is, however, another self-knowledge which is not altogether inwardly directed, this involves the relationship of mind to body, and of both, considered as an entity, to their environment in the rest of nature. Under the influence of neo-Aristotelianism, interest inevitably focuses on the outer world. Natural processes become significant in themselves, and worthy of investigation and explanation. Nature, in fact, under this influence, ceases to be primarily seen as a great repertory of types and becomes a system, or series of systems, explicable in terms of themselves. According to the theory of types, natural phenomena exist principally to throw light on spiritual or moral truth, and this truth has been imprinted in the phenomena by their divine author for the express purpose of enlightening mankind. The result is that nature, in so far as it has any importance at all, serves the inward-turning process of the mind and is of no interest in itself. This view is, of course, incompatible not only with Aristotelianism, but also with much that is Biblical – from the account of creation in Genesis, with its apparent equation of the difference between the sexes with the image of God in which man is created ('to the image of God he created them, male and female he created them', a text whose importance we have already noted),[59] to the interest in the relation of divine Providence to the great natural phenomena of weather and of the earth's geological features,[60] which so often seems to run parallel to the works of Aristotle. We

could certainly take Chaucer's exclamation of praise for the nobleness of the Creator of natural wonders in the *House of Fame* as
giving the quintessence of this view. It is, indeed, abundantly clear
from all that he has to say about Nature, and about her relation to
the Venus who stands for natural passion, that Chaucer's value
for man was not based on any neo-Platonic conception of an exiled
spiritual essence eager to escape from the bonds of the material world,
but on the idea of a creature, in the fullest sense, existing as part of the
physical creation. That certain neo-Platonic elements are synthesized
with Chaucer's Aristotelianism is obvious – and this, no doubt,
would be true of most, if not all, fourteenth-century neo-Aristotelians.

Chaucer's attitude to marriage, as we have seen, is dependent
on his idea of man's place in the natural world – and it is because
of this place that he can include, as a valuable part of man, the love
of kind seen as natural and legitimate sexuality. But it is also dependent on his view of man as the one creature which, by reason of its
unique creation in the image of its Creator, also has a place by right
in the spiritual world. For Chaucer, indeed, as for other medieval
thinkers, the world of nature and the world of the spirit were not
entirely separate, but rather formed a continuum. The difference
between them was that for the Middle Ages the natural world was
restricted to the sphere below the moon, which was subject to change,
that is, it was the world of process and of phenomena, to which
the spirit belongs only while it is in combination with the body.
Above the moon, on the other hand, begins the unchanging realm
which only knows state, and which cannot experience process. This,
as Troilus discovers, is the spirit's true home.

For Chaucer, therefore, there is a sense in which human sexuality,
as an essential part of man's physical nature, shares in that nature's
nobility. There is no sign in his work, however, that he related it, as
mimesis to paradigm, or in any other way, to divine love. For him
the idea of love, both as love of kind and as its destructive
opposite, the blind lust, is always closely linked to Nature and
shares in Nature's potential and Nature's value, as well as Nature's
limitations.

Macrobius's definition of the nobility of man, in the eighth and ninth
chapters of Book I of the *Somnium Scipionis*, closely links it to the
virtues. In chapter ix he says:

Sic enim anima virtutes ipsas conscientia nobilitatis induitur;
quibus post corpus evecta, eo unde descenderat, reportatur.

(For thus the soul, through its perception of its own nobility,
assumes the virtues by which it is brought back, once it has left
the body, to the place from whence it descended.)

As a good neo-Platonist, Macrobius of course has no room for the idea
of a nobility which inheres in the whole nature of man; he places it
unhesitatingly in the exiled soul. In chapter viii, in a passage which, as
we have seen, is a seminal one for the medieval tradition of the virtues
and vices, he defines the virtues under the four main branches of
prudence, temperance, fortitude and justice, with their subdivisions.
As we have said, the *Canterbury Tales* as a whole attempts no such
systematization, but there is no doubt that Chaucer thinks of its
virtuous and vicious characters in a way which is conditioned by the
vices and virtues tradition, which, in one form or another, must have
been very familiar to him. Indeed, it would probably be true to say
that no medieval (or, for that matter, Renaissance) thought on the
goodness or badness of man fails to show the influence of the typical
patterns and approach of this tradition, as it was initiated by such
writers as Macrobius and Prudentius, and as it was developed in
innumerable elaborations of their teachings.[61]

We can see this clearly enough if we consider Chaucer's use of the
theme of true gentility, and his constant recourse to the words
'worthy' and 'gentil', as well as 'noble', to describe his good characters – or, with an ironical reversal of meaning, even his bad ones.[62]
The substance of the short definition he gives us in *Gentillesse* –
'Vertu to sewe, and vyces for to flee' (4) – is repeated with elaborations in the *Wife of Bath's Tale*:

> If gentillesse were planted natureelly
> Unto a certeyn lynage doun the lyne,
> Pryvee and apert, thanne wolde they nevere fyne
> To doon of gentillesse the faire office:
> They myghte do no vileynye or vice.
>
> (*CT* III, 1134–8)

In this tale, of course, there is a certain irony in the fact that this
admirable speech is made by a character not at all 'gentil' and leads

up to a solution of the marriage problem which is a somewhat dubious one. Nevertheless, there is nothing ironical in the description of true nobility – and it would not serve the purpose of the broader irony if there were.

The Wife of Bath links poverty to the theme of *gentillesse*, as does the *Clerk's Tale*, with its emphasis on Griselda's lowly situation as well as on her virtue: 'passynge any wight / Of so yong age, as wel in chiere as dede' (*CT* IV, 240–1). Both aspects are summed up in the exclamation:

> Thus Walter lowely – nay, but roially –
> Wedded with fortunat honestetee
> In Goddes pees lyveth ful esily.
>
> (421–3)

In the *Clerk's Tale* poverty is a school in which Griselda learns to practise virtue in the most comprehensive way, as a maid and finally as a 'widow', while, in between, in her life of rank and wealth, she excels not only in 'wyfly hoomlinesse', but 'eek, whan that the cas required it, / The commune profit koude she redresse' (429–31). There is nothing here which is incompatible with Christian virtue, and, as we have seen, there is much in the tale which has an unusually specific religious orientation – but Griselda's life of virtue is, on the whole, treated from the viewpoint which we found to be the prevailing one in the minor poems: poverty consists in a Stoic withdrawal from superfluity and gives way to concern for the commonweal. The Wife of Bath deals with the topic in a more specialized way, relating it to the purely Christian concept of evangelical poverty:

> The hye God, on whom that we bileeve,
> In wilful poverte chees to lyve his lyf.
> And certes every man, mayden, or wyf,
> May understonde that Jhesus, hevene kyng,
> Ne wolde nat chese a vicious lyvyng.
>
> (*CT* III, 1178–82)

This is the patient poverty which is used to imply much that is still controversial in *Piers Plowman*.[63] By relating it to the nobility of the virtues, Chaucer has removed the controversial overtones. He goes on, moreover, to link it to the Stoic concept of poverty as freedom from worldly 'business':

> Glad poverte is an honest thyng, certeyn;
> This wole Senec and othere clerkes seyn.
> Whoso that halt hym payd of his poverte,
> I holde hym riche, al hadde he nat a sherte.
> (1183–6)

But it is when 'virtuous nobility' is brought into relation with pity that we can see most clearly the influence of the virtues and vices tradition. Pity is a conventional and desired attribute of the lady for writers in the sophisticated tradition of love poetry, who use it to mean no more than her willingness to grant the lover his desire. Chaucer, accordingly, uses it of love, but with a new twist: he always relates it to virtue in a general sense. Thus, in *Wommanly Noblesse*, he begins:

> So hath myn herte caught in remembraunce
> Your beaute hoole and stidefast governaunce,
> Your vertues alle and your hie noblesse . . .
> (1–3)

and looks forward to the time

> . . . whan that your gentilnesse,
> Of my grete wo listeth don alleggeaunce,
> And wyth your pite me som wise avaunce.
> (20–2)

It is hard to say how seriously we should take this poem, but there is no doubt that when Dorigen pities Arveragus because of his 'worthiness', Chaucer is making an important point about the marriage: it is a good one because both partners are virtuous, and this reflects on the nature of their love for each other.

When we come to consider the recurring formula 'pitee renneth soone in gentil herte', the situation is even clearer. We first meet it in the *Canterbury Tales* in the *Knight's Tale*, in a line which is Chaucer's own addition. This stands as a comment on Theseus's decision in the case of Palamoun and Arcite, when he finds them fighting in the grove. The women beg him to be merciful:[64]

> Til at the laste aslaked was his mood,
> For pitee renneth soone in gentil herte.
> (1760–1)

Chaucer then goes on to describe the operation of pity in Theseus's mind in more detail, in a way which makes it clear that there is no question of a mere emotional reaction, but of the tempering of just anger by reason in a kind of debate of the princely virtues in miniature, in which 'ire' (line 1765) – not the vice of *ira*, but righteous wrath – is conquered by another aspect of virtue.

> And though he first for ire quook and sterte,
> He hath considered shortly, in a clause,
> The trespas of hem bothe, and eek the cause,
> And although that his ire hir gilt accused,
> Yet in his resoun he hem bothe excused.
>
> (1762–6)

The whole passage describes Theseus at his most kingly, as he exercises the royal function of justice. In the context, it is clear that 'gentil' is a synonym for 'noble' and does not carry the connotations of the modern 'gentle' (which means 'mild'), while 'pitee' has no connection with love and especially not with anything which could be called 'courtly love', but is a well-known and important facet of the cardinal virtue justice. In fact, we are being shown how *ratio*, a facet of prudence, working on *magnanimitas*, the most important facet of fortitude, reconciles *severitas* and *misericordia*, both facets of justice. The whole episode is organized in terms of the traditional approach to the virtues.[65]

In the Prologue to the *Legend of Good Women*, the formula appears again, and, although it is used of Alceste as the Queen of Love, it refers to the judgement she passes on the poet, not to the conduct of any love affair, and is thus, once more, linked to justice:

> The god of Love gan smyle, and than he sayde:
> 'Wostow,' quod he, 'wher this be wyf or mayde,
> Or queene or countesse, or of what degre,
> That hath so lytel penance yiven thee,
> That hast deserved sorer for to smerte?
> But pite renneth soone in gentil herte:
> That maistow seen, she kytheth what she ys.'
>
> (F, 498–504)

And in what follows, the emphasis falls on 'the gret goodnesse of the queene Alceste', which is, clearly, of a general kind and not restricted to love – its supreme instance is her giving of her life for her husband.

In the *Man of Law's Tale*, too, the same idea, though not expressed in quite the same formula, is related not to love, but to justice and judgement. When Constance stands accused:

> This Alla kyng hath swich compassioun,
> As gentil herte is fulfild of pitee,
> That from his eyen ran the water doun.
> 'Now hastily do fecche a book,' quod he,
> 'And if this knyght wol sweren how that she
> This womman slow, yet wol we us avyse,
> Whom that we wole that shal been oure justise.'
>
> (*CT* II, 659–65)

Here the king tempers justice with a prudent moderation, as well as with pity. When the villain has been miraculously exposed he acts more summarily, and only Constance's perfection feels the pity that his justice calls forth:

> This false knyght was slayn for his untrouthe
> By juggement of Alla hastifly;
> And yet Custance hadde of his deeth greet routhe.
>
> (687–9)

Constance is not showing feminine, or saintly, weakness, but a more complete form of the cardinal virtue.

In the *Squire's Tale*, the same formula is used of Canacee's compassion; and, although her justice is not necessarily in question in the sense of being employed in passing judgement, it is her goodness in a general sense (which would necessarily include the four virtues) which is praised:

> That pitee renneth soone in gentil herte,
> Feelynge his similitude in peynes smerte,
> Is preved alday, as men may it see,
> As wel by werk as by auctoritee;
> For gentil herte kitheth gentillesse.
>
> (*CT* V, 479–83)

It is only when we understand the full force of the formula in the light of these passages that we can see the way in which it is turned against May, as an apt comment on the careless speech in which she decides to satisfy Damyen (*CT* IV, 1982–6). She is not aping *fin' amour*, but demonstrating her total failure in something much more important – in the *gentillesse* which consists in the practice of virtue and the avoidance of villainy.

The scheme of the cardinal virtues, whose influence on Chaucer we have been tracing out, typically includes, under the same heading, what we might now think of as opposites. Thus, righteous anger and pity are both displayed by Theseus and both arise from his justice. In the same way, although poverty and lack of 'business' are an important part of virtue thought of primarily from the viewpoint of prudence, 'magnificence' is nevertheless an important part of virtue thought of from the viewpoint of fortitude.[66] Chaucer is well aware of this and praises the latter virtue with as much enthusiasm, in its appropriate place, as he does patient poverty. His term for it is the same one that he uses for virtue in a general sense: 'noble', 'noblesse'. The standard definition of this virtue is supplied by Cicero:[67]

> Magnificentia est rerum magnarum et excelsarum cum animi ampla quadam et splendida propositione cogitatio atque administratio.

> (Magnificence is the contemplation and execution of great and sublime projects with a certain grandness and splendour of conception.)

This is the 'nobleye' of Cambuskyan (*CT* V, 77); it is shown by the 'noble queen' Dido in her splendid treatment of Aeneas (*Legend of Good Women*, F. 1004) and by Theseus in his preparations for the tournament, when he employs himself 'bisily', in no bad sense, in the building of his 'noble' theatre (*CT* I, 1881 ff.). 'Noble' is, again and again, the appropriate epithet for great works of art or construction. It is used of cities – of both Troy and Carthage – in the 'Legend of Dido' (*Good Women*, F, 936 and 1007); in the *House of Fame*, it is used of the Temple of Venus and of the Goddess Fame herself, in a context in which we may suspect that Chaucer is thinking more about the richness of the design of the figure than of anything else (II, 1409).

Another virtue, which is almost as important for Chaucer as the more general concept of nobleness, is that of truth. This is always, for the Middle Ages, a complex idea. Truth simply opposed to falsehood is virtue opposed to vice, God opposed to the devil; this is the sense that it has in *Piers Plowman*, in the allegory of the Field of Folk and of the Marriage of Meed. But truth in this general sense also implies knowledge and understanding of particular truths, that is, *fides* in the sense of the theological virtue. And this, in turn, involves obligation towards something – a faith to be kept. 'Truth' thus overlaps with 'troth' and *fides* with *fiducia*, which is a branch of fortitude. When, therefore, Chaucer speaks of 'truth' in marriage or of a 'true' wife, he is implying both allegiance to virtue in general and allegiance to the special vows which bind husband and wife together.[68] January hopes to secure both aspects in May, when he tells her that truth (i.e., virtue) will win her the love of Christ as well as increased marriage settlements. In the case of Dorigen we have seen a further extension of meaning to something that we can only render as 'integrity' – a meaning which the poet of *Sir Gawain and the Green Knight* also seems to attach to the word.[69]

Truth, like pity, can be a virtue in lovers, and, to give a single example, Criseyde's use of the term in this limited sense, when she says 'To Diomede algate I wol be trewe,' lends added pathos to her situation, when we remember, as we cannot fail to do, how signally she has failed so far to practise this particular virtue in any sense, whether limited or not.

It is evident that Chaucer's conception of the man or woman who is ennobled by virtue is influenced by traditional ways of thinking. In one tale, and one character, the influence goes, or so I believe, even further and conditions his whole approach to his material. This is the *Physician's Tale*, and the character is Virginia. The story is not one of Chaucer's major successes, but the way in which he handles a popular anecdote from Livy and the not inconsiderable additions he makes to it are interesting.[70]

The long opening section of the tale (the first major addition) is devoted to a description of Nature's pride in Virginia as a perfect example of her handiwork:

> For Nature hath with sovereyn diligence,
> Yformed hire in so greet excellence.
>
> (*CT* VI, 9–10)

Much of this passage, as has often been pointed out, consists of commonplaces. The part played by Nature in the formation of beautiful women is often mentioned by poets. Comparisons to the work of Pygmalion and other sculptors and painters of ancient times are not unusual. The attributes of Nature are those which Chaucer himself lists elsewhere.[71] But the passage as a whole has a depth and seriousness which goes beyond convention and prepares us to approach Virginia's story as something more than a pathetic anecdote. The fact that Chaucer found it worthwhile to write in a passage of this kind proves that the story had its importance for him:

> For He that is the formere principal
> Hath maked me his vicaire general,
> To forme and peynten erthely creaturis
> Right as me list, and ech thyng in my cure is
> Under the moone, that may wane and waxe;
> And for my werk right no thyng wol I axe;
> My lord and I been ful of oon accord.
> I made hire to the worshipe of my lord;
> So do I alle myne othere creatures,
> What colour that they han, or what figures.
>
> (19–28)

This speech clearly defines the worth of the physical creation as consisting in its purpose for the worship of God.

From this passage Chaucer goes straight on to describe the moral virtue of 'this noble creature' – a phrase which tells us beyond possibility of doubt how he regards Virginia and what importance he attaches to her. It has been suggested that in his list of Virginia's virtues Chaucer was influenced by a treatise of St Ambrose, the *de Virginibus*.[72] It is certainly the case that some passages in this work are very like those in which Chaucer describes the way of life and the nurturing of Virginia, but her actual virtues, as Chaucer lists them, belong to a more comprehensive scheme. In her, in fact, Chaucer is not describing dedicated virginity in the particular sense in which St Ambrose takes the subject, but the chastity which belongs both to Nature and to the good Venus, that is, the chastity which, in Nature's plan, necessarily precedes marriage and fruition and which, indeed, continues to find expression in marriage. We have, of course, already seen a development of this theme in the *Parlement of Foules*. This chastity is opposed, in the *Physician's Tale*, to a lechery which is also general in its implications and which, by definition, is contrary to Nature's purpose. Virginia's situation, in fact, is comparable to that of the Lady in *Comus*, but not to the dedicated bride of Christ, whose vows are threatened.

Virginia's virtues, which are described at length in lines 41 ff. (the second major addition), belong to a Macrobian type of schematization, which is not what Ambrose had in mind in the *de Virginibus*, as a glance at his text will show. Chaucer does not formally organize them under the headings of the four cardinal virtues, but he does give Virginia a selection of facets belonging to each of the four. The lists of these subdivisions vary greatly from author to author, and Chaucer, naturally, only gives Virginia a selection – the more militant or princely virtues of fortitude, for example, would obviously not be appropriate to her. It is unlikely that he drew on any one particular source for the list, but, for the purposes of comparison, we can cite Alanus de Insulis, since he is an author Chaucer knew, and his list contains all the separate virtues attributed to Virginia.[73] Chaucer's list, in his own order, is:

chastity (43)
humility (45)
abstinence (45)
temperance (46)
patience (46)
measure (47)
discretion (48)
wisdom (shown in speech) (49)
modesty ('shamefastness') (55)
constancy (56)
perseverance ('ever in business') (56)
sobriety (58–9)
innocence (present throughout by implication, and mentioned
    at 92)

All these are mentioned by Alanus under the appropriate headings of the four cardinal virtues:

Alanus	Chaucer
1. Prudence	
circumspectio	discretion
intellectus, ratio	wisdom
2. Temperance	'attempraunce'
castitas	chastity
abstinentia	abstinence
moderantia	measure
sobrietas	sobriety
pudicitia	modesty
3. Fortitude	
humilitas	humility
patientia	patience
constantia	constancy
perseverantia	perseverance
4. Justice	
innocentia	innocence

Alanus, of course, has other virtues under each heading, but the correspondences show that, while Chaucer is not slavishly copying any scheme of this sort, he has this kind of material in mind. This is shown as much by the characteristic inclusion of terms which are almost synonymous (constancy, perseverance; measure, sobriety) as anything else.

Virginia thus stands as the embodiment of the nobility of man, both in the physical perfection with which Nature has endowed her and in a comprehensive endowment of the moral virtues. Her chastity one of these, but, as we have said, it is a chastity which is in accord with Nature, and it does not exclude the possibility of achieving the perfections appropriate to marriage. Virginia fails to reach these because her life is cut short when she is twelve years old. Unlike the Lady in *Comus*, she does not survive her encounter with lechery.

For Jean de Meun, the story is an illustration of false justice. But Chaucer draws from it a moral which is not, at first sight, so clear:

> Heere may men seen how synne hath his merite.
> Beth war, for no man woot whom God wol smyte

> In no degree, ne in which manere wyse
> The worm of conscience may agryse
> Of wikked lyf, though it so pryvee be
> That no man woot therof but God and he.
> For be he lewed man, or ellis lered,
> He noot how soone that he shal been afered.
> Therfore I rede yow this conseil take:
> Forsaketh synne, er synne yow forsake.
>
> (277–86)

The trouble with this is that it does not appear to fit the story. Appius is not disturbed by his conscience. His wicked life is not 'pryvee': on the contrary, it is so open and obvious to the people at large that:

> . . . right anon a thousand peple in thraste,
> To save the knyght, for routhe and for pitee,
> For knowen was the false iniquitee.
> The peple anon had suspect in this thyng,
> By manere of the cherles chalangyng,
> That it was by the assent of Apius;
> They wisten wel that he was lecherus.
>
> (260–6)

The moral is inexplicable in these terms, but it would be explicable if we could assume that we have been watching an open contest between vice and virtue, between Luxuria and Castitas, in which Luxuria, although victorious for a time, is finally defeated. In spite of the fact that Chaucer assures us that 'this is no fable, / But knowen for historial thyng notable' (155–6), I am not sure that this was not, in fact, the way in which he himself regarded the story and intended his audience to regard it.

The *moralitas*, indeed, suggests that the 'historial thyng' is being presented primarily as an *exemplum*, in human terms, of the war of the vices against the virtues, which was, of all the forms of the tradition, one of the most prolific and popular sources of material for both visual art and poetry in the Middle Ages. In the *Psychomachia* of Prudentius,[74] the epic of the battle in and for man's soul, which collects up so much of the earlier, Classical material and which sets the tone for so much which followed, human figures were already used to illustrate and fill out the personifications. Thus Job fights at Patientia's side (109 ff.). The illustrators were quick to take advantage of this way of emphasizing the human element in the allegory,[75] and from the use of individual human figures it was no great step to the presentation of a complete human story as an *exemplum* of the vice or virtue to be illustrated. When this was done, examples were taken from ancient history as well as from the Bible: for example, in the twelfth century, in two miniatures from Ratisbon, Croesus imprisoned illustrates *opulentia*. Similarly, Alexander's aerial journey was a stock example of arrogance.[76] Livy was often used as a source of moral *exempla* by the Classically minded friars of the later Middle Ages – and, indeed, it is to this use that Jean de Meun and Gower, as well as Chaucer, put the story of Virginia.[77]

Considerations of this kind can help us, I believe, to account for the apparent *volte face* of the *moralitas* to the *Physician's Tale*, but they do not altogether explain Chaucer's treatment of the story. In the illustrations just mentioned, the human story is always explained by the actual presence of the relevant vice or virtue figure, which stands as a personification of the moral content and ensures correct interpretation. The listing of Virginia's virtues and the significance of her name, with the repeated attribution of lechery to Apius, cannot have quite the same effect. Nevertheless, I think that the tale is an instance of what Katzenellenbogen calls 'the mode of thought which proceeds step by step from that which is only valid under certain conditions to that which is universally valid'[78] and also of that equally important mode of thought which seeks for a more accurate and telling exploration of the generalized vices and virtues by showing them as existing in a real world of actual human beings. It is to these two attitudes, as it were pulling at the subject from opposite directions, that medieval allegory owes its peculiar effectiveness, as a form which gains its significance from a tension between the general and the particular, not from the sacrifice of one to the other. It is obvious, however, that in the *Physician's Tale* Chaucer goes further than the average allegorist in the development of his *exemplum*. One reason for this is, I think, the paradoxical one that his main concern is, precisely, with the general theme of the nobleness of man, as exemplified by this particular 'noble creature'. The inclusiveness and importance of this concept necessarily gives to his treatment of the little story a completeness which the ordinary moral *exemplum* does not have. It becomes, in his hands, a self-contained whole of a kind which would normally only be produced by a full sequence of allegorical treatments of the vices and virtues.[79]

Chaucer, in fact, seems poised in this tale between the medieval schematic allegory of the vices and virtues, with its partial illustration in human terms, and the later type of allegory, exemplified by the *Faerie Queene*, in which the content is fully and imaginatively fused with the story. His treatment is obviously not schematic; and yet complete fusion, if we are to read the story in terms of a moral allegory, as the ending seems to invite us to do, is lacking. On the human level, Virginia is destroyed by her encounter with a lecherous man; there is no triumph for her. On the moral level, however, although vice triumphs for a time (just as it did in the *Psychomachia*),[80] it is finally and utterly defeated, and the *moralitas* seems to suggest that this defeat is the internal one of the true *psychomachia*, which takes place within the soul. It is hard to see what else Chaucer meant to imply by his reference to the worm of conscience. But how far all this is successful – and even how far it is, in a strict sense, deliberate – are questions which seem to me hard to answer. My feeling is that Chaucer, who never seems altogether at home with traditional allegory, feels a strong impulse towards it as he handles material which, for an author of his day, has an obvious affinity with the *psychomachia* type of vices and virtues tradition, while, at the same time, he is reaching towards new methods of presentation. Whatever the solution, this little work is interesting because it shows one way at least of bringing together the idea of a nobleness in man which belongs to him as a part of the physical creation and the nobility which is his by right of the good fight he puts up in the conflict of the virtues against the vices.

5

The religious poetry

In the *Retractions*, Chaucer speaks with heartfelt satisfaction of his religious writings:

> But of the translacion of Boece de Consolacione, and othere bookes of legendes of seintes, and omelies, and moralitee, and devocioun, / that thanke I oure Lord Jhesu Crist and his blisful Mooder, and alle the seintes of hevene,

and he passes, without a pause, into a final prayer which, although it is in prose, gives us, I believe, the keynote of his devotional poetry:

> bisekynge hem that they from hennes forth unto my lyves ende sende me grace to biwayle my giltes, and to studie to the salvacioun of my soule, and graunte me grace of verray penitence, confessioun and satisfaccioun to doon in this present lyf, / thurgh the benigne grace of hym that is kyng of kynges and preest over alle preestes, that boghte us with the precious blood of his herte; / so that I may been oon of hem at the day of doom, that shulle be saved. *Qui cum patre et Spiritu Sancto vivit et regnat Deus per omnia secula. Amen.*
>
> (*CT* X, 1086–91)

This is a firmly ordered piece of prose, clear and definite in its rhythms (in marked contrast to much of Chaucer's prose writings), and equally clear and logical in thought and expression. Chaucer first asks for grace to feel contrition and then, in order to further his salvation, for the grace of the other two parts of repentance: con-

186

fession and satisfaction. Christ is addressed in three important and familiar aspects – as king, as priest and as the redeemer who shed His blood on the cross – and this triplet balances the triple division of repentance. The prayer ends with a version of a common liturgical formula; there is, in fact, nothing in it which would be unfitted for liturgical use. We may be reminded of one of Samuel Johnson's prayers by the undoubted and deep sincerity which expresses itself in a form, not precisely impersonal – Chaucer's prayer is fitted, as are Johnson's to the personal occasion which gives rise to it – but which would be as well suited to public as to private use. Like Johnson, Chaucer appears to regard the direct approach to God as a moment of awe and solemnity, unmitigated by tenderness or by the intimacy of mystical fervour. These characteristics – firmness of outline, clearcut doctrinal reference and a sincerity whose seriousness leaves no room for the complexities or ambiguities which are so characteristic of Chaucer's secular writing and which make every line of it so personal to him, are the mark of the religious poetry which survives.

Much, indeed, must be lost, if we can accept the list in the *Retractions*, and there seems no reason why we should not. The lists of his own works which Chaucer gives elsewhere appear to be perfectly reliable. The authenticity of the *Retractions* itself, of course, has been questioned, but the manuscript evidence in its favour is very strong, and the tradition of Chaucer's death-bed repentance arises so early that it seems likely at least to have a basis in fact.[1] It is probable, therefore, that the religious poetry we have – the *ABC*, the scattered passages of prayer or invocation in longer works and the two wholly religious tales, the Prioress's and the Second Nun's – represent a part of his achievement which was important to the poet and his audience, even though it tends to be undervalued today.[2]

If the prayer at the end of the *Retractions* can be taken as representative of the tone and general approach of Chaucer's religious poetry, a passage from the *Envoy to Bukton* could be taken as representative of what it is not like:

> My maister Bukton, whan of Crist our kyng
> Was axed what is trouthe or sothfastnesse,
> He nat a word answerde to that axing,
> As who saith, 'No man is al trewe,' I gesse.
>
> (1–4)

This is not irreverent, but it is not reverent either, nor is the reference to Christ introduced to further any devotional purpose. It is part of a poem, whose special effect we have already described,[3] which gives expression to a complex relationship between Chaucer, his friend and his audience, rather than to any sequence of ideas. In the devotional poems this kind of oblique use of religious material is never permitted to appear.

A good instance of this decorum and single-hearted approach in the religious poetry is the very fine prayer to the Blessed Virgin in the *Prioress's Prologue*. This is well adapted to the immediate purpose. The Prioress asks for help to do justice to her high theme, but there is nothing in the terms in which the Virgin is addressed which would unfit the prayer for general use:

> Lady, thy bountee, thy magnificence,
> Thy vertu, and thy grete humylitee,
> Ther may no tonge expresse in no science;
> For somtyme, Lady, er men praye to thee,
> Thou goost biforn of thy benyngnytee,
> And getest us the lyght, of thy preyere,
> To gyden us unto thy Sone so deere.
>
> (*CT* VII, 474–80)

These lines, in common with the whole of the *Prioress's Prologue*, contain numerous reminiscences of the liturgy, particularly of the Office and the Little Office of the Blessed Virgin.[4] The stanza just quoted is, in fact, built up from two liturgical passages, from the prayer and absolution of Matins:

> Sancta et immaculata virginitas, quibus te laudibus efferam nescio,

and:

> Precibus et meritas beatae Mariae semper Virginis et omnium Sanctorum, perducat nos Dominus ad regna caelorum.

These are blended with a passage from Dante's *Paradiso* expressing a more complex idea:

Donna, se' tanto grande e tanto vali,
  che qual vuol grazia ed a te non ricorre,
  sua disïanza vuol volar sanz' ali.
La tua benignità no pur soccorre
  a chi domanda, ma molte fiate
  liberamente al dimandar precorre.

(Lady, thou art so great, and hast such might
  That whoso crave grace, nor to thee repair,
  Their longing even without wing seeketh flight.
Thy charity doth not only him upbear
  Who prays, but in thy bounty's large excess
  Thou oftentimes dost even forerun the prayer.)
  (*Paradiso*, XXXIII, 13–18; Binyon trans.)

with the result that the whole stanza, though closely modelled on the liturgical texts, has a richer effect.

At the end of her Prologue, the Prioress returns to her immediate purpose of seeking guidance to tell her tale fittingly, with an echo of the opening lines on the showing forth of God's praise through the mouths of babes and sucklings:

But as a child of twelf month oold, or lesse,
That kan unnethes any word expresse,
Ryght so fare I, and therfore I yow preye,
Gydeth my song that I shal of you seye.
  (484–7)

Even here it is only in the last line that the particular application is made; in the body of the Prologue, there is no manipulation of the devotional material for the sake of either the situation or character of the Prioress. Chaucer uses the moral-philosophical material which he derived from a reading of authors not overtly Christian (although he may have believed them to have been so in practice) freely, to fit given situations and characters, manipulating it as, we have seen, with great freedom. He does not appear to feel the same freedom in the case of explicitly Christian, devotional material. The Prioress of the general Prologue may give an impression of religious insincerity or, at best, of a sentimentalized piety.[5] The idea of giving expression to these characteristics through the manipulation of a prayer explicitly addressed to the Blessed Virgin does not seem to have occurred to Chaucer and would probably have been distasteful both to him and to his age. I do not think that we can even see an overreliance on convention in the Prioress's tissue of phrases from the liturgy. There is no reason to believe that for Chaucer or his audience these passages lacked evocative power, and the blending-in of a particularly subtle passage from the *Paradiso*, which Chaucer clearly admires, since he uses it elsewhere,[6] shows that he is not making a mechanical amalgam of familiar phrases.

There is yet another way in which Chaucer's religious poetry is clearly distinguished from his use of moral-philosophical material. In the devotional poetry there is none of the elegance and none of the careful restraint which he brings to a moral-philosophical topic. Questions are not left in the air to be amicably settled by the reader in his own time. The manner and even the vocabulary are quite different. We can compare, for example, the following passage from the Prologue to the *Second Nun's Tale* with *Truth*, which has already been sufficiently quoted:

> And of thy light my soule in prison lighte,
> That troubled is by the contagioun
> Of my body, and also by the wighte
> Of erthely lust and fals affeccioun;
> O havene of refut, o salvacioun
> Of hem that been in sorwe and in distresse,
> Now help.　　　　　　　　(*CT* VIII, 71–7)

This stanza is, in all probability, built up not from reminiscences of the liturgy or of Dante's *Paradiso*, like the rest of her Prologue, but from fragments of Stoic/neo-Platonic philosophizing taken either directly from Macrobius or from a later source, Albericus the Mythographer, which combines Macrobius with similar passages from Servius's commentary on the *Aeneid*, VI, 730–4 (the ultimate source, no doubt, of the figures of the prison and contagion of life).[7] This is, in fact, the kind of material on which *Truth* and other writings like it are based. The mood, however, and the method are quite different. The equable, moderate tone of *Truth* is not present in the *Second Nun's Prologue*. The confident voice which advises moderation – 'Suffyce unto thy good . . .' 'Be war . . .' 'Stryve not . . .' – and which only occasionally rises to a tone of command, is replaced by an urgency which compels us to believe in the immediacy of the troubled state of mind the stanza describes. In fact, in spite of its sources, this is not a discussion of a moral topic in the Senecan manner, but a straightforward act of devotion.

The sense of emotional involvement in this prayer from the *Second Nun's Prologue* is still, however, compatible with the lack of intimacy or privacy which we have noticed in Chaucer's religious writing. It is moving, but it is no more personal – and no less – than the general confession. The prayer at the end of the *Troilus*, with its solemnly patterned language, reproducing the design and something of the cadence of a passage in the *Paradiso* (XIV, 28–30), and with its elliptical constructions which, by slight deviations from normal speech order, contrive to suggest the language of the liturgy, is even more obviously public rather than private:

> Thow oon, and two, and thre, eterne on lyve,
> That regnest ay in thre, and two, and oon,
> Uncircumscript, and al maist circumscrive,
> Us from visible and invisible foon
> Defende, and to thy mercy, everichon,
> So make us, Jesus, for thi mercy digne,
> For love of mayde and moder thyn benigne.
> > Amen.
>
> > (V, 1863–9)

The part played by this prayer in the structure of the epilogue to the *Troilus* has already been discussed,[8] and I have suggested that it is, in fact, appropriate to its context. Nevertheless, it is obvious that it also stands in its own right as an expression of faith and a plea for grace.

Even the prayers which are worked into the *Man of Law's Tale* are handled in a comparable way. This tale, as we have seen, is modelled on the type of popular romance which has a strong religious bias, and the heroine is under the direct protection of God. Her prayers are so far adapted to her special situation and story that they are brief and to the point and avoid any holding up of the action; but the style is still the same serious, impersonal one of Chaucer's other prayers. For example:

> 'Immortal God, that savedest Susanne
> Fro false blame, and thou, merciful mayde,

> Marie I meene, doghter to Seint Anne,
> Bifore whos child angeles synge Osanne,
> If I be giltlees of this felonye
> My socour be, for ellis shal I dye!'
> (CT II, 639–44)

This is closely linked to the immediate situation through the last two lines, and also because, in Constance's peculiar situation, the plea is for 'open miracle' rather than for grace in any more normal or general sense.

Constance's more elaborate prayer to the Virgin, built round the theme of her joys and sorrows (841–54), although, again, it arises from the immediate situation, in which Constance's child is placed in danger, could easily be detached for use as a devotional lyric. There is great poignancy, in the context, in the comparison of Mary's child and Constance's:

> Thow sawe thy child yslayn bifore thyne yen,
> And yet now lyveth my litel child, parfay!
> (848–9)

But, far from being a creative innovation brought into being by the needs of this particular story, this is a familiar motif from the literature of the Complaints of the Blessed Virgin. It is found in poems of the type in which she compares her sorrow with the happiness, or indifference, of the human on-looker. A fifteenth-century English poem[9] has:

> Your childur ȝe dawnse vpon your kne
> With laȝyng, kyssyng and mery chere;
> Beholde my childe, beholde now me,
> For now liggus ded my dere son, dere.

The conclusion, through which Constance makes the application to her own immediate circumstances, is an inversion of another common motif of the Complaints at the Cross. Constance ends:

> 'Rewe on my child, that of thy gentillesse,
> Rewest on every reweful in distresse.'
> (853–4)

Another fifteenth-century English Lament of the Virgin[10] has:

> Yf þu can not wepe for my perplexed heuynesse,
> Yet wepe for my dere sone, which on my lap lieth ded.

In writing this prayer of Constance, Chaucer clearly has in mind the popular devotional form of the *planctus*, which has a general suitability to the story he is telling; but he takes no steps to render it in any sense personal to his heroine. The style appropriate to such lyrics is faithfully reproduced. We do not hear an individual voice.

With this imitation of the *planctus*, Chaucer takes his place within the tradition of the Middle English devotional lyric and, indeed, forms an important bridge between the manner of the earlier fourteenth century and the new styles and methods of the fifteenth.[11] His only complete religious lyric, the *ABC*, is, like many other Middle English religious lyrics, based on the French. It is, by this very fact of close translation, as well as from its style, likely to be an early work. We cannot, therefore, expect to find Chaucer at his best in it, but it is valuable as showing us his idea, early in his career, of what devotional poetry ought to be like. By a tradition which may well be true, it was written for actual use, as a prayer, by the Duchess Blanche whose early death is commemorated in the *Book of the Duchess*.[12]

The *ABC* is a poem – and there are many like it in the Middle Ages – which substitutes a formal device for any thematic development. Its form is provided for by the simple decision to compose twenty-six stanzas, each beginning with a successive letter of the alphabet. Beyond the fact that each is addressed to the Blessed Virgin, there is no consecutive thread running through the poem. Within a stanza, it is true, an idea is sometimes treated in such a way that it gives form and unity to the particular section of the poem in which it occurs. For example, the idea that the sinner who dare not face God may yet find courage to appeal to His Mother, is handled so as to lead up to an effective climax at the end of the quatrain and so as to set the sweetness of the Virgin, described in the first half of the stanza, effectively over against the failings of the sinner, described in the second half:

> Glorious mayde and mooder, which that nevere
> Were bitter, neither in erthe nor in see,

But ful of swetness and of merci evere,
Help that my Fader be not wroth with me.
Spek thou, for I ne dar not him ysee,
So have I doon in erthe, allas the while!
That certes, but if thou my socour bee,
To stink eterne he wole my gost exile.

(49–56)

If we compare the French, we can see that Chaucer has strengthened
and simplified the thematic material, by removing the softer idea
of God as man's brother and concentrating on a harsher confrontation of justice and mercy. The result is much tauter than the rather
meandering French stanza:[13]

Glorieuse vierge mere
Qui a nul onques amere
Ne fus en terre ne en mer,
Ta douceur ores m'apere
Et ne sueffres que mon pere
De devant li me jecte puer.
Se devant li tout vuit j'apper
Et par moy ne puis eschapper
Que ma faute ne compere.
Tu devant li pour moy te per
En li' moustrant que, s'a li per
Ne sui, si est il mon frere.

Thematic structure of this kind, however, is restricted to the stanza,
and only the general subject of praise or appeal to the Virgin holds
the poem as a whole together. This is not the case with the later
prayers and invocations which occur as a part of longer works.
It is illuminating to compare two versions of the figure of the burning
bush, one from the *ABC* and one from a mature, free-hand work,
the *Prioress's Prologue*. In the *ABC*, the handling, as with all the types
and figures of the Virgin, is diffuse. At times, it is not even syntacti-
cally clear, and the material is laid out so that, instead of a unified
image, containing and illuminating the paradox, we are told first
what Moses saw, then what he thought and then what we ought to
think:

Moises, that saugh the bush with flawmes rede
Brenninge, of which ther never a stikke brende,
Was signe of thin unwemmed maidenhede.
Thou art the bush on which ther gan descende
The Holi Gost, the which that Moises wende
Had ben a-fyr; and this was in figure.
Now, ladi, from the fyr thou us defende
Which that in helle eternalli shal dure.

(89–96)

The French, here, is less ambitious, but clearer. It begins by stating that what Moses saw was 'in figure', then describes what he saw and then makes the application. Chaucer's attempt at a closer organization is here not happy:[14]

Moyses vit en figure
Que tu, vierge nete et pure,
Jesu le filz Dieu conseüs;
Un bysson contre nature
Vit qui ardoit sans arsure.
C'es tu, n'en suis point deceüs,
Dex est li feus qu'en toy eüs;
Et tu, buisson des recreüz
Es, pour tremper leur ardure.
A ce veoir, vierge, veüs
Soie par toy et receüs
Oste chaussement d'ordure.

In the *Prioress's Prologue*, the figure is differently treated:

O mooder Mayde! O mayde Mooder free!
O bussh unbrent, brennynge in Moyses sighte,
That ravyshedest doun fro the Deitee,
Thurgh thyn humblesse, the Goost that in th'alighte,
Of whos vertu, whan he thyn herte lighte,
Conceyved was the Fadres sapience,
Help me to telle it in thy reverence!

(CT VII, 467–73)

The same antiphon that lies behind de Guilleville's treatment of the burning bush is behind this – translated in the *Lay Folk's Prymer* 'Bi þe buysch þat Moises siȝ unbrent, we knowen þat þi preisable maydenhede is kept'[15] – but here Chaucer has condensed the ideas, forcing the opposites into close juxtaposition – 'mooder Mayde', 'mayde Mooder', 'unbrent, brennynge' – so that the paradox itself becomes the theme of the stanza, and each different aspect of it is set before us directly, without pause for interpretation. The mother who remains a maid; the fire which does not consume; the Spirit which, far from enforcing Mary's virginity, is itself forced by her humility to make the descent from heaven; the Conception which is physical and actual and which yet results in the containing within the physical and actual of something whose scope can only be embraced by an abstract term – 'the Fadres sapience' – all these are welded together and left, as a brilliant organic whole, to make their own impact on the reader without further intervention by the poet.

In comparison, the two stanzas on the Conception in the *Second Nun's Prologue* are slightly more diffuse; but they show the same clear grasp and steady development of the central paradox. In this case the contrast is between the nature and attributes of the Deity and those of the humanity which he assumes in Mary:

> Thow Mayde and Mooder, doghter of thy Sone,
> Thow welle of mercy, synful soules cure,
> In whom that God for bountee chees to wone,
> Thow humble, and heigh over every creature,
> Thow nobledest so ferforth oure nature,
> That no desdeyn the Makere hadde of kynde
> His Sone in blood and flessh to clothe and wynde.

> Withinne the cloistre blisful of thy sydis
> Took mannes shap the eterneel love and pees,
> That of the tryne compas lord and gyde is,
> Whom erthe and see and hevene, out of relees,
> Ay heryen; and thou, Virgine wemmelees
> Baar of the body – and dweltest mayden pure –
> The Creatour of every creature.

> (*CT* VIII, 36–49)

These lines clearly illustrate the absolute quality of Chaucer's religious writing, in contrast to his more contextual use of philosophical material. We know nothing of the Second Nun, so that the question of the suitability of these lines to her character does not arise. We do know, however, that they are a fairly close rendering, with some condensation, of the prayer which Dante considered fitting to be spoken by St Bernard in the ultimate sphere of Paradise, when the illumination of heaven had been added to that which he enjoyed on earth.[16] Such a prayer and such illumination could hardly be made dramatically appropriate to an anonymous nun without considerable building up; but, it is obvious, Chaucer is not here devising a passage suitable to a specific pilgrim. He is reproducing some of the greatest religious poetry he knew.

The fact that Chaucer had read Dante and had understood and could reproduce his special blend of the unswerving line of purely intellectual argument with imagery precisely and vividly realized, separates much of his religious poetry from all other English writing of this kind, both before and immediately after him. The *ABC*, presumably written before he came under Italian influence, reproduces the familiar, fourteenth-century mode of writing, in which imagery is discursively presented and in which there is little clear thematic development. Each image or figure, in poetry of this type, stands alone, and one image cannot take fire from another. A good instance of this kind of writing is William of Shoreham's poem on the Blessed Virgin, 'Marye, maide, milde and fre'.[17] Here the types and figures of the Virgin are set out in a list, without any attempt at connection or systematic development. The stanza containing the figure of the burning bush will show the style:

> Thou art the boshe of Sinai,
> Thou art the righte Sarray;
> Thou hast ibrought ous out of cry
> Of calenge of the Fende;
> Thou art Cristes owene drury
> And of Davies kende.
>
> (19–24)

This way of writing certainly continued into the fifteenth century – as good a Chaucerian as Dunbar, for example, used it in his poem addressed to the Blessed Virgin, *Ane Ballat of our Lady*:[18]

> Hale, sterne superne! Hale, in eterne,
>   In Godis sicht to schyne!
> Lucerne in derne for to discerne
>   Be glory and grace devyne;
> Hodiern, modern, sempitern,
>   Angelicall regyne!
> Our tern inferne for to dispern
>   Helpe, rialest rosyne.
>   *Ave Maria, gracia plena!*
>   Haile, fresche floure femynyne!
> Yerne us, guberne, virgin matern,
>   Of reuth baith rute and ryne.
>   (1–12)

In spite of the rigours of the 'aureate' style and the virtuosity, rarely found in fourteenth-century lyric, which never allows the rhythm to flag, this is the old method of discursive imagery.

On the whole, however, fifteenth-century poets, when they are at their best, show that they have discovered the principle of thematic development in the short poem – the form which comes from within, instead of the device imposed from without – and they therefore use imagery in a new way. We have only to think of the major form of the Complaint of the Blessed Virgin which, in the early fourteenth century, tends to be narrative and expository but which becomes, by the fifteenth, a coherent development of a selected theme. The poem from which we have already quoted, which is built round the contrast between the joy of earthly mothers in their children and the sorrow of the Mother of God in hers, is a case in point.[19]

There are, it is true, instances in the earlier lyric of imagery organically and imaginatively used, but they are isolated, and the technique of the poet seems incomplete and curiously hesitant. A good example comes from a poem which has a schematic form comparable to the *ABC* – in this case an acrostic of the Angelic Salutation:[20]

> And the fruit, þat to alle gode
> Frouering is, and ek hem strongeþ,
> And soules helþe and liues fode
> Þat worschipeliche hit vnderfongeþ,

Ripede in þin herte blode,
Ase appel þat on the tre hongeþ
So dede vpon rode
He to wham folk cristene longeþ.

(97–104)

The bringing together of the apple which hung on the tree of life
and of knowledge with the fruit of the tree of the Cross, in terms of
an apple ripening in Mary's heart's blood (which, again, brings
together the conception and birth and the death of her Son), is
striking and evocative, but the reader needs to help the poet.
This density of meaning has not all been brought effectively to bear
in the actual lines before us. In contrast, we can turn to the assured
handling of an image, whose implications are also multiple, by
Lydgate in one of his most successful short poems, 'Lat no man
booste of conning nor vertu':[21]

It was the Roose of the bloody feeld,
Roose of Jericho that grew in Beedlem,
The five rooses portrayed in the sheeld,
Splayed in the baneer at Jerusalem;
The sonne was clips, and dirk in every rem,
Whan Christ Jesu five welles list uncloose
Toward Paradis, called the rede strem –
Of whos five woundes prent in your hert a roose.

(57–64)

Lydgate has realized that the total movement of the poem must be
organized so as to carry the reader with and through the densely
packed imagery.

When the fourteenth century does achieve a comparably com-
pelling movement, it is in a manner more like that of Langland
than like that of Chaucer and his followers. Rolle, for instance,
can often bring off a paradox in a way which reminds us of Langland's pregnant line. For example, from the *Ego Dormio*:[22]

A wonder it es to se, wha sa understude,
How God of mageste was dyand on the rude.

In the same way, Langland exploits the cumulative roll and beat
of his long line:

The lorde of lyf and of liȝte tho leyed his eyen togideres.
The daye for drede with-drowe and derke bicam the sonne.

(B, XVIII, 59–60)

William Herebert's poem on the theme 'Quis est iste qui venit de Edom' has the same kind of cumulative energy, arising from the exploitation of the rhythmic possibilities of a long line treated as a whole. It has, too, an imaginative power which is not short of Langland's:

> What ys he, thys lordling, that cometh vrom the vyht
> Wyth blod-rede wede so grysliche ydyht,
> So vayre y-coyntised, so semlich in syht,
> So styflyche ȝongeth, so douhti a knyht?
>
> Ich hyt am, Ich hyt am, that ne speke bote ryht,
> Chaunpyoun to helen monkunde in vyht.

The poem goes on to develop the image of the wine press to the bitterly triumphant conclusion:[23]

> Ich habbe y-trodded the uolk in wrethe and in grome,
> Adreynt al wyth shennesse, y-drawe doun wyth shome.

Although the movement is quieter, we find the same imaginative energy, and the same sense of an irresistible progression in the movement of the verse, in Langland's use of the same image:

> For I, that am lorde of lyf, loue is my drynke,
> And for that drynke to-day I deyde vpon erthe.
> I fauȝte so, me threstes ȝet, for mannes soule sake;
> May no drynke me moiste, ne my thruste slake,
> Tyl the vendage falle in the vale of Iosephath,
> That I drynke riȝte ripe must, *resureccio mortuorum*.

(B, XVIII, 363–8)

This kind of imagination, and this kind of verse movement, is foreign both to Chaucer and to the fifteenth century. It represents, perhaps, the greatest independent achievement of English religious poetry in the earlier period, but it is not transmissible to a later generation. What is transmissible is the newer synthesis of intellectual argument and illuminating image which Chaucer developed to best effect under the influence of Dante.

The *Second Nun's Tale* is Chaucer's simplest and most wholehearted treatment of a saint's legend.[24] In it he grasps the essence of the hagiographical approach and presents for our consideration, in full seriousness and reverence, a special case of the intervention of divine Providence in the natural world. This intervention, at once so unique and amazing and yet so common and expected in the world of such a legend, is the object of the story, and the human participants exist only as a part of the medium in which the divine act works itself out. All specifically and individually human characteristics are lost.

Thus, the opening of the tale is organized so as to lead up as swiftly and economically as possible to the miraculous appearance of the angel. Cecilia is presented in terms of the ideal, with no touch of realism or individuality:

> This mayden bright Cecilie, as hir lif seith,
> Was comen of Romayns, and of noble kynde,
> And from hir cradel up fostred in the feith
> Of Crist, and bar his gospel in hir mynde.
> She nevere cessed, as I writen fynde,
> Of hir preyere, and God to love and drede,
> Bisekynge hym to kepe hir maydenhede.
>
> (*CT* VIII, 120–6)

When the time of her marriage comes, she is shown advancing to it at the same unhurried pace and with the same clear confidence:

> And whan this mayden sholde unto a man
> Ywedded be, that was ful yong of age,
> Which that ycleped was Valerian,
> And day was comen of hir marriage,
> She, ful devout and humble in hir corage,
> Under hir robe of gold, that sat ful faire,
> Hadde next hire flessh yclad hire in an haire.

And whil the organs maden melodie,
To God allone in herte thus sang she:
'O Lord, my soule and eek my bodye gye
Unwemmed, lest that it confounded be.'
(127–37)

Her prayer is not so much a petition as a statement. The steady
flow of the verse, varied only by the strong, emphatic pauses at
the beginning, carries us on over contrasts which are never allowed
to become conflicts. In the same way, Cecilia makes not an appeal,
but a statement to her husband. If he does not respect her virginity,
the angel who cares for her will straightway kill him:

'And in youre yowthe thus ye shullen dye.'
(158)

The tranquil certainty of divinely ordered cause and effect is not
disturbed by the slightest intervention of human emotions. There is
no clash between human and divine love, no regrets, no promise
of pity, merely a steady sober progression to the moment of revelation,
when the angel appears with the two flowery crowns.

The rest of the legend proceeds in the same untroubled way, with
the emphasis as much on conversion by doctrine (in, for example,
Cecilia's explanations in lines 320 ff.) as by marvels. Indeed, the
sobriety in the presentation of the marvels, and the care to back
each one up by insistence on the fundamentals of the Christian faith,
gives the tale a dignity sometimes lacking in hagiographical literature. For example, Valerian is presented with a book:

And on his book right thus he gan to rede:
'O Lord, o feith, o God, withouten mo,
O Cristendom, and Fader of alle also,
Aboven alle and over alle everywhere.'
(206–9)

We seem to have a more vivid sense of a Christian heroic age,
in which dogma and miracle are thought of as going hand in hand,
than is often the case in writing of this kind. This impression is
enhanced by the light sketching in of the pagan convert's first
reactions to the strange world of Christianity. Valerian's brother
thus receives the explanation of the miraculous flowers:

Tiburce answerde, 'Seistow this to me
In soothnesse, or in dreem I herkne this?'
'In dremes,' quod Valerian, 'han we be
Unto this tyme, brother myn, ywis.
But now at erst in trouthe oure dwellyng is.'

(260–4)

The paradox is not handled so as to induce the slightest sense of
conflict, but is presented as confident, even triumphal, assertion.

The contrast between the Christian life and the Christian expectation is more sharply put when Tiburce expresses his horror that he
should be taken to Urban, and here Chaucer allows something
more like actual life to show through the legendary structure.
Tiburce's fears are real fears. The persecution of the faithful is
as actual as their ultimate reward:

Tiburce answerde and seyde, 'Brother deere,
First tel me whider I shal, and to what man?'
'To whom?', quod he, 'com forth with right good cheere,
I wol thee lede unto the Pope Urban.'
'Til Urban? brother myn, Valerian?'
Quod tho Tiburce, 'woltow me thider lede?
Me thynketh that it were a wonder dede.

Ne menestow nat Urban', quod he tho,
'That is so ofte dampned to be deed,
And woneth in halkes alwey to and fro,
And dar nat ones putte forth his heed?
Men sholde hym brennen in a fyr so reed
If he were founde, or that men myghte hym spye,
And we also to bere hym compaignye.

And whil we seken thilke divinitee
That is yhid in hevene pryvely
Algate ybrend in this world shul we be!'

(302–18)

Cecilia's answer is simple and firm:

'But ther is bettre lif in oother place,
That nevere shal be lost, ne drede thee noght.'

(323–4)

The series of martyrdoms which follow are related in the usual hagiographical manner, without appeal to the emotions of fear or pity. We are to feel wonder at the greatness of the victory and admiration for the victor. Cecilia's farewell words to the two brothers could stand as a conclusion to the tale as a whole – or to any legend of this type:

> 'Ye han for sothe ydoon a greet bataille,
> Youre cours is doon, youre feith han ye conserved.
> Gooth to the corone of lif that may nat faille;
> The rightful Juge, which that ye han served,
> Shal yeve it yow as ye han it deserved.'
>
> (386–90)

The final description of her own death merely drives home the same point. It is related entirely without emotion or reference to pain. The purpose of the narrative is not to provoke any of the reactions which could be associated with the contemplation of actual suffering. The point is to present one more great witness to divine truth. To modern sensibility, Cecilia teaching the people 'half deed, with hir nekke ycorven there' is not attractive. But we place the emphasis wrongly. The point is that she still, after all that the tormentors can do, continues to bear irrepressible witness to God's truth and to carry out the purpose of His particular intervention and suspension of the laws of nature in her case. This is the wonder and triumph of the tale; and, in Chaucer's hands, through the steady progress of the narrative and the soberly collected cadences of his verse, we can only feel that it has been well achieved.

The same impossibility of silencing the voice of the Christian witness is the theme of the *Prioress's Tale*; but the poem as a whole presents a much more complex problem than does the *Second Nun's Tale*. For one thing, it is much more closely integrated into the plan of the *Canterbury Tales*. As we have said, we know nothing of the Second Nun; her prologue, even apart from its lapse into the male gender, is not particularly suitable to an anonymous English female religious, with its sounding echoes of St Bernard's prayer in Dante's Paradise. The tale itself is suitable enough, but it has no reflections of the teller, since the teller has not been endowed with an image to reflect, and its handling, with its strong, steady, restrained progress perhaps suggests a masculine rather than a feminine narrator, at any rate if we contrast it with the softer line of the other tales told by women – the *Wife of Bath's Tale*, with its tendency to calculated digression, and the *Prioress's Tale*, in which softness has been carried to a point which sometimes troubles modern taste.

This is, in fact, the crux of the matter. Are we to see in the *Prioress's Tale* a religious work, a saint's legend told primarily, if not wholly, for its own sake and with a view to its own scale of values, or are we to see a skilful adaptation of a familiar medieval genre, a pastiche built up with the sole object of displaying to advantage (or, in some views, disadvantage) the character of the Prioress?[25]

Either view, taken to extremes, would probably be equally false. The saint's legend, as a genre, does not appeal greatly to modern taste. When it is unmistakably in question, as in the *Second Nun's Tale*, an easy solution is to drop the tale quietly from Chaucer's works. It does not show him at his incomparable best; we have enough without it – we can leave it unread. The *Prioress's Tale*, however, is too evidently good for this treatment, and it is also too evidently a part of the *Canterbury Tales*. Therefore, it is read; but modern taste tends to favour the suppression of the religious element and to search for subtleties of a non-religious kind, connected with the characterization and even satirization of the Prioress. On the other hand, to dismiss the Prioress entirely and to treat the tale as an isolated legend would be equally disproportionate. It is evident that between the *Second Nun's Tale* and the *Prioress's Tale* something has happened, and that that something is the growth of the concept of the *Canterbury Tales* as a framework in which individual tales can keep their identity but are yet affected by their place in the whole. Therefore, although we cannot read the *Prioress's Tale* wholly and exclusively in the light of what we know about the Prioress, we cannot keep her out either. The tale is fitted to the teller through a certain contrived simplicity and deliberate restriction of scope (in which it is in contrast to the *Second Nun's Tale*); but nothing within it, and nothing that we know about Chaucer as a religious poet, could possibly lead us to think that he presents it with anything but sincerity, or that we hear any other voice than his in the final prayer:

> Preye eek for us, we synful folk unstable,
> That, of his mercy, God so merciable
> On us his grete mercy multiplie,
> For reverence of his mooder Marie –
>
> (687–90)

or that we are not to take at its face value the reaction of the company:

> Whan seyd was al this miracle, every man
> As sobre was that wonder was to se.
>
> (691–2)

Nevertheless, there are basic differences in the narrative art of Chaucer's two saints' legends. The *Prioress's Tale*, for one thing, is naturalistically presented. Instead of the grand, flat stylization of Cecilia's offer to her husband of a choice between love and death, as tranquilly accepted by him as it is offered, there is minute attention to motivation and to the logical development of the action. The one suspension of normal cause and effect in which the miracle consists is carefully pointed up for what it is – an interruption of natural law by the direct intervention of God's hand. This is not indicated through the grand paradox of the awakening from the dream of life, but by exact statement:

> 'My throte is kut unto my nekke boon,'
> Seyde this child, 'and, as by wey of kynde,
> I sholde have dyed, ye, longe tyme agon.
> But Jesu Crist, as ye in bookes fynde,
> Wil that his glorie laste and be in mynde,
> And for the worship of his Mooder deere
> Yet may I synge *O Alma* loude and cleere.'
>
> (649–55)

The two stages of the narrative – the events leading up to the killing of the child, and those leading up to the discovery of his body – are carefully laid out, with great attention to probability and to the exact order of events. The child's devotion to the Virgin is accounted for by his mother's early teaching: 'For sely child wol alday sone leere' (512). This devotion grows, as he first hears and then learns the song '*Alma Redemptoris*', until he sings it at all possible moments because 'On Cristes mooder set was his entente' (550). Through this habit he provokes the Jews and comes to his ugly death:

> This cursed Jew hym hente, and heeld hym faste,
> And kitte his throte, and in a pit hym caste.

> I seye that in a wardrobe they hym threwe
> Where as thise Jewes purgen hire entraille.
>
> (570–3)

The sense of shock at this brutality is conveyed by the personal intrusion into the narrative of 'I seye'. This is the highest point of pathos in the first part of the narrative. The extreme youth and innocence of the child have been repeatedly emphasized – 'litel' is the prevailing epithet used of him (503, 509, 516, where it is carried over even to the book from which he learns, and 552) – and the whole narrative helps to build up the sense of his childish and partial comprehension of the devotion he pays to the mother of God. Neither he nor the child from whom he learns his song understand the Latin. His teacher, the slightly elder child, says apologetically 'I lerne song, I kan but smal grammeere'. Nevertheless, these fumbling attempts to learn of something beyond his comprehension culminate in clear, direct contact with what he seeks:

> The swetnesse hath his herte perced so
> Of Cristes mooder, that to hire to preye,
> He kan nat stynte of syngyng by the weye.
>
> (555–7)

This is the real miracle, and it is from this point that the story begins to unfold on two levels of reality: on the one hand we have the childish, uncomprehending little boy, perfunctorily butchered; on the other, the martyr who becomes an important witness to the reality of the Christian faith. The Prioress moves immediately from one plane to the other. After describing the death she continues:

> O martir, sowded to virginitee,
> Now maystow syngen, folwynge evere in oon
> The white Lamb celestial – quod she –

Of which the grete evaungelist, Seint John,
In Pathmos wroot, which seith that they that goon
Biforn this Lamb, and synge a song al newe,
That nevere, flesshly, wommen they ne knewe.

(579–85)

This effectively shifts attention from the 'litel body sweete', which
is later buried, to the blessed soul, which takes its place among the
virgin followers of the Lamb.

The same plan is followed in the next section of the narrative.
First the natural reactions of the mother, which send her out to
search for her son, are realistically described:

This poure wydwe awaiteth al that nyght
After hir litel child, but he cam noght;
For which, as soone as it was dayes lyght,
With face pale of drede and bisy thoght,
She hath at scole and elleswhere hym soght,
Til finally she gan so fer espie
That he last seyn was in the Juerie.

With moodres pitee in hir brest enclosed,
She gooth, as she were half out of hir mynde,
To every place where she hath supposed
By liklihede hir litel child to fynde.

(586–96)

When the body is found, through its miraculous singing, there is
the same immediate transition to the child's translated state:

This gemme of chastite, this emeraude,
And eek of martirdom the ruby bright . . .

(609–10)

The rest of the tale is taken up with the explanation of the miracle,
spoken by the child as though he still lived, and with a return to the
earlier mood of pathos and tenderness:

'Wherfore I synge, and synge moot certeyn,
In honour of that blisful Mayden free,
Til fro my tonge of taken is the greyn;
And after that thus seyde she to me:
"My litel child, now wol I fecche thee,

Whan that the greyn is fro thy tonge ytake.
Be nat agast, I wol thee not forsake."'

(663-9)

The so-called 'sentimentality' of the *Prioress's Tale* arises from the
fact that the miracle consists in the divine intervention in ordinary
insignificant events and persons; the commonplace and the uncomprehending are taken up into the world of the spirit. The tale
is thus a perfect *exemplum* of the statement in its prologue that the
Blessed Virgin sometimes anticipates men's prayers. An imperfect
intention and a childish, only half-comprehending state are changed,
through her mediation, into the perfection of martyrdom and the
fullness of knowledge in the heavenly life in the train of the Lamb.
In the *Second Nun's Tale*, on the other hand, the miracles affect heroically significant figures who are marked out for martyrdom from the
beginning and, indeed, are quite incomprehensible considered from
any other viewpoint. Thus, although the result is a pathos and tenderness which seem particularly appropriate to the Prioress, her feelings,
as they are displayed by her tale, are hardly to be equated with her
tears over trapped mice and little dogs. The other pilgrims are not
represented as sharing these; but they are sobered and silenced by
her tale. If we feel that the tale is too soft or its contrasts too crude,
we are, I think, merely demonstrating the difference between four-
teenth- and twentieth-century sensibility. We cannot share the tears
which 'trikled doun as reyn' when the little clergoun finally gives
up the ghost any more than we can weep with Petrarch over Griselda,
but we need not therefore doubt the genuineness of these displays
of emotion or try to read an extreme of subtlety into a moment in
which the fourteenth century was probably at its simplest and most
sincere.

6

Aftermath:
the noble rethor poet

If we were now, in conclusion, to attempt a brief characterization of Chaucer's poetry, we could only fall back on Dryden's famous phrase 'God's plenty'. Everything is there: high seriousness as well as high comedy; a subtly complex organization of diction and rhythm, as well as the plainest of plain writing where that is appropriate. Philosophical ideas are handled with freedom and understanding, while direct observation of the world around is sharp and precise. Yet, of all this richness of poetic achievement and poetic variety, which Dryden – and, we may surely assume, Spenser before him – had no difficulty in perceiving, Chaucer's immediate followers, or so we are often told, valued only the poet's most formal flights of rhetoric, in which they found encouragement for their own peculiar development of the 'aureate style'.[1]

Was it really the case that the writers of the fifteenth and early sixteenth centuries failed to appreciate, or even understand, more than a fraction of what Chaucer had done, while, in the years that followed, he quietly took his place, without any apparent revolution of feeling, as a familiar and established part of the main stream of English poetry?[2] The question is usually answered in the affirmative, because, it is said, the English Chaucerians were too stupid – 'dunces' according to C. S. Lewis, although with some qualification – to recognize anything else in their master. The Scottish Chaucerians, who were, manifestly, not dunces, are usually allowed a more perceptive appreciation of the English poet, although they too are thought to overemphasize the importance of 'rhetoric'.[3]

A close look at the facts does not really support judgements of this kind. For one thing, there is far greater variety of style in the fifteenth century than these critics seem to assume, and a much greater exploitation of Chaucer's plainer ways of writing.[4] For another, although there are striking differences, in the kinds of poetry undertaken and the kind of audience aimed at, between Chaucer and his followers, the change is not one which can usefully be defined in terms of 'stupidity' or 'dullness'. And, finally, we need to ask what, precisely, the many panegyrics in praise of Chaucer really meant. They are, as a rule, phrased in terms which seem to us unnecessarily elaborate and contrived; and therefore, we feel, they must correspond to an admiration for elaboration and contrivance in the poet praised. A closer look, it seems to me, suggests that this is not necessarily the case.

First among the 'stupid' poets comes Lydgate, with an immensely bulky *oeuvre* composed, for the most part, in metres which we may understand as little as Spenser understood Chaucer's.[5] Even if we did understand them, it is doubtful if we should be able to claim that Lydgate is a consistently good poet. Setting aside the problem of their scansion, his lines are too numerous and too repetitive; too many of his works are mere versifications of material for which there was a demand, but which he does not feel the need to treat, more than occasionally, in a way which rises above verse and into poetry. Yet to be an indifferent or an uneven poet is not necessarily to be an incompetent critic. What seems to me striking about the immense bulk of Lydgate's work is not incompetence or stupidity, but the overwhelming testimony it provides to an eager and, indeed, almost insatiable appetite for something which it might be better to call 'letters' rather than poetry. In this respect, perhaps the only age which provides an apt parallel is that of the Victorians, in which books – and especially long books – similarly flourished because they were enjoyed for a wide variety of reasons by a wide audience. The fifteenth century seems to have had similarly wide interests and to have been delighted by factual reading matter of all kinds as well as by what we should call 'imaginative' works; and its industrious writers were ready and willing to cater for every aspect of taste. Inevitably, the very width of interest and the capacity to cope effortlessly with quantity, as was the case with the Victorians, tended to encourage a lowering of standards of finished and detailed workmanship. Thus we find in the best of the Victorian novelists the same surprising tolerance of bad, or at the least mediocre, writing as we do in the fifteenth-century providers of literature in bulk. Lydgate, undoubtedly, reflects an audience much more easily pleased than Chaucer's could ever have been: one which had acquired the habit of books and could take the latest production in its stride, very much as we tend to do today, without too anxious weighing of its absolute merits. If this is literary stupidity, we must accuse the whole Victorian age and, no doubt, our own as well of stupidity of an exactly similar kind.

In fact, the fifteenth-century taste in books, though catholic, was far from stupid, if we can judge from the importance of what they helped to transmit to writers of the following centuries. It is true that it is not always their version which survives, but we can ask whether new ones would have been undertaken without their help in keeping interest alive. To give only a few examples of works of this seminal kind, Lydgate himself was responsible for a version of de Guilleville's *Pèlerinages* and also of the *Secreta Secretorum*.[6] In the latter work and in the *Fall of Princes*, he dealt with much material that was of great importance to the Elizabethans.[7] He also provided versions of the stories of Troy and of Thebes – the two points at which Classical epic and romance met in a meaningful way. Here, too, he was transmitting a branch of European romance on which Chaucer had drawn, but which does not seem to have penetrated into England before the fourteenth century. In addition, he wrote a great deal of what we can only call 'album-poetry'[8] – occasional poems which, although they lack Chaucer's characteristic finish and urbanity, still have their own importance. Writing of this kind fosters the taste for poetry as a social art and keeps open the soil in which it can flourish in more serious forms.

Lydgate, of course, was not alone in activities of this kind. Important translations and compilations were undertaken by numerous other writers.[9] A reading of Caxton's publisher's list, for example, will show the same instinct for an important or representative book, for material worth preserving, even in an inferior form. We can pick out such names as Chaucer himself, Gower and Malory; works of the indefatigable adapter and popularizer, Christine de Pisan; the *Recuyell of the Histories of Troy*; the *Mirror of the World*; the *Golden Legend*; a translation of the French romance version of the *Aeneid*; Classics and near-Classics (works by Cicero and Boethius); Aesop's *Fables*; as well as books about chess and health.

We cannot, certainly, hold Chaucer responsible for the growth, which Caxton fostered, of the reading public in the fifteenth century nor for the change of taste between that century and the preceding one. Many factors are involved, some of them social rather than literary or cultural in any strict sense. Nevertheless, we can certainly see Chaucer, together with some of his contemporaries, especially Gower, as influential in helping to establish a new attitude to poetry in English.

The literary activities of the fifteenth century, although they are broadly based and therefore tend to lack that exquisiteness of achievement which would demand a more sensitively perceptive audience, were very far from being stupid. In another way, too, they showed appreciation of an important part of fourteenth-century achievement, especially that of Chaucer and Gower: they continued to foster interest in and knowledge of Classical antiquity, with its inevitable effect on all aspects of cultural life and, especially, on the conception and the evaluation of poetry. We have already discussed Chaucer's attitude to antiquity and the important part it played in his development as a poet. The influence of Gower as a transmitter of Classical legends, in some ways even greater than that of Chaucer, has recently been emphasized by J. A. W. Bennett.[10] We have also had occasion to refer to the importance of certain English Friars in this connection: it is notable that Beryl Smalley frequently compares their activity with the typically 'Renaissance' attitude to the Classics of Boccaccio or Petrarch.[11] The fifteenth and early sixteenth centuries in England continued the process. Lydgate's interest in antiquity has recently been demonstrated by Alain Renoir.[12] Caxton, as we have seen, included translations of Classical works in his list, and the literary activity of the Scottish Chaucerians finally produced what is still one of the best translations of the *Aeneid* in the English language – that of Gavin Douglas. Somewhat earlier, Henryson wrote a version of the story of Orpheus and Eurydice, and modelled his fables on Aesop's. Boethius's *de Consolatione Philosophiae* was again translated, and so was another old favourite, Cicero's *de Amicitia*, while Skelton broke new ground with the *Diodorus Siculus* and Lord Berners with the *Meditations* of Marcus Aurelius. Works like Christine de Pisan's *Othéa* were also translated and remained influential for a long time.[13]

We can see something of the value a poet like Lydgate placed on the classical past if we read, for example, his 'Exclamacion of the deth of Alcibiades'.[14] It is the honour and prowess, the royal nobility, which emerge as important – to give a romanticized version, perhaps, of the ideal leader, but also one which clearly derives from an idea of princely magnificence which has links with Aristotle and Cicero, as well as with the political realities of Lydgate's own time:

> Alcibiades is passed into fate
> Liht of knihthod lith clipsed in the shade:
> The Parchas sustren to soone sette his date
> Of hih noblesse to make the laurer fade.
> Lacedemonoys of his deth were glade:
> Funeral fyr his bodi hath deffied,
> For hih prowesse his soule stellefied.
>
> (3676–82)

After this it is not surprising to find that it is Duke Humphrey's *virtue* in studying the Classics which is praised, not merely his industry:

> His corage neuer doth appalle
> To studie in bookis off antiquite,
> Therin he hath so gret felicite
> Vertuously hymsilff to ocupie.
>
> (*Fall of Princes*, I, 395–8)

Once again, it would be a gross oversimplification to attribute solely to Chaucer and his contemporaries this lasting feeling for the importance of the Classics. Nevertheless, it is, I think, true to say that without their activities Classical material could not so easily, nor so early, have been accepted as suitable matter for English poetry – or if it had been, it might have been used in accordance with other purposes and patterns of thought. We can certainly see, in Lydgate's praise of Classical heroes, a continuation of the attitude, and even the phrasing, of Chaucer in the *Knight's Tale* and the *Troilus*; and, although the individual works produced during the fifteenth century may not always have been very striking in themselves, the resultant widening of the whole basis of poetry is of importance. It is not, and this must be emphasized, a question of a Humanistic attitude to Classical learning – whether or not this appeared in the fifteenth century remains a matter for debate – it is rather one of the whole nature and scope of poetry.[15]

The writers who praised Chaucer were, thus, not merely representative of a highly specialized and transitory fashion in English literature, nor of narrow interests as far as subject-matter is con-

cerned. Most of them, at one time or another, used what we now call
the 'aureate style', but such flights of rhetorical and verbal elaboration were by no means characteristic of their work as a whole.
Lydgate, at one end of the period, and Dunbar at the other, for
example, wrote 'aureate' works, but both also cultivated other styles.
What was characteristic of these and of many other writers was
participation in an energetic drive to provide a widening public
with reading matter in quantity and in variety. This they did with
considerable shrewdness and appreciation of the best books for the
purpose. In the process, many of them go out of their way to testify
to their admiration of Chaucer and to the debt they think they owe
him. If we now examine what they say, we shall, I think, see that
they show the same shrewdness and ability to grasp essentials here
as they do in other literary matters.

There is no doubt that most of the praise which is showered on
Chaucer during the fifteenth century relates to his style. Nevertheless,
there is also praise of his matter. For his immediate contemporary
Usk, he was 'the noble philosophical poete'.[16] A little later, Hoccleve
asks:

> . . . who was hier in philosophie
> To Aristotle in our tonge but thow?

and Caxton calls him 'the noble and grete philosopher'.[17] Thomas
Feylde, writing at the beginning of the sixteenth century, has praise
for Chaucer, Gower and Lydgate which covers their subject-matter –
and which shows how the term 'rhetorician' can have a very
general sense and refer as much to the handling of content as to the
details of expression:[18]

> C[h]aucer floure of rethoryke eloquence
> Compyled bokes pleasaunt and meruayllous.
> After hym noble Gower, experte in scyence,
> Wrote moralytyes herde and delycyous.
> But Lydgate's workes are fruytefull and sentencyous.
> Who of his bokes hathe redde the fyne,
> He wyll hym call a famus rethorycyne.

There is no reason to doubt the sincerity or (allowing for a little complimentary hyperbole) the good sense of such praise of Chaucer's matter. His poetry is, as we have seen, often philosophical in tone and content, and it would be odd if those who came after him failed to appreciate the fact, since they certainly continued to show interest in philosophical-moral works of this kind. If there is a difference, it is that some of the material which Chaucer had used structurally, with the full force of a familiar philosophical argument behind it, becomes for his successors little more than an accepted part of the imagery of poetry. Lydgate, for example, uses the philosophical chain in the *Life of Our Lady* merely as part of a circumlocution for God, whom he describes as:

> . . . the Prince and the worthy Kyng
> That all enbraseth in his myghty cheyne.
>
> (ii, 772–3)

It would be impossible to say whether this is the chain of the elements, the Homeric chain of being or the chain of love. But even if some Chaucerian topics of this kind tend to lose their force, it cannot be denied that Lydgate handles the larger units of his romance narratives to express ideas and ideals, just as Chaucer had done before him.[19]

The general tone and the particular language which the fifteenth century used to praise Chaucer's poetic art are well represented by the following passage from the *Life of Our Lady*:[20]

> The noble rethor Poete of breteine
> That worthy was the laurer to haue
> Of p[o]etrie and the palme atteine.
> That made firste to distille and reyne
> The golde dewe droppis of speche and eloquence
> In-to oure tounge thourgh his excellence,
> And founde the flourys first of rethoryk
> Oure rude speche oonly to enlumyne,
> That in oure tunge was neuer noon him like.

Phrases like 'the rethor Poete', 'speche and eloquence', 'the flourys . . . of rethoryk', 'to enlumyne', recur again and again, and it is not surprising that they have passed unquestioned as implying nothing more than a preoccupation with elaboration of diction, with 'fine writing', at the expense of subject-matter. They could, indeed, hardly have been better chosen to mislead us and to appear to describe what we admire least in poetry. In the same way, Dunbar, to take another example, praises Chaucer in terms which are even more elaborate:

> O reverend Chaucere, rose of rethoris all,
> As in oure tong ane flour imperiall,
> That raise in Britane evir quho redis rycht,
> Thou beris of makaris the tryumph riall;
> Thy fresch anamalit termes celicall
> This mater coud illumynit have full brycht:
> Was thou noucht of oure Inglisch all the lycht,
> Surmounting eviry tong terrestriall
> Alls fer as Mayis morow dois mydnycht?
>
> (*Golden Targe*, 253–61)

Yet Dunbar's own work, in which he frequently uses other and far less elaborate styles, suggests a full and true appreciation of Chaucer's achievement. It is hardly satisfactory to suppose that, in spite of critical denseness, Dunbar arrived at this result by a happy chance of genius.

Dunbar wrote his praise of Chaucer in the early years of the sixteenth century. Somewhat earlier, Caxton had produced criticism which, it is generally agreed, is excellent. Miss Spurgeon, who considered that 'the comments on Chaucer which have any pretension to be called literary or aesthetic criticism' before the middle of the sixteenth century 'consist purely of praise of a very simple and vague kind, the vagueness and general nature of the remarks being their most striking feature',[21] still singles out Caxton as 'on the whole, amongst all Chaucer's contemporaries and successors during the fifteenth century, the most discriminating . . . the remarks of both writers [the other is the author of the *Book of Courtesy*, to which we shall presently come] sound curiously modern as to the qualities they specially single out for approval.' These qualities are: 'Chaucer's vivid powers of description, his felicitous use of words, his freedom from long-windedness'.[22] Yet the man who appreciated these 'unrhetorical' qualities in Chaucer not only thought the passage from Lydgate's *Life of Our Lady* worth printing, but also expressed his own views in terms just as high-flown as Lydgate's and, as a matter of fact, borrowed from him.[23] Much the same may be said of the author of the *Book of Courtesy*. The stanza in which he praises Chaucer with so much discrimination comes after one phrased with all the elaboration we dislike in Lydgate or Dunbar.

It must, of course, be remembered, before we try to resolve these apparent contradictions by a closer examination of the actual words used by the fifteenth- and early sixteenth-century writers, that we are never, even in Caxton's prefaces, dealing with actual critical works, but only with writing which is either panegyric or apologetic in intent. Chaucer himself, as we shall see, provided a pattern for the praise of dead poets, and he also makes a number of his characters apologize, in terms more or less serious, for lack of rhetorical skill[24] – a kind of apology which Gower feels the need to offer in his own person.[25] These passages, in which a contrast of the alleged feebleness of the present generation of writers with the great ones of the past is implicit, are imitated by later poets as an acceptable *topos*. Nevertheless, although much is, no doubt, conventional, the continued popularity of praise of a great English poet, rather than of the masters of a Classical past, does suggest a genuine interest in the more immediate problems with which writers in English are faced and leads to a kind of critical approach which, even if it remains elementary, is none the less real and fosters the emergence of a certain critical vocabulary.

The most important part of this vocabulary is, obviously, the term 'rhetoric' itself, together with the other words and phrases associated with it. As we have seen, in considering Thomas Feylde's contribution, it is by no means safe to assume a limited sense for the term 'rhetorician'. It has, indeed, been recognized for some time now that it is not always possible to interpret medieval references to rhetoric as applying only to the use of the figures and tropes enumerated in the treatises on the subject. Manly's view, in 'Chaucer and the Rhetoricians', of rhetoric as simply ornamentation will no longer hold.[26] Even Baldwin, who says, clearly thinking on the same lines as Manly, 'a rhetoricated poetic . . . is always a perversion', allows that 'in the fourteenth and fifteenth centuries the English word rhetoric denoted style generally, whether in prose or in verse'.[27] Dorothy Everett goes further and emphasizes the more general senses and, especially, the 'composing function' of rhetoric:[28]

Aftermath: the noble rethor poet

I believe that, for a number of English poets of the late
fourteenth century, *rhetorica* still had some of its old 'composing
function'. In particular, I think that it can be shown that
Chaucer dealt with certain problems of presentation and
organisation in ways which are traceable, though certainly
not always directly, to rhetorical teaching.

Some such general sense as this is needed to make sense of Feylde's
praise of the 'pleasant' and 'marvellous' in Chaucer's work and,
even more, of that of the 'fruitful' and 'sententious' in Lydgate's.

'Flowers of rhetoric' can certainly mean the figures and tropes, the
'colours' described in the treatises; and, as at any rate the more
difficult of these were generally agreed to be only appropriate to
the high style, it is likely that mention of them does imply a lofty
poetic flight. Chaucer himself clearly associates the 'colours' with
such a style in, for example, the words of the Host to the Clerk:

> Youre termes, youre colours, and youre figures,
> Keepe hem in stoor, til so be that ye endite
> Heigh style, as whan that men to kynges write.
> *(CT* IV, 16–18)

Gower, in his discussion of rhetoric in the *Confessio Amantis*,
distinguishes between the different styles and purposes of rhetoric.
In the long section devoted to the subject in Book VII, he does
not refer to the colours or figures. The reason is that he is concerned,
at this point, not with poetry as such, but with rhetoric as the lore
which teaches

> Hou that he schal hise wordes sette,
> Hou he schal lose, hou he schal knette,
> And in what wise he schal pronounce
> His tale plein withoute frounce.
> (1591–4)

For this purpose of the most effective presentation of a specific
subject-matter, a plain style is appropriate – and therefore good
rhetoric. Gower uses the verb 'to colour', in this context, only of
delusively persuasive speaking:

> Thei spieken plein after the lawe,
> But he the wordes of his sawe
> Coloureth in an other weie.
>
> (1623–5)

Here again, he is concerned with basic presentation, not ornamentation.

At the end of the *Confessio Amantis*, however, Gower does use the word 'peynte', in a conventional apology for his own lack of art, in a way which suggests that he associates the colours of rhetoric with an exalted style in poetry. He speaks of his book's 'lak of curiositee':

> For thilke scole of eloquence
> Belongith nought to my science,
> Uppon the forme of rethoriqe
> My wordis forto peinte and pike,
> As Tullius som tyme wrote.
>
> (VIII, 3115–19)

And he goes on to speak of his 'rude wordis and pleyne'.

The *Court of Sapience*[29] similarly contrasts the colours of rhetoric with a 'dull and blunt' style:

> Who so thynketh my wrytynge dull and blont
> And wolde conceyue the colours purperate
> Of Rethoryke, go he to triasunt
> And to Galfryde, the poete laureate;
> To Januens, a clerke of grete astate
> Within the fyrst parte of his gramer boke;
> Of this mater there groundely may he loke.

The final reference to the 'gramar boke', the textbook of the medieval schools which contained much rhetorical teaching, suggests that the tropes and figures are meant here.[30]

When, therefore, Chaucer is praised for his use of the colours or flowers of rhetoric, it is probable that the writer has in mind his use of the high style, appropriately adorned with the more difficult figures. We cannot, however, conclude that this is all that is meant; and more general praise of rhetoric, without qualifications, is likely to refer to the presentation of subject-matter in the most appropriate way, which would, of course, include the low or plain style.

This, as we have seen, is, for Gower, the meaning of the rhetoric taught by Cicero; and Gower is careful to distinguish rhetorically effective oratory from poetry. There are signs of a similar distinction among Chaucer's fifteenth-century critics, as, for example, in the *Regement of Princes*, where Hoccleve praises him in separate terms for his 'rhetoric', his 'philosophie' and his 'poesie':

> Deth, bi thi deth, hath harme irreparable
> Vnto vs doon; hir vengeable duresse
> Despoiled hath this land of the swetnesse
> Of rethorik; for vnto Tullius
> Was neuer man so lyk amonges vs.
>
> Also, who was hier in philosophie
> To Aristotle, in our tonge, but thow?
> The steppes of virgile in poesie
> Thow filwedist eeke, men wot wel y-now.
>   (2082–90)

After this, it is difficult to be sure whether such praise as John Walton's of Osney is only for general poetic excellence or also for skill in the Ciceronian art, when he addresses himself:[31]

> To Chaucer that is floure of rethoryk
> In englisshe tong and excellent poete . . .

For other writers, however, it is clear that rhetoric and the 'eloquence' or 'well-saying', which are often used as synonyms, have the more general sense of 'good style', 'good writing' or 'good poetry'.[32] The *OED* does not note this sense for 'speech', but it was in fact a further synonym for fifteenth-century writers. We have already seen Lydgate using the phrase 'speech and eloquence', and the *Court of Sapience* has 'fragraunte in speche, experte in poetrie'.[33] This use of 'speche' is in keeping with Chaucer's own in the *Book of the Duchess*, 919–20:

> 'And which a goodly, softe speche
> Had that swete, my lyves leche!'

This does not mean merely that the lady had a pleasing voice, as the rest of the passage shows. It will be worth quoting this description at length, since in it Chaucer uses terms which were to become essential parts of the fifteenth-century critical vocabulary – 'eloquence', 'facounde'[34] – and uses them in association with truth, simplicity and, above all, fitness of language:

> And which a goodly, softe speche
> Had that swete, my lyves leche!
> So frendly, and so wel ygrounded,
> Up al resoun so wel yfounded,
> And so tretable to alle goode
> That I dar swere wel by the roode,
> Of eloquence was never founde
> So swete a sownynge facounde,
> Ne trewer tonged, ne skorned lasse,
> Ne bet koude hele – that, by the masse,
> I durste swere, thogh the Pope hit songe,
> That ther was never yet throgh hir tonge
> Man ne woman gretly harmed;
> As for her [ther] was al harm hyd –
> Ne lasse flaterynge in hir word,
> That purely hir symple record
> Was found as trewe as any bond,
> Or trouthe of any mannes hond.
>
> (919–36)

We can compare the description of Virginia's eloquence, which is a sign of her wisdom:

> Hir facound eek ful wommanly and pleyn,
> No countrefeted termes hadde she
> To seme wys; but after hir degree
> She spak, and alle hir wordes, moore and lesse,
> Sownynge in vertu and in gentillesse.
>
> (*CT* VI, 50–4)

These passages show not only praise of simplicity, and its association with truth, but the even closer association of style – the manner of using words – with subject matter.

Lydgate, too, associates eloquence and well-saying with simplicity and truth to nature in the passage which introduces his own invasion of the Canterbury pilgrimage. He praises the poet of the tales in which each man speaks 'lik to his degre', and, therefore, some 'boystously, in her teermes rude', in these words:

> Floure of Poetes thorghout al breteyne
> Which sothly hadde most of excellence
> In rethorike and in eloquence . . .
> Of wel seyinge first in oure language.

A beginning which may sound to us like the praise of ornament and elaboration, but which is followed by a passage[35] as perceptive and appropriate to Chaucer's actual achievement as anything Caxton ever wrote – in fact, of course, it provided Caxton with a model:

> Of eche thyng keping in substaunce
> The sentence hool, with-oute variance,
> Voyding the Chaf, sothly for to seyn,
> Enlumynyng the trewe piked greyn
> Be crafty writinge of his sawes swete.

Not only does Lydgate show his appreciation of the churls' tales as examples of Chaucer's poetic skill, he also shows that he has made a careful study of their style, and, in the exchange with the Host which he includes in his Prologue, he is careful to imitate the colloquialisms, oaths, frequent references to parts of the body or to commonplace objects ('a gret puddyng or a rounde hagys') which are characteristic of the speech of the low characters in the *Canterbury Tales*. We can, I think, also detect an attempt to reproduce the cadences of actual speech – an effect which Chaucer achieves so effortlessly and convincingly – for example, in lines like:

> Which spak to me, and seide anon, 'daun Pers,
> Daun Domynyk, Dan Godfrey, or Clement,
> Ye be welcom newly into kent,
> Thogh youre bridel haue neither boos ne belle . . .'
>
> (83–6)

Lydgate's actual tale, of course, like that of Chaucer's Monk, is written in a style suitable both to his own standing and to the subject-matter.

After this it is easy to see why the stanza in the *Book of Courtesy*, so highly praised by Miss Spurgeon, comes after one even more liable to be misunderstood than Lydgate's *Commendacioun*. This praises Chaucer in the following terms, so elaborate in themselves that it is hard to realize that they do not relate to a similar elaboration in the master's own style:[36]

> O fader and founder of ornate eloquence
>   That enlumened hast alle our breteyne,
> To soone we loste thy laureate scyence.
>   O lusty lyquour of that fulsom fontayne:
>   O cursid deth, why hast thow that poete slayne,
>   I mene fader chaucer, maister galfryde?
>   Alas the whyle that euer he from vs dyde!

We must presently look more closely at the precise meaning of the words 'enlumen', 'ornate', 'fulsome'. For the moment it is enough to note that, after this beginning, which may well seem 'fulsome' to us in a sense other than that intended by the writer, we read on:

> Redith his werkis ful of plesaunce:
>   Clere in sentence, in langage excellent.
> Briefly to wryte, suche was his suffysaunce,
>   Whateuer to saye he toke in his entente;
>   His langage was so fayr and pertynente
>   It semeth vnto mannys heerynge,
>   Not only the worde but verely the thynge.
>
>   . . . his hole entente
>   How to plese in euery audyence,
>   And in our tunge was welle of eloquence.

The adjectives of praise are 'clear', 'brief', 'pertinent'; and the supreme achievement of the 'eloquence' so elaborately described in the first stanza is summed up as the fitting of appropriate language to the matter to be expressed.

Caxton has a very similar idea of 'noble makyng and wrytyng', for which he uses as a synonym 'wel-sayeng':[37]

> And so in alle hys werkys excellyth in myn opynyon alle other
> wryters in our Englyssh. For he wrytteth no voyde wordes but

alle hys mater is ful of hye and quycke sentence. To whom
ought to be gyuen laude and preysyng for hys noble makyng
and wrytyng. For of hym alle other haue borowed syth and
taken, in alle theyr wel-sayeng and wrytyng.

Caxton has just been praising the 'grete wysedom and subtyl
vnderstondyng' of the *House of Fame*, that is, its content; and,
indeed, his whole tendency in this passage is to link style to content:
'he writeth no voyde *wordes*, but alle hys *mater* is ful of hye and quycke
sentence'. He repeats these phrases in his Proheme to his edition of the
Canterbury Tales. Here we find the same mixture of appreciation of
Chaucer's achievement, in terms which we can easily understand
and approve, and what appears to be praise of his more ornamented
style, which we have already seen in the *Book of Courtesy* and in
Lydgate:[38]

We ought to gyue a synguler laude vnto that noble and grete
philosopher Gefferey Chaucer, the whiche for his ornate
wrytyng in our tongue maye wel haue the name of a laureate
poete. For to fore that he by his labour enbelysshyd, ornated
and made faire our englisshe, in thys Royame was had rude
speche and incongrue, as yet it appiereth by olde bookes
whyche at thys day ought not to haue place ne be compared
emong ne to his beauteuous volumes and aournate writynges.

He goes on to praise:

Many a noble historye as wel in metre as in ryme and prose,
and them so craftyly made that he comprehended hys maters
in short quyck and hye sentences eschewyng prolyxyte, castying
away the chaf of superfluyte and shewyng the pyked grayn
of sentence, vttered by crafty and sugred eloquence. Of whom,
emong all other of hys bokes, I purpose temprynte by the grace
of god the book of the tales of cauntyrburye in whiche I fynde
many a noble hystorye of euery astate and degre. Fyrst rehercyng
the condicions and tharraye of eche of them as properly as
possyble is to be sayd.

It will by now be clear that we cannot take the praise of 'rhetoric'
and its synonyms – 'eloquence', 'speche', 'well-saying' – in any simple

way as praise of an elaborately ornamented style. Nor does such praise signify lack of interest in subject-matter. In fact, what the fifteenth- and early sixteenth-century writers appear to admire most in Chaucer is, precisely, his ability to suit style to subject-matter; and they also appreciate the fact that his subject-matter is extremely varied. In praising this ability, however, besides using the general terms 'rhetoric', etc., they are apt to use figurative language of a kind which inevitably suggests to us a much more limited meaning of 'rhetoric': that of ornamented style. As this sense does not, as we have seen, fit the general tenor of the longer passages – especially those of Lydgate, Caxton and the *Book of Courtesy* – we need to consider whether this exuberant terminology really does bear the sense it appears to do at first sight.

The first in importance of these critical metaphors is, probably, that of 'gold' and its synonym 'aureate', since this has assumed considerable importance for modern critics, through Lydgate's use of it and for its association with what we now call the 'aureate style'. Lydgate, for example, praises Chaucer for the 'golde dewe droppis of speche and eloquence', in the *Life of Our Lady*, and this phrase has often been interpreted as referring to Chaucer as the source for the aureate way of writing – it is, indeed, often further assumed that most fifteenth-century writers felt that this was a debt they owed to Chaucer.[39]

The actual word 'aureate' may well have been coined by Lydgate. It is first recorded as used by him in, as we shall see, a variety of different ways. The 'aureate style', as the phrase is used nowadays, is more limited in meaning. Its characteristics are an elaborate diction, involving many difficult Latin words which are new to English and, indeed, often only partly adapted to it.[40] There is no sign that Lydgate himself restricted 'aureate' to this particular way of writing or that he associated it especially with Chaucer. Modern critics of the style have generally concentrated on what they call its 'artificiality' and have seen it as a manifestation of the weakness of poor craftsmen, who tried to disguise poverty of subject-matter by a meretricious dressing-up of language. So, for example, Renoir says (and his remark could easily be paralleled from other critics): 'Aureate diction seeks effect for its own sake and prefers Latinate words to their Anglo-saxon equivalents'.[41] This is, I think, to miss the point, as Renoir's own example shows. He quotes in support of his definition the beginning of Dunbar's *Ane Ballat of Our Lady*, 'Hale, sterne superne'. It is certainly true that the total effect of this poem is odd and perhaps overdone, but it is not true that all the Latinate words have Anglo-Saxon equivalents. 'Eternal', 'maternal', 'angelical', 'feminine', are words for which we still find a use, although we have settled for a different termination. Moreover, Dunbar is certainly deliberate in his aim to reproduce in English the peculiar dignity and effectiveness of the Latin hymns to the Blessed Virgin, as an extension of the poetic capabilities of the language. This is, thus, not an attempt to give ordinary material importance through the style; it is, on the contrary, an attempt to raise the style to the level of important material of a particular kind; and at this level 'motherly' and 'wommanly' would not serve the poet's purpose. In fact, it is, I think, true to say that diction of this kind is part of a widespread movement to increase the capabilities of the English language. Thomas Warton sums up the situation well:[42]

> On the whole I am of opinion, that Lydgate made considerable additions to those amplifications of our language, in which Chaucer, Gower, and Occleve led the way.

We can, I believe, see that much of the diction which is typically 'aureate' is not, in fact, perverse overornamentation, but a practical solution to a particular problem, if we realize how much of it is actually translator's language. Chaucer himself deals with the problem of adapting the idiom of his own language to a completely different one in different ways. He is able to take French more or less for granted because, as we have seen, by his day the vocabulary, idiom and even the verse cadences of that language had been absorbed into a kind of literary *koinê*. Italian is more difficult, and we can see him adapting Dante in a more adventurous way in, for example, the *Second Nun's Prologue*, where he has 'noble' as a verb, 'cloister' in a figurative sense and various sounding phrases which are new to English: 'the eterneel lyf, and of the feend victorie' 'the eterneel love and pees'; 'the tryne compas'. The last of these probably owes as much to the Latin of the hymns as to Dante, and the same may be true of the figurative use of 'cloister'.[43] The result was probably striking enough to a contemporary audience, and still makes its mark on us as English of an obviously serious and elevated kind. In an earlier work, the *ABC*, we can see a less successful, but still interesting, attempt to achieve a somewhat similar effect. Here Chaucer evidently found the easy style of the French original too low for the subject, and he turns to the phraseology of Latin hymns to produce a language more worthy of it. Thus, for example, where the French has 'Dame es de misericorde', Chaucer raises the Virgin's rank to 'Queen of misericorde' (25) on the model of Latin phrases like 'Regina misericordiae', 'gratiae', etc. Similarly, the French 'esperance' becomes 'hope of refut' (32), on the model of Latin 'spes salutis', and in line 109 Chaucer introduces the word 'ancille' from the Latin 'ancilla (domini)', a word which is not in the French. In the same way, Lydgate weaves many phrases from Latin sources into the texture of *A Balade in Commendation of Our Lady*,[44] for example: 'fructif olyve' = 'oliva fructifera' (38); 'redolent cedyr' = 'cedrus redolens' (39); 'light without nebule' = 'lux nubila pellens' (53); 'braunchelet of the pigment-tre' = 'virgula pigmenti' (44). Dunbar's *Ballat*, too, has numerous reminiscences of various Latin hymns.[45]

Even if we cannot share their taste, we must nevertheless accept that the stiff but gorgeous embroidery of the medieval Latin liturgical poetry in praise of the Blessed Virgin appealed strongly to the imaginations not only of lesser poets of the fifteenth century, but also to Chaucer himself; and they clearly felt that it was worthwhile to try to reproduce these effects in their own language. It is in this particular area that the special characteristics of the 'aureate style', as we define it today, appear to be most marked. But, as J. Norton-Smith points out, Lydgate shows a strong interest in innovation in vocabulary throughout his work, in all the different styles he uses.[46] We are, in fact, in the presence of a phenomenon which is later typical of Renaissance writers and critics: the feeling that the vernacular is worthy to take its place as the language of letters, but that, to enable it to do so effectively, it needs enriching. This is a feeling which can hardly fail to arise as soon as poets become aware of the dignity and importance of their calling – and, as we have seen, this is an attitude which was certainly fostered by Chaucer and his contemporaries, so that it is not surprising that their followers inherit it along with much else.

A common result of this new self-consciousness of poets is, in England, a feeling of dissatisfaction with the rhyming powers of the language, in contrast to French or Italian. Thus Lydgate remarks in the *Troy Book* (II, 168): 'In ryme Ynglisch hath skarsete'. This was to be common complaint of Elizabethan poets, and it is not surprising that Lydgate's early seventeenth-century adapter still takes it over as a perfectly natural statement:[47]

> For as you know, the English tongue is harsh,
> And wanteth words to make up perfect rime.

Obviously, it is in the rhyming position that words with romance or Latin endings are most useful. In the passage just quoted Lydgate rhymes 'skarsete' with 'coryouste'. And in the *Temple of Glass*, which is in no way aureate, he uses the following in the rhyme position, in one stanza (489–95): 'visitacioun', 'subieccioun', 'transmutacioun', 'reuerence', 'excellence' – all polysyllabic, but none, it must be noted, unfamiliar or unnecessary today. There are no other learned words in the stanza, so that it is clear that the rhyme words are specially affected.

It is, of course, true that the piling up of unfamiliar words does make for a style which is, and was intended to be, a 'high' one; and such passages are quite distinct from those in which occasional Latinate words lend copiousness to a diction otherwise predominantly English. That Lydgate and his contemporaries drew a firm distinction between the two is suggested by the use by John Metham of a phrase which is really much more apt than 'aureate style'. This is 'half-changed Latin', and it occurs in a passage of praise of Lydgate:[48]

> Eke Jon Lydgate, sumtyme monke off Byry,
> > Hys bokys endytyd with termys off retoryk
> And halff chongyd Latyne, with conseytys off poetry
> > And craffty imagynacionys off thingys fantastyk;
> > And eke hys qwyght her schewyd, and hys late werk,
> How that his contynwauns made hym both a poyet and a clerk.

Whether or not he was responsible for the introduction of the word 'aureate' into the language, Lydgate was certainly fond of it. Numerous examples of his use of it will be found in the Appendix, 'Aureate Diction', to Norton-Smith's edition of his poems.[49] Norton-Smith distinguishes four senses:

1. 'colours of rhetoric', that is, the figures appropriate to the high style, in the phrase 'aureate colours' (*Fall of Princes*, VIII, 80–1).

2. 'The spoken sound of eloquent language.' This interpretation is, I think, more doubtful. For example, when Lydgate says, in *Mumming for Mercers*, 'Throughe that sugred bawme aureate they called weren poetes laureate' (34–5), he means, I think, no more than 'through the excellence of their writing, their good style'. In the *Troy Book*:

> His tale gan with sugred wordis swete
> Making the baum outward for to flete
> Of rethorik and of elloquence,
>
> > (IV, 5202–4)

he uses the same metaphor of persuasive presentation, not of any special elaboration in style.

3. 'Rhetorical inspiration giving rise to eloquence, associated with "licour"', ('influence' or 'dew'). This is supported by a quotation from *St Edmund*:

> Send doun of grace thi licour aureat
> Which enlumynyth these rethoriciens,
>
> > (221–2)

and in the envoi Lydgate adds a reference to:

> Off Mercurye the aureat influence
> The tenlumyne dystylled skarsly doun.
>
> > (12–13)

Here, if it were not for the word 'rhetoriciens', the natural way of interpreting these lines would be as referring in a general sense to what we should call 'poetic inspiration'. This concept, of course, would not have been so far weighted on the side of content – and especially of emotional content – for Lydgate as it would be for us. Nevertheless, allowing for the fact that, for him, a poet's activity would be, typically, to order words, there seems no reason not to associate the lines with this activity in its most general aspects and to understand 'rhetoriciens' here in its very common sense of 'good writers', 'poets'.

4. Lastly, Norton-Smith points out passages in which 'aureate licoure' refers to the actual ink which Lydgate hopes will flow freely from his pen. The point of this is, obviously, that he wishes to deal appropriately with a subject worthy of rubrication, that is, of the actual use of red or gold letters in an actual manuscript. For example, in *St Margarete* he says:

> O gemme of gemmes, vyrgyn of most renoun,
> Thy lyf to write be thou my socoure,
> And shede of grace the aureate lycoure
> In-to my penne . . .
>
> (54–7)

Here, Lydgate is once more playing with the idea of inspiration in a general sense and of the achievement of a style suitable to the subject-matter. After this analysis it is surprising to read Norton-Smith's conclusion that 'The evidence makes clear the essentially decorative nature of Lydgate's concept of eloquence – the art of applying the *colores rhetorici*'.[50]

Apart from the general tenor of the contexts in which Lydgate uses the term 'aureate', the imagery he associates with it supports a more general meaning, in keeping with the more general senses of 'rhetoric' and 'eloquence' which we have been discussing. These images are 'sugar', 'balm', 'licour' and 'dew'. As Lydgate uses them, 'balm', 'licour' and 'dew' all stand for a healing, enlivening, cordial liquid which is distilled either by a plant in the process of its growth, and as the cause of growth, or by a heavenly body as it sheds its influence (also associated with growth) on the earth.[51] Sugar – in 'sugred', etc. – refers to the sweetness of the plant substances and also to something which is a medicine and preservative in its own right.[52] When we remember that this is also true of Lydgate's central image of gold itself, we can see that this imagery forms a close nexus, linking the ideas of growth, health, vigour, in a totality of meaning which, while Lydgate certainly has style in mind, is more appropriate to the expression of an idea of poetry as a whole and, more particularly, of that relation of style to content which is needed to make an effective statement of the work as a whole. This is particularly obvious in the case of the quotation from *St Margarete*. Here, as in the hymns to the Virgin, it is not just a case of dressing up an old subject, but of finding a way of writing which will give the most

complete expression to the matter in hand. It would be going too
far to claim that Lydgate is ever completely successful in this
quest or to assume that he fully understood any need for what
we might call an 'organic' unity of manner and matter, but we
cannot escape the fact that he uses organic and cosmic metaphors to
express what ideas he has of the relation between the two.

Another important critical metaphor, and one which is, perhaps,
less likely to mislead us is that which relates to light – 'enlumine'
'illuminate'. We are still accustomed to use this word in figurative
senses. Chaucer himself uses this image, in a sounding line, in his
praise of Petrarch in the *Clerk's Prologue*:

> Frannceys Petrak, the lauriat poete,
> Highte this clerk, whos rethorike sweete
> Enlumyned al Ytaille of poetrie,
> As Lynyan dide of philosophie,
> Or lawe, or oother art particuler.
> (*CT* IV, 31–5)

I quote the lines in full because, in their praise of and lament for a
dead poet and in their concentration on the content of poetry –
implied by the comparison with the other informative arts – as well
as its language, its 'rethorike sweete', they set the tone for much
that was later to be written about Chaucer himself.

Lydgate certainly picks up the word 'enlumyne'. He uses it in the
Siege of Thebes:

> Enlumynyng the trewe piked greyn
> Be crafty writinge of his sawes swete.
> (56–7)

and in the *Life of Our Lady*:

> And founde the flourys first of rethoryke
> Oure rude speche oonly to enlumyne.

Chaucer's magnificent line meant, I believe, 'to cast lustre on the
whole of Italy' or 'to shed an illuminating light, an enlightening

radiance over', or perhaps both; and by *rethorike* he certainly meant to refer to the ordering of the material of poetry. In the *Siege of Thebes*, the meaning is clearly more limited, but it still relates to subject-matter – 'the trewe piked greyn'. As we have seen, this image, in the fifteenth century, belongs to the *topos* of the praise of brevity. The whole line would thus mean 'writing with admirable and luminous brevity'. It is, however, possible that Lydgate has the other sense of the image in mind, that of the real, worthwhile matter of poetry as distinct from its pleasant appearance – the 'chaff'.[53] In this case the meaning would be 'using his art as a poet to ensure the reader's full understanding of the true meaning of his poetry'. In either case, Lydgate is putting the emphasis on matter rather than manner – or, rather, is regarding manner as the expression of matter, not its decoration. In the *Life of Our Lady*, it is the English language itself which is 'illuminated', and, if we interpret the 'flourys of rethoryke' in a general sense, rather than as the figures and tropes, the meaning will be 'to make expressive, capable of being used for the laying-out and organizing of a poet's subject-matter'.

In the *Book of Courtesy*, in a passage already quoted, there is a close imitation of Chaucer's praise of Petrarch in the lines:

> O fader and founder of ornate eloquence
> That enlumened hast alle our bretayne.

Just as Chaucer's own lines in praise of Petrarch associate his eloquence with meaning and compare his skill with that of philosophers and lawyers, so the *Book of Courtesy* regards Chaucer's own 'ornate eloquence' as the power to order language so as to give the fullest expression to meaning. In the next stanza he is stated to be 'clere in sentence'.

Much has been written about the idea of light and illumination in medieval aesthetic theory,[54] and it is not necessary to go into detail here. It will be enough to recall that it always relates to the revelation of the order, harmony and proportion which produces beauty in a work of art. St Thomas Aquinas's well-known definition cannot be bettered. The clarity of the beautiful, he says is: 'The shining forth of the form of a thing, either of a work of art or of nature . . . in such a manner that it is presented to the mind with all the fullness and richness of its perfection and order.'[55]

St Thomas thus relates the ordering power of art to the order of created things. For St Ambrose, too, the part played by light in the creation is comparable to the *illuminatio* of art. He speaks of the part played by illumination in the revelation of the perfection of the natural world – an illumination which is, in fact a realization of order and form: 'Invisible also was the earth, because the light which illumined the world did not yet exist, nor did the sun. . . . And justly is the earth called invisible, because it was without order, not having as yet received from its Creator its appropriate form and beauty.'[56]

Illumination is, thus, an important part of the creative process; and we can see that speculation on the meaning of Genesis, as well as the study of Classical authors, lies behind the medieval aesthetic doctrine of light.

Critical metaphors such as these, however, are not the only problem. Terms which seem more straightforward in that they have little or no metaphorical content can be equally misleading. 'Ornate', which is very commonly used of a writer's style, is a good example. It is, as verb and adjective, a favourite word of praise for writers of the fifteenth century.[57] In the same way, the Latin treatises like to use the word 'ornare' and its derivatives. Now, in these treatises 'ornare' means 'to embellish', that is to present a given material in such a way as to make it more pleasing. Curtius notes that, in practice, 'ornare' is often no more than the equivalent of 'amplificare',[58] and Manly, who renders *ornatior* as 'more beautiful', makes it clear that, for the Latin writers, the means of adding beauty to subject-matter are amplification or abbreviation.[59] Since both these belong to the ordering and laying out of material, that is, to the organizing function of rhetoric, it is clear that 'ornare' also has reference to this function, and that, although it sometimes refers to a more ample or more ambitious treatment, it can also refer to a short, pregnant – 'hye and quycke' – one.

This is, indeed, to give the term rather more meaning than Manly meant to imply. Support for the fuller sense, however, comes from another context in which the idea of 'ornation' plays an important part. This develops from the summing up of the work of the six days of creation in Genesis 2:1 – in the Vulgate: 'Igitur perfectus sunt caeli et terra et omnis ornatus eorum.' The beginning of the book of Genesis was much pondered in the Middle Ages, and indeed beyond, on the basis of patristic treatments. One of the most important of these, that of St Ambrose in the *Hexameron*, to which we have already had occasion to refer,[60] will speak for all. In the first place the adornments of the earth are not its ornaments in any superficial sense, but its visible form: this contrasts with ὕλη, the first matter:[61]

> When the foundation of the earth has been laid and the
> substance of the heavens stabilized – these two are, as it
> were, the hinges of the universe – he added: 'And the earth
> was void and without form'. What is the meaning of the word
> 'was'? Perhaps that men may not extend their hypothesis to
> refer to something without end and say: 'See how matter, the
> so-called ὕλη of the philosophers, did not have a beginning
> according even to the divine Scriptures.'

What the 'forms' are is shown a few pages later:[62]

> And perhaps they may say: 'Why did not God, in accordance
> with the words, "He spoke and they were made," grant to the
> elements at the same time as they arose their appropriate
> adornments, as if He, at the moment of creation, were unable
> to cause the heavens immediately to gleam with studded stars
> and the earth to be clothed with flowers and fruit?' That could
> very well have happened. Yet Scripture points out that things
> were first created and afterwards put in order.

The adornments of the earth are, in fact, its visible appearance with all that lives, or moves, or exists in inanimate form; that is, all its parts and constituent elements. Thus, 'to create and afterwards to beautify' is to form, and then to organize and dispose in due order and proportion – and this is the meaning of beauty. For St Ambrose, as for many after him, God the Creator is, above all, an artist. He is the good Architect who 'lays the foundation first, and afterwards, when the foundation has been laid, plots the various parts of the building, one after another and adds thereto the ornamentation', that is, realizes the design.[63] He is also[64] the 'divine Artist and eternal Craftsman: What artist is not indebted to Him?' 'God willed it that we be imitators of Himself, so that we first make something, and afterwards beautify it'.

'Ornare' thus means, in this context at least, to make beautiful by the giving of outward form to a design in such a way that the separate parts are properly disposed: it does not mean, in a narrow sense, to impose decoration on an existing whole. Ornate and its derivatives were certainly used in this fuller sense in English in the fifteenth century. Caxton has: 'thus, in sixe dayes was heven and erthe made and alle the ornation of them'.[65] The *OED* has numerous examples from the fifteenth, sixteenth and seventeenth centuries in which 'ornate', or 'ornately', are used of language. A careful study of these suggests that the definition 'ornamentally', 'elegantly', 'with decoration', is not always appropriate. In many cases, 'a manner suited to the occasion', that is, with 'eloquence' or 'well-saying', in the more general sense, would be better. For example, the quotation from George Ashby (*c.* 1460) requires the meaning 'eloquently' in a general sense: 'A king sholde enfourme his sone . . . to speke ornatly with equite.' And for Speed, in 1611, the associations of the word are not those of decoration: 'He rehearsed them the same matter againe . . . so well and ornately, so evident and plaine'. Even when ornate does refer to a higher style, the idea of the fitness of language to subject-matter is paramount, as in the *OED* quotation for 1538 under 'ornate', ppl. a.: 'because the mater ben so vyle it may nocht have an ornate style.' It is notable, too, that when Bacon still uses the standard phraseology of the fifteenth century to praise 'eloquent orators', he certainly has not mere ornamentation, but rather effectiveness in style, in mind, as the achievement of their 'sugared and ornate eloquence'.

Another word which may well mislead the modern reader when it is used in praise of Chaucer's writing is 'fulsome'. The meaning of this word was already changing in the fourteenth century. Chaucer himself uses it in the *Squire's Tale*, in conjunction with 'prolixity' to describe a faulty style: 'The savour passeth ever the lenger the more, / For fulsomnesse of his prolixitee' (*CT* V, 404–5), and this became the normal sense by the seventeenth century.[66] It is doubtful, therefore, whether Chaucer himself would have appreciated the compliment when the author of the *Book of Courtesy* speaks of his poetry as 'the lusty lyquour of that fulsome fontayne'. What is actually meant, however, is merely 'copious', 'abundant'. In the same way Barclay writes of 'fulsome fieldes' – rich, abundantly yielding land.[67] Lydgate was particularly fond of this word. He has the 'fulsome well' in the *Life of our Lady* and also in the *Secrees*. He also writes (again in the *Life of Our Lady*) of the 'fulsom light of heuenly influence'. In these phrases, 'fulsom' indicates a plenitude, poured out in the form of water, or in emanation from the heavenly bodies, which is equally applicable to the divine work of creation, as it is displayed in nature, and to the work of the human artist.

We can now see that the contrast between such words of praise as 'ornate' and 'fulsome' and the frequent praise of Chaucer's brevity is not as great as it might seem. Miss Spurgeon was inclined to see in the latter a discerning innovation. The discernment is, I think, there, but not the innovation. As we have said, this was an established *topos* in the Middle Ages.[68] But whereas the praise of terseness, which derives ultimately from Classical authors, easily degenerates into a meaningless formula in which *brevis* is a term of general approbation, the English fifteenth-century writers restore meaning to the *topos* by relating it closely to content and, for some of their most telling phrases, by direct recourse to the original Classical sources. It will be unnecessary to repeat the relevant passages, mainly from Lydgate, Caxton and the *Book of Courtesy*, since they have already been quoted, but we can note that Lydgate, for example, when he writes of 'the sentence hool, withouten variaunce', is probably translating Horace, *Ars Poetica*, 23: 'simplex dumtaxat et unum'. Horace was referring to the clear and consistent representation of an object – a wine jar or pitcher – that is, to the content of a poem. For Lydgate, similarly, 'sentence' can only refer to subject-matter.

Again, Caxton's 'hye and quycke sentence' may be reminiscent of the *Ars Poetica*, 25–6, where Horace, writing of the dangers of extremes of style, uses the words 'nervi . . . animique' for the characteristics of a desirable style. The whole tenor of Caxton's praise is, indeed, very similar to this passage of the *Ars Poetica*. Horace says that, in trying to be brief, one must avoid obscurity; on the other hand, one must not seek smoothness at the expense of force. Caxton maintains that Chaucer combined brevity with strength and sublimity, a smooth style with clear sense: 'shewyng the pyked grayn of sentence, vttered by crafty and sugred eloquence.' These are meaningful phrases, and, in their close linking of manner and matter, they give new life and significance to an old *topos*.

The fifteenth and early sixteenth centuries, we may surely conclude, showed a much deeper and wider appreciation of Chaucer's art than has sometimes been allowed. They did have a good deal to say about his style (although they also frequently commented on his subject-matter); but they did not restrict themselves to praising one kind of style, and they appreciated plainness and brevity as well as high rhetoric. What they are all agreed on is the novelty of what Chaucer was doing. They considered that he had altered the status of the English language by making it richer and more copious, and better able to express a wide range of important content. This, indeed, is the crux of the matter. Excitement about language is meaningless without excitement about content. There would be no need to extend the actual medium of poetry unless it had become desirable and necessary for it to contain a larger and more exacting range of subject-matter. The new dignity of poetry is, certainly, the dignity of consummate craftsmanship, which fits it to take its place with the other arts, but it is also dependent on a new ability to give expression to 'noble histories' – a phrase (no doubt picked up from the *Knight's Tale*) which is used of Chaucer's work.[69]

This enthusiasm for the new copiousness and expressiveness of the language of poetry is couched in terms which may seem strange to us; the metaphors and flights of fancy of fifteenth-century critical terminology are, indeed, more nearly adapted to the writers' feelings of excitement over the new vistas which they felt had opened up for poetry than to the accurate description of what had actually happened. Nevertheless, analysis of some of their key terms does, I think, show that they relate not to the superficial decoration of the subject matter, but to its presentation in terms of the most appropriate language, with the emphasis on the close unity of style and content.

It is, of course, true that many of the fifteenth-century poets who show the greatest excitement and sense of change did not themselves produce poetry of a very high order of inspiration. Nevertheless, there were good poets among them in Scotland and among the English Chaucerians – for example the poets of the *Flower and the Leaf* and the *Assembly of Ladies* – to say nothing of many who cultivated the lyric. Nor can we dismiss Lydgate's work as inconsiderable. We can certainly see in it, as in that of many of his contemporaries, a continued ferment of interest in and experimentation with the language, besides a preoccupation with what we have described as important subject-matter. It is true that fifteenth-century experiments with language were largely lexicographical – and this, after all, was also the case with the rather similarly preoccupied Elizabethan poets, with only a few great exceptions. The kind of idiomatic syntactical flexibility which Chaucer was able to introduce into the metrical arrangements of poetry is not much developed. But with all its hesitations, its apparently halting cadences and its occasional pursuit of a Latinity which never integrated into English (as well as of much new vocabulary which did), the fifteenth-century's understanding of the change which had come over poetry in Chaucer's hands is an essential link with the centuries which followed, and as much a part of the development of English poetry as a whole as the 'noble rethor poet's' own contribution to his art.

Notes

Cross references to the present volumes are given in bold type.

1 The *Knight's Tale*

1 For the existence of an earlier, pre-*Canterbury Tales* version of the *Knight's Tale*, see Robinson, p. 669 (general note to the *Knight's Tale*).

2 *Ibid.*, p. 669, col. 2, for references to the main discussions of Boccaccio's sources.

3 For Chaucer's use of the *Teseida*, see *Sources and Analogues*, ch. 2, and R. A. Pratt, 'Chaucer's use of the *Teseida*', *PMLA* LXII (1947), pp. 598 ff.

4 Critics have varied in the degree of differentiation which they detect between them. For the moderate view that they are 'significantly differentiated' but not 'individualized', see R. Frost, 'An Interpretation of Chaucer's *Knight's Tale*', *RES* XXV (1949), pp. 290 ff., where references to other opinions are also given.

5 See **pp. 28 ff.**

6 Cf. the dual aspect of Venus in the *Parlement* and also **pp. 25 ff.**

7 This aspect of Virgil's epic is made the basis of an illustration of the fall of Troy as related by Aeneas, which is found as early as 1502 in the form of a woodcut, in the Grüninger Virgil, Strassburg. This is more magnificently reproduced in Limoges enamel dated 1525–30 (see **I, Plate II**). The various gods Aeneas mentions in Book II are all depicted as playing their parts in the action. Venus is shown immediately behind Aeneas, advising him – she seems, indeed, almost to grow out of his more dominating figure. Jupiter is shown through the purely Christian iconography of the hand of God coming through a cloud and scattering lightning: he is thus, for this artist, as so often for Chaucer, placed, as Providence, on a different footing to the other gods.

8 Curry, *Medieval Sciences*, pp. 119 ff.

9 *Ibid.*, pp. 119 and 120.

10 *Thebaid*, I, 124.

11 Quoted and translated in Saxl, Panofsky and Klibansky, *Saturn and Melancholy*, p. 261. See Ficino, *Opera Omnia* (Basle, 1576), p. 534.

12 The importance of the theme of order in the *Knight's Tale* has often been pointed out. For a recent study see Paul G. Ruggiers, *The Art of the Canterbury Tales* (Madison, Milwaukee and London, 1967), pp. 151 ff., where references are given to earlier discussions.

13 In England this is clearly reflected in *Piers Plowman*. See P. M. Kean, 'Love, Law and *Lewté* in *Piers Plowman*', *RES* N.S. XV (1964), pp. 241 ff.

14 For Langland's use of the term 'conqueror' in relation to the ideas of kingship and justice, see P. M. Kean, 'Justice, Kingship and the Good Life in the Second Part of *Piers Plowman*', in S. S. Hussey, ed., *Piers Plowman: Critical Approaches* (London, 1969), pp. 106 ff.

15 Robertson, *Preface*, pp. 264 ff.

16 This corresponds to the first three lines of st. lxxxv, Book II, of the *Teseida*, but the Italian is less specific:

> Mentre li Greco i lor givan cercando,
> e rivistando il campo sanguinoso,
> e' corpi sottosopra rivoltando . . .

17 See **I, pp. 165 ff.**

18 See, however, Robinson, note to line 1167, where it is pointed out that Gower uses 'positive law' to refer to ecclesiastical restrictions on marriage (*Mirour de l'Omme*, 18469 ff.). If this is the sense here, 'in ech degree' may refer to degrees of kinship. This would, however, only mean that Arcite places the chief disrupting effect of love within the institution of marriage, which normally stands for the maximum unity and order (see further **pp. 48–52**).

19 In III, pr. ii. For a full comparison of the two passages see Bennett, *The Knight's Tale*, 117–18.

20 Book I, m.v. Details in Bennett, *The Knight's Tale*, notes to lines 445 ff.

21 *Teseida*, IV, especially st. xxviii.

22 See Bennett, *The Knight's Tale*, note to 503–20 and Robinson, note to 1372, for details and references.

23 A detailed discussion of melancholy as an illness is given in Saxl, Panofsky and Klibansky, *Saturn and Melancholy*, especially in the first two chapters.

24 Cf. *de Consolatione*, IV, pr. vi and m. vi. Chaucer uses the same material in *Troilus*, V, 1541 ff.

25 Providence and prescience are discussed and distinguished by Boethius in *de Consolatione*, V, pr. iv. Providence belongs to a chain of causality (cf. IV, pr. vi); prescience does not (V, pr. iv, beginning). Neither, as Boethius argues at length, are incompatible with free will.

26 Boccaccio could, no doubt, have seen the remains of an actual Roman building. He could also have used the description given by Vitruvius,

de Architectura, V, iii, 3 (a work well known in the Middle Ages as well as in the Renaissance), or that of Isidore of Seville, *Etymologiæ*, XVIII, xlii–li (cf. the description of the Circus, XVIII, xxviii–xxxi).

27 See Paul Frankl, *The Gothic: Literary Sources and Interpretations through Eight Centuries* (Princeton, 1960); and George Henderson, *Gothic* (London 1967), pp. 19 ff. On Chaucer's buildings in the *House of Fame* (his most elaborate contributions to the fashion) see Bennett, *Chaucer's Book of Fame*, pp. 113 ff.

28 E.g., Westminster Abbey, rebuilt under Henry III; Westminster Palace, with many elaborate and magnificent murals (see Henderson, *Gothic*, p. 38). Royal patronage of the arts continued under Richard II on a scale sufficient to justify a modern art historian's comparing him to the Duc de Berri (Henderson, p. 35). A brief account of notable buildings in Chaucer's London is given by D. W. Robertson, *Chaucer's London* (New York, 1968); unfortunately, many dates and factual details are inaccurate.

29 Architects are often shown in visual representations with geometrical instruments. See Henderson, plates 2 and 3. Vitruvius also stresses the importance of geometry, for example in Book I, i, of the *de Architectura*.

30 *Cligès*, ed. A. Micha (Paris, 1957), 5317–18.

31 See Henderson's discussion in 'The Gothic Artist', *Gothic*, ch. 1. Vitruvius also stresses the versatility needed by the architect (*de Architectura*, I, i.).

32 *Cligès*, 5316 ff.

33 Quoted in Henderson, *Gothic*, p. 22.

34 *Hexameron*, I, ii, 27, and I, ii, 25. The idea of the artificer-creator is, of course, Platonic. Cf. Cornford, *Plato's Cosmology* (London, 1937), p. 26. It would be possible to equate Theseus's circular theatre, more precisely, with the zodiac and the temples with the positions of the planets in a real configuration (see North, 'Kalenderes Enlumyned', pp. 150 ff.). If Chaucer had intended this, however, one would expect Saturn to have been included, since his relation to Venus is so important in the action – to say nothing of Jupiter. The *Knight's Tale*, it seems to me, owes its peculiar character and structure to a treatment of the gods which blends the idea of planetary power and pagan deity, and not to the kind of purely astronomical allegorizing which Chaucer used in the *Complaint of Mars*.

35 Good examples are reproduced in Saxl, Panofsky and Klibansky, *Saturn and Melancholy*, plates 31–4, 36–42. See also plates 77, 78, 100, 116 in M. Hussey, *Chaucer's World: a Pictorial Companion* (Cambridge, 1967). Chaucer also uses literary sources for his descriptions of the gods and probably draws indirectly on Petrarch's *Africa*, via the *Libellus de deorum imaginibus*, ascribed to Albericus. See W. H. Ernest, 'Descriptions of Pagan Divinities from Petrarch to Chaucer', *Speculum*, XXXII (1957), pp. 511 ff. See also J. M. Steadman, 'Venus' Citole in Chaucer's *Knight's Tale* and Berchorius', *Speculum*, XXXIV (1959),

pp. 620 ff.; B. Nye Quinn, 'Venus, Chaucer and Peter Bersuire', *Speculum*, XXXVIII, pp. 479 ff.

36 Chaucer is probably drawing on Statius, *Thebaid*, VII, 40 ff., where the carter is, more heroically, a charioteer. If the change is deliberate, it must be intended to support the more realistic treatment of epic-heroic material which we so often find in the *Knight's Tale*. It is possible, however, that Chaucer actually has a chariot in mind, since medieval illustrators often rendered the Classical chariot as a kind of farm cart.

37 This detail is in the *Teseida*.

38 For example, in the careful attention paid to the hours (those appropriate to the various planets) at which the votaries offer their prayers.

39 Hanging, breaking on the wheel and punishment in the stocks are common features of the Children of Saturn illustrations.

40 Probably because labourers of all sorts are subject to Saturn. Otherwise a revolt would seem more appropriate to Mars.

41 The Saturnian man is repeatedly characterized as treacherous. See Saxl, Panofsky and Klibansky *Saturn and Melancholy*, especially pp. 127 ff.

42 Diseases, especially epidemic ones, were thought to be due to stellar forces. Hence, of course, the term 'influenza'. Arcite provides an instance of disease induced by Saturn.

43 Cf. especially *de Consolatione*, IV, vii: 'Omnem', inquit, 'bonam prorsus esse fortunam'. See also Chaucer's own *Fortune*.

44 See Saxl, Panofsky and Klibansky, *Saturn and Melancholy*, pp. 151 ff. The essential goodness of the planets was also part of Stoic doctrine. Cf. Cicero, *de Natura Deorum*, II, xx.

45 For the identification of Saturn with the Sun, see Saxl, Panofsky and Klibansky, *Saturn and Melancholy*, p. 155, n. 96.

46 See **I, pp. 73 ff.** and **II, pp. 43 ff.**

47 See Saxl, Panofsky and Klibansky, *Saturn and Melancholy*, p. 157, n. 102.

48 Saxl, Panofsky and Klibansky, *Saturn and Melancholy*, p. 169.

49 Thomas Wright, ed., *de Natura Rerum* (London, 1863; Rolls Series), p. 41.

50 On this etymology see Saxl, Panofsky and Klibansky, *Saturn and Melancholy*, p. 177.

51 The Saturn page in the early prints shows the merging of ideas (see **Plate I**). Saturn is an old man, muffled up in flowing garments: he carries the symbolical scythe, but the genealogy itself implies an euhemeristic interpretation. For an account of Boccaccio's methods in the *de Genealogia*, see C. G. Osgood, *Boccaccio on Poetry* (Princeton, 1930; reprinted New York, 1956), pp. xvi ff.

52 Curry, *Medieval Sciences*, pp. 130 ff.

53 See, e.g., A. T. P. Byles, ed., *The Book of Fayttes of Armes and Chiualrye*, EETS, 189 (1937), p. 9, on the caution with which war should be regarded by the king. In *Sir Gawain and the Green Knight*, King Arthur is

criticized by his court for unnecessarily exposing Gawain to danger (674 ff.).

54 Curry, *Medieval Sciences*, pp. 139 ff.

55 See *OED* 'Transmutation', 2.

56 The idea that man is a stranger in the world and life a journey is also a Stoic one. Seneca uses it, for example, in the *Consolatio ad Marciam*.

57 This long lapse of time is Chaucer's addition.

58 Full citation of the passages from Boethius which are used by Chaucer will be found in Bennett, *Knight's Tale*, pp. 146–7.

59 See **I, pp. 73 ff.**

60 This is the 'entrechaungeable mutacioun' (Chaucer's translation) of the elements in the *de Consolatione*, IV, pr. vi (see **I, p. 189**).

61 *Wanderer*, lines 64–5. Both this poem and the *Seafarer* show an interest in ideas concerning the organization of the physical world. Both (*Wanderer*, 62–3; *Seafarer*, 80 ff.) subscribe to the common view that it and all its inhabitants were undergoing gradual diminution – in contrast to the theory derived from Aristotle's system of compensatory changes (see **pp. 45–7**).

62 The argument for the existence of God from the perception of order and causality in the universe is derived in part from Plato, especially in the *Timaeus*, in part from Aristotle. Cicero was probably the most important link in its transmission to the later Middle Ages. He used the argument to refute the Epicurean thesis of a random universe in which the concept of Providence was impossible. See *de Natura deorum*, II, xxx.

63 See **I, pp. 71 ff.**

64 *F.Q.*, VII, especially 17 ff. The argument is even more fully deployed in Book V, ii, 39 ff.

65 I owe this reference and the one to Aristotle, which follows, to Miss E. G. W. Mackenzie.

66 The *consolatio* has recently been explored in relation to the *Pearl* by I. Bishop, *The Pearl in its Setting* (Oxford, 1968); on the use of 'consolatory topics' in the *Knight's Tale*, see pp. 21 ff. J. E. Cross 'On the Genre of the Wanderer', *Neophilologus*, XLV (1961), p. 69, notes that the fall of cities is a consolatory topic, and we must allow for a certain overlap between *solacia* and the philosophical argument on mutability.

67 At the end of the *Wife of Bath's Tale*, Chaucer ironically repeats the phrase 'parfit joye' of the Wife's conception of an ideal marriage. See **p. 153.**

68 It was generally agreed that virginity was the highest way of life for the individual, since this was the life lived by Christ on earth. Nevertheless, it is important to remember that the three possible ways of life – virginity, marriage and widowhood – were all valued, and chastity played a part in each (see the *Parson's Tale*, *CT* X, 940 ff.).

69 *CT* X, 882, and see **Plate III.**

70 St Ambrose, xi, 50, *de Paradiso*, in J. J. Savage, trans. *St. Ambrose: Hexameron, Paradise, and Cain and Abel* (New York, 1961), pp. 328–9.

71 St Augustine, *The Good of Marriage*, C. T. Wilcox, trans., *St. Augustine: Treatises on Marriage and other Subjects* (New York, 1955), p. 9.

2 The *Canterbury Tales*: the problem of narrative structure

1 A full discussion of the frame device will be found in *Sources and Analogues*, I, pp. 1 ff.

2 Dante, Boccaccio and Petrarch all wrote of poetry in a general way (but did not concern themselves with questions of structure) in works which Chaucer may have known. Apart from these, there were only the more technical treatises on rhetoric, to one of which, that of Geoffrey of Vinsauf, he refers and which he must therefore have read. These, of course, were mainly concerned with details of style, in the use of figures of speech, and only cursorily with larger questions of organization. The most detailed modern work on medieval aesthetics is that of E. de Bruyne, *Études d'esthétique médiévale*, 3 vols. (Bruges, 1946). See also Dorothy Everett, 'Some Reflections on Chaucer's "Art Poetical" ', in *Essays on Middle English Literature*, pp. 149 ff., and the references there given. Chaucerian narrative structure has recently been discussed by R. M. Jordan, *Chaucer and the Shape of Creation* (Cambridge, Mass., 1967). See also R. O. Payne, *The Key of Remembrance* (New Haven and London, 1963).

3 The short narrative presents few problems, as it necessarily implies a closer structure. For the relation of narrative form to length and the suggestion that medieval romances are best classified by taking length and scope into account, see D. Mehl, *The Middle English Romances of the Thirteenth and Fourteenth Centuries* (London, 1968).

4 See **I, pp. 28–9.**

5 *OED* 'Tenor', sb.[1], I. 1.

6 For Humanist poets like Boccaccio or his countryman Salutati, the poetry itself, with which Classical authors clothed their versions of the stories, was valuable. It seems likely that Chaucer shared their viewpoint. On the division between the Humanists and the Moralists, who were only interested in what could be made of the content of Classical poetry, see R. H. Green, 'Classical Fable and English Poetry in the Fourteenth Century', in D. Bethurum, ed., *Approaches to Medieval Literature* (New York and London, 1960), pp. 110 ff. The fourteenth century was often critical of the content of Classical narrative. Chaucer shows knowledge of the historical criticism applied to the versions of the story of the Trojan War which lead to the condemnation of Homer (see **I, pp. 28–9, 164 ff.**). He was not alone in considering the relation of the various Dido stories to the facts, although he does not seem to have known – or perhaps did not care to use – the historical 'research' which

proved her to have been a virtuous widow who resisted the charms of
Aeneas, or even showed that she never met him, since she could be
proved to have lived three hundred years earlier. Petrarch held the
first, the Englishman John Ridevall the second of these views. See
Beryl Smalley, *English Friars and Antiquity in the Early Fourteenth Century*
(Oxford, 1960), pp. 130–1 and 293.

7 As, e.g., in Salutati's *de Laboribus Herculis*. Boccaccio, too, in the
de Genealogia, provides figurative interpretations of many of the stories;
although this work is primarily an encyclopaedia of Classical mytho-
logy, it is an interpretative encyclopaedia.

8 See 'Classical Fable and English Poetry'. Many examples of the
allegorization of Classical stories are given in Smalley, *English Friars
and Antiquity*; see especially the chapter on Thomas Waleys's attitude to
the classics, pp. 102 ff.

9 Cf.:   And shortly, outher he wolde lese his lif,
             Or wynnen Emelye unto his wyf.
             This is th' effect, and his entente pleyn.   (*CT* I, 1485–7)

Here, 'effect' is used of the purpose which is to shape Palamoun's
future course.

10 For example, Dorigen supports the contention that a woman had
better die than be dishonoured by a long list of Classical heroines
(*CT* V, 1399 ff.); and in the *Nun's Priest's Tale* appeals are made to
Classical (and Biblical) examples as well as to the verses of 'Daun
Burnel the Asse'.

11 *Heroides*, I, vii. Ovid makes Dido refer to the voices of the nymphs in
the cave, but not to Venus and Juno, and only with scepticism to the
divine order which summons Aeneas to leave her (lines 95–6, 139 ff.).

12 See **pp. 4–5.**

13 Although the term 'coniunx' is only used of Dido's first marriage, and
she finally offers herself to Aeneas on any terms:

             'si pudet uxoris, non nupta, sed hospita dicar;
             dum tua sit, Dido quidlibet esse feret.'   (167–8)

14 It certainly fails as an effective summary of the *Aeneid* and hardly
achieves a successful abstraction of part of Virgil's material (as Ovid
does). Chaucer has not really solved the problem of combining his two
sources. The white swan passage, for example, from *Heroides*, I, vii, 1–3,
is abruptly tacked on at the end, as if, glancing back, he found it too
good to miss, but did not care to integrate it effectively into his version.

15 This topic is developed at length in the *Roman de la Rose*, 20817 ff. (cf.
the discussion of art *versus* nature in lines 16005 ff.). Chaucer also uses it
in the *Physician's Tale* in a way which shows that he understood its
implications (see **pp. 179 ff.**).

16 The possible stylistic influence of Chrétien, direct or indirect, is discussed by Muscatine, *French Tradition*, Ch. 2.

17 Except, perhaps, in the *Squire's Tale* (see **pp. 64–5**).

18 *Sources and Analogues*, XX, pp. 486 ff.; see also the discussion in chapter 1 above.

19 *Ibid.*, p. 490; full references in notes 1–3, pp. 490–1.

20 See H. L. Savage, *The Gawain Poet* (Chapel Hill, North Carolina, 1956), pp. 31 ff.; J. A. Burrow, *A Reading of Sir Gawain and the Green Knight* (London, 1965), pp. 71 ff.

21 *Sir Gawain and The Green Knight*, 1178–9, 1319, 1468–9, 1560–1.

22 See North, 'Kalenderes Enlumyned', p. 151.

23 E.g., *Sir Percevall*, 1057–60, 1121–5; *Ywain and Gawain*, 869–70; *Eger and Grime*, 721–2. Examples could be multiplied.

24 For the probable scope of the *Squire's Tale*, see *Sources and Analogues*, XIII, pp. 357 ff.

25 Cf. *OED* 'Process', sb. 4 and 5 ('a course or method of action'), both well attested for the fourteenth century.

26 See **pp. 7 ff.**

27 For Chaucer's knowledge and use of English lyric, see also **pp. 87–8.**

28 See Robinson, notes, for references. Dorothy Everett, 'Chaucer's Good Ear', in *Essays on Middle English Literature*, pp. 140–1, suggests that *Partonope* is likely to have been written in imitation of the *Knight's Tale*, as far as these lines are concerned.

29 Lines 3525 ff., and see R. M. Smith, 'Three notes on the *Knight's Tale*', *MLN*, LI (1936). Passages like these, which seem to preserve something of the actual movement of the alliterative line, are rare; but many romances use alliterative phrases in passages describing fighting, partly, no doubt because of such natural collocations as: 'helm', 'hauberk', 'hew'; 'shaft', 'shield'; 'spark', 'spring'; or, if the initial letter alone is accepted as sufficient (which it would not have been in O.E. verse), 'sowrd', 'spear', 'smite'. Some of these occur, for example, in *Guy of Warwick*, a romance which normally avoids alliteration: e.g., Auchinleck MS, 1442, 1485–6, 1506–67, 1961; and cf. Auchinleck MS, 1403–4, 1962.

30 This method goes back to OE battle poetry. Cf. *Battle of Maldon*, 108–10; *Judith*, 220 ff.; *Finn Fragment*, 28 ff. In ME it is found, e.g., in *Ipomedan*, 7811 ff., 7988 ff.; *Alliterative Morte Arthure*, 2807, 2910–11, 4113 ff., 3615 ff. (adapted to a sea battle); *Guy of Warwick*, Auchinleck MS, 1403–4, Caius MS, 2181 ff.

31 *Guy*, Auchinleck MS, 1393, 1979, 1983, 2967; Caius MS, 2187; *Havelok*, 2328–33.

32 A different interpretation of the function of the framing passages will be found in Jordan, *Chaucer and the Shape of Creation*, pp. 161 ff.

33 Chaucer may also be remembering Boccaccio's introductory *sonetto*, which gives the general argument for the whole poem. This passes straight from Arcita, as the subject of Books IX, X and XI, to Emilia, as that of the last book.

34 See **pp. 18–19.**

35 See **pp. 5 ff.**

36 For the characteristics of the 'Breton lay' see Bliss, ed., *Sir Orfeo*, pp. 36 ff.; Mehl, *Middle English Romances*, pp. 40 ff.

37 On this point see further **pp. 96 ff.**

38 See **pp. 96 ff., 148 ff., 157 ff.**

39 This is certainly the case with *Piers Plowman*, which becomes more intelligible as critics concentrate increasingly on the development of the poet's thought, rather than on the attempt to discover the kind of consecutive structure which would be normal for realistic narrative. In the same way, the *Roman de la Rose* may seem 'spoilt' by Jean de Meun unless the structural function of the so-called digressions is understood.

40 How far we can see, in the *Confessio Amantis*, consistent allegory, rather than a sequence of tales bound together by a framing device, is debatable. J. H. Fisher, *John Gower* (London, 1965), pp. 135 ff., has recently argued for an 'inner consistency in purpose and point of view' not only in the *Confessio Amantis*, but in all three of Gower's major poems, which, he suggests, can be read as one continuous work.

41 R. A. Pratt and Karl Young, 'The Literary Framework of the Canterbury Tales', in *Sources and Analogues*, I, pp. 1–81.

42 The episode of the daughters of Minyas in Ovid's *Metamorphoses* (IV, 1–415) is an important prototype here. The stories are told for sheer entertainment; the frame provides the occasion, and brings the tellers together. See *Sources and Analogues*, pp. 9 ff.

43 This is, for example, the case with Boccaccio's *Ameto*, which Chaucer may have known, where all the stories are to be about the experiences in love of their tellers.

44 The most important are, of course, the *Decameron* of Boccaccio and the collection of *novelle* made by Sercambi. It is, however, impossible to prove that Chaucer knew either. See *Sources and Analogues*, pp. 13 ff.

45 So, for example, F. Tupper, 'Chaucer and the Seven Deadly Sins', *PMLA* XXIX (1914), pp. 93 ff., argued that the tales were intended to treat systematically the seven deadly sins. See Robinson, notes, p. 650, for further references. Two more recent critics have, in different ways, argued for a similarly consistent moral purpose in the plan of the *Canterbury Tales*. These are B. F. Huppé and Trevor Whittock, both of whose books are entitled *A Reading of the Canterbury Tales* (respectively, New York, 1964, and Cambridge, 1968).

3 The *Canterbury Tales*: Chaucerian comedy

1 There are, of course, other comic elements in these poems which have already been discussed. The figure of the Dreamer, too, might well be included among their comic ones.

2 See **pp. 123 ff.**

3 In the case of the Man of Law and of the Physician, for example, much of the criticism of their characters and activities is stock material. For details, see Robinson, notes.

4 Walter Raleigh, *Some Authors* (Oxford, 1923), p. 5, quoted in Lawlor, *Chaucer*, p. 105, in an illuminating chapter 'Tales and Tellers'.

5 There is a further stylistic nuance here in the use of alliteration in the last two lines. By this Chaucer reminds us of the tradition of alliterative writing and suggests some of its weighty seriousness as applied to social criticism.

6 Muscatine, *French Tradition*, p. 59 ff.; although, as we have seen (**I, pp. 22–3**), the selection of realistic and practical descriptive detail is also characteristic of much earlier romance writing.

7 See **chapter 6.**

8 See **p. 164.**

9 The Harley Lyrics are close to the mood and the actual wording of Nicholas's pleas; cf. G. L. Brook, ed., *The Harley Lyrics* (Manchester, 1948), pp. 44, 33.

ʒef me shal wonte wille of on,
Þis wunne weole y wole forgon,

and:

Bote he me wolle to hire take,
For te buen hire owen make,
Longe to lyuen ichulle forsake,
Ant feye fallen adoun.

10 There is a suggestion here of the sophisticated form of the *aubade*, which Chaucer, of course, uses seriously in the *Troilus*. Here, however, the flatness and triteness of the formulae suggest a more popular version.

11 The Prologue to the tale describes the Summoner's anger with the friar, and this is allowed to enter into the tale itself. Thomas's revenge is the result of his pent up anger with the intolerable friar, who reacts with the same vice. It does not, however, follow that Chaucer intended to use this device systematically in the *Canterbury Tales*.

12 See Everett, 'Chaucer's Good Ear', in *Essays on Middle English Literature*, p. 145.

13 This is so convincingly carried out that a modern critic has, or so it seems to me, momentarily found himself inside the story. Cf. Ruggiers, *The Art of the Canterbury Tales*, p. 82, where he associates the Monk's sudden flush (an involuntary acknowledgement of the implications of his equivocal speech to the Merchant's wife) with modesty – which is to take it, literally, at its face-value.

14 A useful and moderate discussion of the problems involved in an attempt to assess the 'coherence' of the *Canterbury Tales* will be found in Lawlor, *Chaucer*, pp. 109 ff.

15 It is, of course, true that the personality of the Knight is of great importance in his tale not only as a reinforcement of the viewpoint of

Theseus, but also as a living exemplification of some, at least, of the 'noble' aspects of the story. It may well be, too, that the peculiar limitations of the Prioress's religious sensibility are reflected by her choice of subject and handling of it in her tale – though I find this a more doubtful proposition (see **pp. 205 ff.**).

16 The Summoner's vice of anger has already been mentioned. In the same way, the Merchant's preoccupation with his own misfortunes in marriage contributes to the near-obsessiveness of his tale. The Wife of Bath's interest in marriage, which extends to her tale, is also a personal one, and the Pardoner is implicated in his tale in a peculiarly complex way (see **pp. 97 ff.**).

17 See **pp. 128–9.**

18 *CT* VI, 960 ff., and *CT* II, 1170 ff. The latter is the epilogue to the *Man of Law's Tale*. Although its position in the series is very uncertain (see Robinson, notes, pp. 696–7), there seems no reason to doubt the authenticity of the exchange between the Parson and the Host. The second speech, telling the Parson not to preach here, is attributed in most MSS to the Squire, to whom it seems inappropriate. The minority attributions of this speech to the Shipman or the Summoner seem likely to reflect Chaucer's second, and better, thoughts.

19 The heroine of *Le Bone Florence of Rome* is typical of this type of semi-hagiographical figure. Not only does she beat out the teeth of a would-be ravisher with a stone, found conveniently by her bed, but she brings upon a seaman, who makes an attempt on her virtue, first a storm at sea and secondly a hideous disease.

20 See **p. 122.**

21 See **pp. 173–5.**

22 Perhaps most fully and recently by Whittock, *A Reading of the Canterbury Tales*, pp. 77 ff.

23 For the various sources on which Chaucer might have drawn, see *Sources and Analogues*, pp. 207 ff.

24 Not given as a source in *Sources and Analogues* (see pp. 333 ff.).

25 For a recent discussion which throws much light on figures of this kind, see Tuve, *Allegorical Imagery*, pp. 173 ff.

26 Although verbal reminiscences of the *Roman* are few. See *Sources and Analogues*, pp. 409–11, where the passages closest to the *Pardoner's Prologue* are reprinted.

27 *Piers Plowman*, B, II, 52 ff.

28 Although to be successful such figures need to be presented as fully and strikingly concrete. Rosemond Tuve points out that an essential part of allegory of this kind, is 'the spate of colloquial specificity, by means of which the abstraction shines through as a living form' (*Allegorical Imagery*, p. 175).

29 The question of Chaucer's authorship of the fragmentary English translation is still unsettled (for references see Robinson, notes, pp. 872–3). Fragment C has always been considered least likely to have been written by him, since (like B) it contains non-Chaucerian dialect

forms. Its rhythms, too, although they have some affinity to the *House of Fame*, seem, for the most part, un-Chaucerian.

30 For a recent discussion of these movements, with full references to earlier studies, see Gordon Leff, *Heresy in the Later Middle Ages*, 2 vols. (Manchester, 1967).

31 For Langland, see R. W. Frank Jr, *Piers Plowman and the Scheme of Salvation* (Newhaven, 1957), pp. 45 ff. It has been suggested, notably by Morton W. Bloomfield, *Piers Plowman as a Fourteenth Century Apocalypse* (New Brunswick, N.J., 1961), that Langland was influenced by Joachimite ideas – a thesis which I do not find fully convincing. It seems clear, at any rate, that such an influence was not felt by Chaucer.

32 *Roman de la Rose*, Chaucerian version, C, 7127 ff.

33 Jean de Meun devotes lines 4221–6900 to Reason's attempt to convert L'Amant.

34 Luxuria (often identified with Venus) as a naked woman swimming in the sea goes back to the *Mythologies* of Fulgentius. She is transmitted through the *Ovide Moralisé* (C. de Boer, ed. [Amsterdam, 1938], V, p. 402). Cf. Seznec, *La Survivance des Dieux Antiques*, plate 31. Robert Holcot reproduces the idea in one of his 'pictures'; see Smalley, *English Friars and Antiquity*, p. 175.

35 This latter passage is usually accepted as genuine, since the MS authority is good, but as cancelled, because of its overlap with the passage quoted above. See Robinson, p. 755, for details and references.

36 The venom and directness with which he goes straight to the Pardoner's most obvious weak point in lines 952–5 are in keeping with his later admission that his prevailing sin, like that of the Summoner, is *ira*: 'For I am perilous with knyf in honde' (VII, 1919). Chaucer has not drawn a simple figure of a genial host in Harry Bailey.

37 Curry, *Medieval Sciences*, pp. 54 ff.

38 This is clearly seen in the confessions of the sins in *Piers Plowman*; the device of the confession, indeed, presupposes a kind of consciousness in the vices of their converse. In the same way, the motif of the abandonment of the soul by its vices, often used in the morality plays, depends on acknowledgement of the fact that they stand opposed to their corresponding virtues.

39 See **pp. 148 ff., 157 ff.**

40 *The Book of Courtesy*, st. 49 (quoted in Spurgeon, *Chaucer Criticism and Allusion*, p. 67).

4 The *Canterbury Tales*: major themes

1 T. W. Craik, *The Comic Tales of Chaucer* (London, 1964), p. xiv.

2 *Piers Plowman*, B, XIII, 272 ff.

3 See **I, pp. 81 ff.**

4 I would therefore modify a little the view of Barbara Bartholomew, *Fortuna and Natura: A Reading of Three Chaucer Narratives* (The Hague, 1966). She sees Fortune and Nature as fundamentally and permanently opposed.

5 For a recent study of the medieval genre of the saint's life, see Rosemary Woolf, 'Saints' Lives', in E. G. Stanley, ed., *Continuations and Beginnings: Studies in Old English Literature* (London, 1966), pp. 37 ff. The date of the *Man of Law's Tale* is uncertain, and I do not necessarily suggest that it was written later than the *Knight's Tale*. The astronomical evidence for date is examined by North in 'Kalenderes Enlumyned', pp. 426 ff; he would place it late, in 1394, although he regards the evidence as doubtful.

6 See Mehl, *The Middle English Romances*, pp. 120 ff.

7 The horoscope is fully discussed by North, 'Kalenderes Enlumyned', p. 426.

8 See **p. 120.**

9 *Troilus*, III, 1819. There is poignancy in Chaucer's persistent use of words meaning rest and stability in reference to a love which is necessarily as transient as the natural world of which it forms a part. There may also be a more particular philosophical implication in his use of such formulae (see **pp. 174–5**).

10 Cf. *Truth*, 8–10, and see **I, pp. 40–2.**

11 This is, of course, the substance of Boethius's complaint against Fortune (see **pp. 12–14**).

12 Chaucer uses this topic, in relation to the inevitable reversal brought about by death in the *Knight's Tale*, in Theseus's speech on the First Mover: 'He moot be deed, the kyng as shal a page' (*CT* I, 3030). The crowned king is often depicted attached to Fortune's wheel in MS illustrations.

13 The figure of Griselda brings together the Stoic virtue of patience in adversity and the Christian virtue of patience which is a branch of fortitude, that is, of persistence, in a general way, in the Christian life. (Much relevant material is collected by Tuve, *Allegorical Imagery*; see Virtues and Vices, Patience, and Fortitude in her Index.) In *Piers Plowman*, the allegorical figure Patience has reference to the living of the Christian life in general. For something nearer the Stoic view, in which Patience is opposed to the assaults of particular vices, see, e.g., the illustration to a ninth-century *Psychomachia* from Leyden University Library reproduced as plate V of A. Katzenellenbogen, *Allegories of the Virtues and Vices in Medieval Art* (London, 1939); this dominating, militant (and male) figure is shown standing, self-sufficient and unharmed by the slings and arrows of the small and ineffectual looking Vices.

14 The topic of the three states of human life, and the perfection appropriate to each, is handled at length in *Piers Plowman* B, XVI, 60 ff. All discussions are based on I Cor. 7.

15 See his note to this line. Salter, *Chaucer: The Knight's Tale and the Clerk's*

Tale, pp. 48–9, notes several Biblical echoes in the *Clerk's Tale*, but does not comment on this one.

16 E.g., in Rolle's *Meditations on the Passion*, I, 54–5 (H. E. Allen, ed., *English Writings of Richard Rolle* [Oxford, 1931], p. 21).

17 Isaiah 53:7: 'He shall be led as a sheep to the slaughter and shall be dumb as a lamb before his shearer, and he shall not open his mouth.'

18 The fourth book of Thomas à Kempis's *Imitation of Christ* has much, especially concerning the soul's need for endurance and patience *vis-à-vis* its divine lover, which is of interest in relation to the *Clerk's Tale*, as have many other works on mystical love. The differences, however, between such works and Chaucer's poem are as striking as the similarities.

19 R. M. Wilson, ed., *Sawles Warde* (Leeds, 1938), p. 2. The English writer follows, with some modifications, Hugh of St Victor, *de Anima*, xiii (reprinted in *Sawles Warde*, p. 3).

20 See Henderson, *Gothic*: the discussion on 'Gothic for Art's Sake' (ch. 3) is illuminating. For a contrary view of the significance of secular decoration in the religious art of this period see Robertson, *Preface*, passim.

21 This was not the only possible view. St Augustine considered that free will consisted in the ability to do either evil or good, and he appears to have been followed by Langland (*Piers Plowman* C, XVII, 193–4). See the discussion by A. V. C. Schmidt, 'Langland and Scholastic Philosophy', *Medium Aevum*, XXXVIII (1969), pp. 134 ff.

22 Brook, ed., *Harley Lyrics*, p. 44.

23 'Mysgovernaunce', *CT* VIII, 2012. Of Lucifer, the Monk says:

> For though Fortune may noon angel dere,
> From heigh degree yet fell he for his synne.
> (2001–2)

24 As, for example, Robertson (*Preface*, pp. 251–2) seems to do. J. D. North ('Kalenderes Enlumyned', pp. 418 ff.) finds an underlying astronomical allegory in the poem. But this, too, seems unconvincing.

25 The emphasis at the beginning is on the political (and, of course, missionary) aspects of the marriage (see especially 232 ff.); and Constance's son Maurice does, in fact, become a good and Christian emperor (1121 ff.). On the whole, however, the political implications of the marriage are subordinate to the Christian ones in this tale.

26 This is especially obvious at the beginning, when failure to marry is cited as a fault in Walter as a prince. He finally marries in answer to the pleas of his people (92 ff.) and carefully chooses a wife capable of furthering the 'commune profit' (431).

27 See G. L. Kittredge, 'Chaucer's Discussion of Marriage', *MPh* IX (1911–12), pp. 435 ff. This was the pioneer study, to which many have since been added. Some of the most important contributions are conveniently listed by R. Schoeck and J. Taylor, *Chaucer Criticism*, I (Notre Dame, Ind., 1960), p. 158, n. 1; Kittredge's article is also reprinted in this book.

28 See **pp. 49–52.**

29 It is, of course, the case that much of L'Ami's advice is cynical, and even this is double-edged: L'Amant can take it one way, we can take it another.

30 With the proviso, of course, that the *Knight's Tale* does make considerable play with the 'service' of love – an irrational proceeding (according to Theseus) and a contributory factor to the discords which are finally resolved by the marriage.

31 Used, e.g., in the *Knight's Tale*, 1164, where Chaucer is quoting Boethius: 'Quis legem det amantibus?' (*de Consolatione* III, m. xii, 47). See also *Troilus*, IV, 618, and the Chaucerian *Roman*, 3432 ff. Closest to the *Franklin's Tale* is L'Ami's dictum 'Car il couvient amour mourir / Quant amant veulent seignourir', which Chaucer doubtless had in mind.

32 *Roman*, 4221 ff. On the place of *amicitia* in love and marriage, see Gervase Mathew, 'Ideals of Friendship', in J. Lawlor, ed., *Patterns of Love and Courtesy: Essays in Memory of C. S. Lewis* (London, 1966), pp. 45 ff.

33 J. J. Parry, ed., *The Art of Courtly Love by Andreas Capellanus* (New York, 1941), p. 102. The women speakers in the dialogues generally show a common sense which points up the unscrupulous logic of the men who try to seduce them. 'Courtly' in Parry's title renders 'honeste'.

34 *Ibid.*, p. 103.

35 A phrase which may carry sophisticated connotations: the implication here is of a law compatible with marriage and the 'law of Kind', instead of the reverse. Andreas Capellanus makes frequent reference to the laws or rules of love, e.g., I, dialogue v, where they are listed (*ibid.*, pp. 81–2), and Marie de Champagne's letter (*ibid.*, p. 107).

36 *Roman*, 14471 ff.

37 E.g., *Roman*, 12761 ff., 12857 ff.

38 Huppé, *A Reading of the Canterbury Tales*, p. 135.

39 At line 163 'Up stirte the Pardoner', but only to make a personal application of her words to himself. The Summoner (832 ff.) merely seizes on a chance to quarrel with the Friar. He is, evidently, satisfied with the 'disport' provided and resents interruptions.

40 *Roman*, 9091 ff.

41 See **I, pp. 168 ff.** and **II, pp. 175–8.**

42 See **pp. 165 ff.**

43 See **I, pp. 170–1.**

44 *Somnium*, I, viii and ix.

45 Macrobius seems to have transmitted the popular scheme of the four cardinal virtues to the Middle Ages. His own source was Plato, *Republic*, IV, 427 E. For further subdivisions of the original four, Macrobius cites Plotinus, 'On the Virtues' (i.e., *Enneads*, I, ii). As is often the case with Macrobius's citation of sources, this is misleading, and he seems to have been using Porphyry (see Stahl, *Macrobius: Commentary on the Dream of Cicero*, pp. 120–1, notes 2–5, where full

references are given). For abundant illustration of the importance of the *Somnium*, I, viii to the medieval vices and virtues tradition see Tuve, *Allegorical Imagery*, pp. 57 ff. The vices and virtues section of the *Parson's Tale*, of course, derives from a thirteenth-century treatise, the *Summa Vitiorum* of Raymund of Pennaforte.

46 A. J. Denomy, *'Fin' Amors:* The Pure Love of the Troubadours: Its Amorality and Possible Sources', *Medieval Studies*, VII (1945), p. 176. This islolated quotation, however, does not do justice to Denomy's numerous analyses of the ideas involved in 'courtly love'. See, for example, 'The Two Moralities of Chaucer's *Troilus and Criseyde*', *Transactions of the Royal Society of Canada*, third series, XLIV, 2 (1950), pp. 35 ff. (reprinted in Schoeck and Taylor, *Chaucer Criticism*, II, pp. 147 ff.). The warning given by Mrs D. R. Sutherland ('The Language of the Troubadours', *French Studies*, X [1956], p. 212) on the need to take into account the reticence necessarily practised by poets composing for polite circles is relevant here. Critics need not now share the surprise of, e.g., W. G. Dodd (*Courtly Love in Chaucer and Gower*, [Harvard, 1913], p. 5) at the emphasis placed on sensuality by Andreas Capellanus in his definitions of love (see Parry, pp. 28 ff.).

47 Lewis, *Allegory of Love*, p. 12. The other three are humility, courtesy (which rather begs the question), and the religion of love, by which Lewis meant 'a rival, or parody of the real religion' (p. 18). It will be clear from the discussion of Chaucer's philosophical position in the *Parlement*, the *Troilus* and the *Knight's Tale* that this last 'mark' could have little meaning for him.

48 Colin Hardie, 'Dante and the Tradition of Courtly Love' in *Patterns of Love and Courtesy*, pp. 26 ff.

49 Dronke, *Medieval Latin and the Rise of European Love-Lyric*, I, especially ch. 2 ('The Background of Ideas'), pp. 57 ff.

50 Lewis, *Allegory of Love*, pp. 14 ff. Cf. Dronke, *op. cit.*, p. 6.

51 Étienne Gilson, *La Théologie Mystique de Saint Bernard* (Paris, 1947), p. 215.

52 Dronke, *Medieval Latin and the Rise of European Love-Lyric*, I, p. 6, where he writes of 'the accord of human and divine love' and (in note 2) of 'the belief of the poets in the identity of the two loves'.

53 Lewis, *Allegory of Love*, p. 154.

54 *Roman*, 6945 ff.

55 R. J. Menner, ed., *Purity, Yale Studies in English*, LXI (New Haven and London, 1920).

56 In the story of Balshazzar's Feast in *Purity*, 1357 ff.

57 See Menner, ed., *Purity*, xxvii ff. References to clothes, architecture, etc., in this group of poems suggest a date late in the fourteenth century.

58 Phyllis Hodgson, ed., *The Cloud of Unknowing*, EETS, 218 (1944).

59 See **p. 49.**

60 See also **pp. 44 ff.,** e.g., in parts of the Psalms, Job and Wisdom.

61 See Dom O. Lottin, *Psychologie et Morale aux xiie et xiiie siècles*, 6 vols.

(Paris, 1942–60); Tuve, 'Allegory of Vices and Virtues', *Allegorical Imagery*, ch. ii; Katzenellenbogen, *Allegories of the Virtues and Vices*. See also Morton W. Bloomfield, *The Seven Deadly Sins* (East Lansing, Michigan, 1952).

62 Cf., e.g., the telling use of the epithets 'noble' and 'free' of January (*CT* IV, 2069).

63 Cf., e.g., Langland's development of the theme in the discussion of the poverty of the Friars and of the good and bad Need (*Piers Plowman*, B, XX).

64 Just as the Theban Women did, earlier in the poem, using a variant of the same formula:

> Som drope of pitee, thurgh thy gentillesse
> Upon us wrecched wommen lat thou falle.
>
> (*CT* I, 920–1)

65 As Robinson's note to *CT* I, 1761 (pp. 675–6) shows, the Italian poets were fond of the dictum that love is at home in the 'gentle' heart. (See also Bennett, *Knight's Tale*, p. 128, note to 903, and *Selections from John Gower* (Oxford, 1968), p. 150, note to 1451.) The Italian formula probably owes its structure to Ovid:

> Quo quisquis maior, magis est placabilis irae,
> Et facilis motus mens generosa capit.
>
> (*Tristia* III, v, 31–2)

Ovid's sense actually suits Chaucer's meaning better than does that of the Italian poets. Pity, as an important part of justice, is implied in Cicero's discussion in the *de Officiis*, I, vii ff., in which he lays stress in humaneness. *Misericordia* features in the lists of the parts of justice in, e.g., Guillaume de Conches and Alanus de Insulis. *Humanitas* is in Macrobius's list. Gower includes pity as one of the 'Five Points of Policy', i.e., the kingly virtues, in the *Confessio Amantis*, VII.

66 *Magnificentia* is already a part of fortitude in Cicero. It remains, e.g., even in lists like Alanus de Insulis's lengthened one, which also includes the apparently opposite virtue of *humilitas*.

67 *De Inventione*, II, liv. Cicero obviously bases this definition on Aristotle (some relevant passages from the *Ethics* and *Rhetoric* are collected by Tuve, *Allegorical Imagery*, pp. 58–9). Cicero's definition was well known and influential. It is quoted, for example, by Aquinas in his section on *magnificentia* in the *Summa Theologica*, II, II, cxxxiv, ii.

68 Thus Dorigen promises to be 'youre humble trewe wyf' (*CT* V, 758), and the hag in the *Wife of Bath's Tale* says that she will be 'also good and trewe / As evere was wyf, syn that the world was newe' (*CT* III, 1243–4).

69 See the discussion in Burrow, *A Reading of Sir Gawain and the Green Knight*, pp. 42–50.

70 See *Sources and Analogues*, pp. 398 ff.

71 For details and references see Robinson, notes to this passage.

72 The relevant part of this text is conveniently reproduced in *Sources and*

Analogues, pp. 407–8. It is noteworthy that the virtues Chaucer ascribed to Virginia are part of her natural endowments (cf. Canacee's virtuous compassion, of which it is said 'Nature in youre principles hath set', *CT* V, 487). The natural tendency of the human mind to virtue is an important part of the topic from early times. Cicero, for example, makes much of it in the *de Officiis* (e.g., I, iv, vii and xix). Cf. *Confessio Amantis*, V, 2594–5, where Nature endows the Lady with both 'beaute' and 'bounte' (i.e., 'goodness').

73 Alanus, *De Virtutibus et de Vitiis et de Donis Spiritus Sancti*, in Lottin, *Psychologie et Morale*, VI.

74 J. Bergman, ed., *Aurelii Prudentii Clementis Carmina*, Corp. Script. Eccles. Lat., LXI (Vienna and Leipzig, 1926), pp. 165 ff.

75 As, for example, in the Bamberg Apocalypse (A.D. 1001–1002), where Abraham is associated with God-fearing obedience, Moses with Purity and David with Penitence, and in the *Psychomachia*, where Job is associated with Patience (see Katzenellenbogen, *Allegories of the Virtues and Vices*, p. 15).

76 *Ibid.*, pp. 57–8.

77 Smalley, *English Friars and Antiquity*, e.g., 104–5, 124–5.

78 Katzenellenbogen, *Allegories of the Virtues and Vices*, p. 3, n. 1 (I have slightly modified the English translation).

79 Such as that described in *ibid.*, ch. 3 ('The Virtue and Vice Cycle of Notre-Dame').

80 *Psychomachia*, V, 310 ff.

5 The religious poetry

1 For a summary of the evidence and references to various discussions of it, see Robinson, notes.

2 The *Man of Law's Tale*, the *Clerk's Tale* and to some extent the *Physician's Tale* are, of course, written from a specifically Christian standpoint and contain much material that can only be described as religious. Nevertheless, they seem to me to be concerned primarily with the development of themes which are not, strictly speaking, devotional ones, and I have therefore included them in the preceding chapter, rather than in this one.

3 See **I, p. 32.**

4 See Robinson, notes, for further references.

5 She has been variously interpreted. Views range from the comparatively mild strictures of E. T. Donaldson ('Chaucer the Pilgrim', *PMLA*, LXIX [1954] 928 ff.), who at least finds her 'a perfect lady', if an imperfect nun, to those of B. F. Huppé, for whom the ladylike perfection only exists to throw into relief the religious failings (*A Reading of the Canterbury Tales*, pp. 33–4).

6 In the *Second Nun's Prologue*; see next note and **pp. 196–7.**

7 For details see Robinson, notes, and *Sources and Analogues*, pp. 664 ff., where the relevant passages are printed in full.

8 See **pp. 162 ff.**

9 Carleton Brown, ed., *Religious Lyrics of the Fifteenth Century* (Oxford, 1939), no. 7, pp. 5–8.

10 *Ibid.*, no. 8, pp. 8–9.

11 Chaucer, however, is not mentioned as a religious poet in the latest book on the subject: Rosemary Woolf, *English Religious Lyric in the Middle Ages* (Oxford, 1968).

12 For the evidence, see Robinson, notes.

13 De Guilleville's poem is printed in W. W. Skeat, ed., *Works of Geoffrey Chaucer* (Oxford, 1926), I, pp. 261 ff.; for these lines see p. 264.

14 *Ibid.*, p. 266.

15 H. Littlehales, ed., *Lay Folk's Prymer*, EETS, O.S., 105 and 109 (1895–1897), p. 24.

16 *Paradiso*, XXXIII, 1 ff. For Chaucer's treatment of this passage and his blending-in of reminiscences of other religious texts, see *Sources and Analogues*, pp. 664 ff.

17 See R. T. Davies, ed., *Medieval English Lyrics* (London, 1963), no. 34, p. 103.

18 W. Mackay Mackenzie, ed., *The Poems of William Dunbar* (Edinburgh, 1932), no. 82, p. 160.

19 *Religious Lyrics of the Fifteenth Century*, no. 7.

20 Carleton Brown, ed., *Religious Lyrics of the Fourteenth Century* (Oxford, 1924), no. 131, p. 233.

21 In abridged form in *Medieval English Lyrics* no. 97, p. 193. Cf. H. N. MacCracken, ed., *The Minor Poems of Lydgate*, II, EETS, O.S., 192 (1934), pp. 780 ff.

22 *Ego Dormio*, 235–6, in *English Writings of Richard Rolle*, p. 68.

23 *Religious Lyrics of the Fourteenth Century*, no. 25, pp. 28–9.

24 In several places Chaucer states that his intention is only to give a faithful rendering of a version of Cecilia's legend (24–5, 78–83 and cf. 124). For the probability that he did, indeed, follow a single source, see *Sources and Analogues*, pp. 667 ff.

25 One of the most ingenious, and tempting, interpretations is that of R. J. Schoeck, 'Chaucer's Prioress: Mercy and Tender Heart', reprinted in *Chaucer Criticism*, I, pp. 245 ff. Schoeck contends that Chaucer condemns anti-Semitism through the tale, by presenting the Prioress as a character incapable of taking a liberal, and truly Christian, view of her material. This is, perhaps, to confuse the ugly, and certainly false, propaganda story which lies behind the tale with Chaucer's creation, and certainly, I am afraid, to force on the poet an enlightenment which was not granted to him. References to most of the other important discussions of the tale will be found in Schoeck's article.

6 Aftermath: the noble rethor poet

1 The phrase is a modern one, although 'aureate' was used as a term of praise for fine writing, especially by Lydgate. For its meaning see also **pp. 226–32.** For the limitations of the appreciation of Chaucer by his followers see, e.g., Spurgeon, *Chaucer Criticism and Allusion*, I, pp. xciii–xciv; G. H. McKnight, *Modern English in the Making* (New York, 1928), p. 46; and Lewis, *Allegory of Love*, pp. 162 ff., where the same assumption is made with greater subtlety. Muscatine, *French Tradition*, p. 244, seems to return to an oversimplified view, as does Alain Renoir in his definition of aureate diction in *The Poetry of John Lydgate* (London, 1967), pp. 136 ff. Lydgate's most recent editor, John Norton-Smith, on the other hand, emphasizes the variety of Lydgate's styles, of which the so-called 'aureate' is only one (*John Lydgate: Poems* [Oxford, 1966], pp. xi–xii).

2 Thus, even C. S. Lewis, who places Chaucer's love poems within the mainstream of English poetry, considered the *Canterbury Tales* 'sterile' (*Allegory of Love*, p. 163). Muscatine goes further and sees Chaucer as so distinctively a 'high-gothic' poet as to be effectively cut off from the future – or so he seems to imply when he writes that even Spenser 'looks back to him from a distance of two centuries and emulates him only faintly' (*French Tradition*, p. 245). Such statements, however, seem to me out of keeping with the actual words of sixteenth-century authors when they write of Chaucer.

3 Thus Dunbar's 'Chaucerian' quality is admitted by Muscatine, but with the excusing comment that he 'writes a full century later' (*French Tradition*, p. 244).

4 The English Chaucerians – the poets of the *Flower and the Leaf*, of the *Assembly of Ladies*, and of the *Court of Love* – utilize to the full their master's simple, easy conversational style and show no tendency to emulate his more 'rhetorical' way of writing.

5 According to Puttenham, *Art of English Poesie* (London, 1589), p. 50, Lydgate was a poet that 'wrate in good verse'. Modern critics have disagreed, but there have been some recent attempts to re-examine and explain his practice; see W. F. Schirmer, *John Lydgate*, pp. 70 ff. and the references there given, and James G. Southworth, *Verses of Cadence* (Oxford, 1954) and *The Prosody of Chaucer and his Followers* (Oxford, 1962).

6 On the importance of the *Pèlerinages* and their long continued circulation, in one form or another, see Tuve, *Allegorical Imagery*, pp. 145 ff. The *Secreta* was influential not only in its own right, but also through numerous encyclopaedic works which drew on it – for instance, that of Bartholomeus Anglicus, which was popular in Chaucer's day and which was retranslated and printed in the sixteenth century.

7 Material of this kind reappears, for example, in the *Mirror for Magistrates*, in the *Faerie Queene* and in Shakespeare's history plays.
8 Much of his secular poetry on love and other subjects comes under this heading. See McCracken, ed., *Minor Poems of Lydgate*, II.
9 E.g., Gilbert of the Haye, *Buke of the Law of Armys*, *Buke of the Governaunce of Princis* (a *Secreta Secretorum* version); Hoccleve, *Regement of Princes*; Stephen Scrope, *Epistle of Othéa*, *The Book of Noblesse* and Cicero's *Of Old Age*; Tiptoft, Cicero's *de Amicitia*; *The Declamacion of Noblesse*; Trevisa, Bartholomeus Anglicus's *de Proprietatibus Rerum*; John Walton, Boethius's *de Consolatione Philosophiae*.
10 *Selections from John Gower* (Oxford, 1968), pp. xi ff.
11 Smalley, *English Friars and Antiquity*, e.g., pp. 130 f.
12 Renoir, *The Poetry of John Lydgate*, especially chs. 3 and 5.
13 See Tuve, *Allegorical Imagery*, pp. 33 ff.
14 Lydgate, *Fall of Princes*, III, 3655 ff.
15 It would be far beyond the scope of this chapter to attempt to distinguish the attitudes and approaches of the Renaissance or of fully developed Humanism from those of the close of the Middle Ages. My purpose is only to indicate how far some books remained popular from the fourteenth to the sixteenth century and how an interest in both European and Classical literature, which Chaucer and his contemporaries initiated, remained an important one for English poets. I am not concerned with the general effects of this interest, but with its influence on poetry.
16 *Testament of Love*, iii and iv, in Skeat, ed., *Works of Geoffrey Chaucer*, VII, p. 123.
17 Hoccleve, *Regement of Princes*, 4988–9, quoted in Spurgeon, *Chaucer Criticism and Allusion*, I, p. 22; Caxton, Proheme to the *Canterbury Tales* (quoted in Spurgeon, p. 62).
18 Quoted in Spurgeon, *Chaucer Criticism and Allusion*, I, p. 70.
19 See Renoir, *Poetry of John Lydgate*, especially ch. 8.
20 Quoted in Spurgeon, *Chaucer Criticism and Allusion*, I, p. 19. This is, for example, quoted by Muscatine (*French Tradition*, p. 244) in support of the contention that 'most of his followers see him only as the poet of high style'.
21 Spurgeon, *Chaucer Criticism and Allusion*, I, p. cxxxi.
22 *Ibid.* I, p. xiv.
23 See **pp. 224-5.**
24 The significance of these passages is discussed by Everett, 'Some Reflections on Chaucer's "Art Poetical"', in *Essays on Middle English Literature*, pp. 150 f.
25 E.g., *Confessio Amantis*, VIII, 3116 ff.
26 Warton Lecture on English Poetry, XVII (British Academy, 1926), passim and, especially, p. 10.
27 C. S. Baldwin, *Medieval Rhetoric and Poetic* (New York, 1928), pp. 292, 295.
28 Everett, 'Some Reflections on Chaucer's "Art Poetical"', in *Essays on*

Middle English Literature, p. 153. The same problem is discussed in relation to sixteenth-century poetry and criticism by Rosemond Tuve, *Elizabethan and Metaphysical Imagery* (Chicago, 1947); see especially note B to ch. 2, p. 411. Cf. also McKnight's remarks (*Modern English in the Making*, pp. 46 f.), on the meaning of 'rhetoric' and 'eloquence' for fifteenth-century writers.

29 Quoted in Spurgeon, *Chaucer Criticism and Allusion*, I, p. 17. Galfryde, here, is, almost certainly, not Chaucer but Geoffrey of Vinsauf, whom Chaucer himself mentions as 'deere maister soverayn' (*CT* VII, 3347).

30 The more difficult of these would, of course, only be appropriate to the high style. We cannot, however, always be certain that the *colores rhetoricae* refer to ornaments of style. They were often used, from Quintilian onwards, in their Ciceronian sense to refer to the treatment of the material from a particular speaker or writer's point of view (see Everett, 'Some Reflections on Chaucer's "Art Poetical"', in *Essays on Middle English Literature*, pp. 152–3, and the references there given).

31 Quoted in Spurgeon, p. 20.

32 See *OED* 'Rhetoric', and cf. Baldwin, *Medieval Rhetoric and Poetic*, p. 292. In the plural, 'rhetorikes' (and sometimes 'eloquences') meant 'figures of rhetoric'.

33 And Dame Rhetoric in this poem teaches the art of 'endyting' in a general way.

34 'Eloquence' and 'well-saying' are generally preferred to 'facounde', but the adjective 'facundious' is sometimes used of good style (e.g., Hawes, *The Booke Called the Example of Vertu*, quoted in Spurgeon, p. 66; Henry Bradshaw, *The Holy Lyfe and History of St Werburge*, quoted in Spurgeon, *Chaucer Criticism and Allusion*, I, p. 71).

35 A. Erdman, ed., Prologue, *Siege of Thebes*, EETS, E.S., 108 (1911), 40–7, 53–7.

36 F. J. Furnivall, ed., *Book of Courtesy*, EETS, 32 (1868), stanzas 48–50.

37 Epilogue to the *Book of Fame*, quoted in Spurgeon, *Chaucer Criticism and Allusion*, I, p. 61.

38 *Ibid.* (pp. 61–2). The figure of the chaff and grain seems to be limited, as far as English writers are concerned, to the *topos* of the praise of brevity. See **p. 233.**

39 He is called 'the aureat poete' by an unknown writer in a fifteenth-century MS (see Spurgeon, *Chaucer Criticism and Allusion*, I, p. 45). Dunbar (*Golden Targe*, 263) applies the term to Gower and Lydgate, praising their 'tongis aureate'.

40 For typical modern descriptions of the aureate style see Renoir, *Poetry of John Lydgate*, p. 137, and Norton-Smith, ed., *Lydgate: Poems*, pp. xi and 192 ff.

41 Renoir, *Poetry of John Lydgate*, p. 137.

42 Thomas Warton, *History of English Poetry* (London, 1778 and 1781), p. 349.

43 For detailed references to the sources of this passage, see Robinson, notes, and cf. **pp. 196–7.**

44 See Norton-Smith, ed., *Lydgate Poems*, no. 8 and accompanying notes.
45 Mackenzie, ed., *Poems of William Dunbar*, p. 160. Parallels from Latin sources are pointed out in his notes.
46 Norton-Smith, ed., *Lydgate: Poems*, pp. xi–xii.
47 *The Life and Death of Hector* (London, 1614), See Renoir, *Poetry of John Lydgate*, pp. 138 ff.
48 In *Amoryus and Cleopes* (*c.* 1458–9), in H. Craig, ed., *The Works of John Metham*, EETS, O.S., 132 (1906), lines 2192–7.
49 Norton-Smith, ed., *Lydgate Poems*, pp. 192–5.
50 *Ibid.*, p. 194.
51 'Balm' is usually associated with spice plants, either as a fragrance or as a liquid. 'Licour' is the life-bearing sap of the plant (as in Prologue, *CT* I, 3–4). For more detailed discussion of this particular complex of imagery, see Kean, *The Pearl: An Interpretation*, especially pp. 53 ff.; for 'dew', see pp. 142–4.
52 Some of these associations are still present as late as the seventeenth century, when 'sugar's uncorrupting oil' is still a pregnant image. Already in the sixteenth century, however, other senses were coming to the fore. Shakespeare has 'to sugar o'er his villainy', and both Sidney and Daniel use 'to sugar' in the sense of a 'to disguise' or 'palliate'. (See *OED* 'Sugar', sb. and v.) Once the idea of excessive sweetness, insipidity, is added, the reversal of meaning is complete, and 'sugary verses' comes to mean the exact opposite of what it would have meant in the fifteenth century.
53 Medieval writers sometimes use the 'chaff', or husk, to refer to the literal sense of poetry, and the 'kernel', or grain, to mean the allegorical or moral sense. For a discussion of this usage see Robertson, *Preface*, pp. 316–17. It does not appear to me that allegory is as regularly involved in the use of this image as Robertson assumes.
54 E.g., de Bruyne, *Etude d'Esthétique Mediévale*, III; and Tuve, *Elizabethan and Metaphysical Imagery*, p. 29 and the references there given.
55 See K. E. Gilbert and H. Kuhn, *A History of Esthetics* (New York, 1939), pp. 135–44.
56 Savage, trans., *St. Ambrose: Hexameron*, p. 28.
57 Hoccleve used it as well as Caxton (see, e.g., Spurgeon, *Chaucer Criticism and Allusion*, I, p. 21), and it remained popular for a long time. Cf. the citations in Spurgeon from John Rastell, 1520 (p. 73) and from the work of an unknown writer printed in 1525 (p. 75).
58 Curtius, *European Literature and the Latin Middle Ages*, p. 492.
59 The British Academy, *Chaucer and the Rhetoricians*, Warton Lecture on English Poetry, VII (1926), p. 10.
60 See **p. 24.**
61 Savage, trans., *St. Ambrose: Hexameron*, p. 26.
62 *Ibid.*, pp. 28–9.
63 *Ibid.*, p. 26. On the idea of God as the good Architect, see also **pp. 23–5.** As far as aesthetic criticism was concerned, Geoffrey of Vinsauf's version is influential (see E. Faral, *Les Arts Poétiques* (Paris, 1923),

p. 198). On Chaucer's probable knowledge and use of this passage, see Bennett, *Parlement*, pp. 4–5. But it is Boccaccio, as Osgood notes, who really restores meaning to the idea of creating and afterwards beautifying, and who relates the meaning of *ornare* to the realization of the work as a whole. 'This fervor of poesy is sublime in its effects: it impels the soul to a longing for utterance; it brings forth strange and unheard-of creations of the mind; it arranges these meditations in a fixed order, adorns [*ornare*] the whole composition with unusual interweaving of words and thoughts' (Osgood, *Boccaccio on Poetry*, p. 39). The final phrase shows that *ornare* refers to content as well as to style. It is perhaps worth noting that for Puttenham the 'ornament' of the figure of speech still has a composing function; he calls it 'the instrument wherwith we burnish our language, fashioning it to this or that measure or proportion' (*Art of English Poesie*, III, iii, pp. 142–3).

64 Savage, trans., *St. Ambrose: Hexameron*, pp. 23, 29.

65 *Golden Legend*, 37/1.

66 *OED* 'Fulsome', a.7.

67 See *ibid.* a.1. The sense 'overgrown', rank, and so 'offensive' were also, however, present from an early period. Confusion with ME 'fulsum' from *ful* = 'foul' is possible.

68 See Curtius, *European Literature in the Latin Middle Ages*, pp. 487 ff. Skelton (Alexander Dyce, ed., *Poetical Works of John Skelton* [London, 1843]) is thus not necessarily showing a new attitude to poetic style when he says that:

> Chaucer, that famus clerke,
> His termes were not darke
> But plesaunt, easy, and playne,
> No word he wrote in vayne.
> (*Phillip Sparrow*, 800–3)

69 Caxton writes of 'many a noble historye' (Proheme to the *Canterbury Tales*). *Troilus*, according to Wynkyn de Worde's title of 1517, is 'noble . . . hystory'. In Berthelet's address to the Reader at the beginning of his 1532 edition of the *Confessio Amantis*, the Troilus becomes 'the whiche noble warke'.

Index

Index

Index

Index

Index

Index

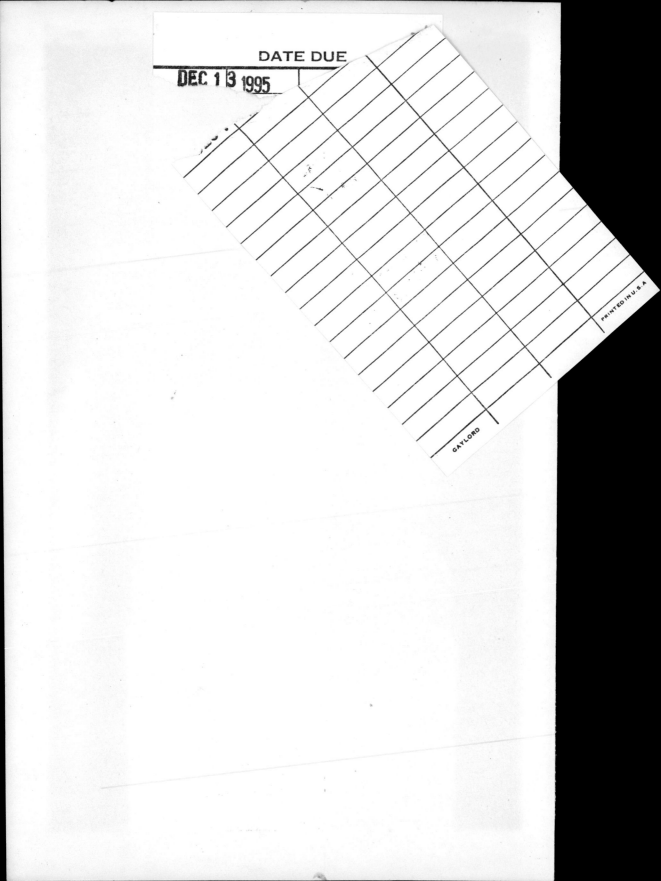

GAYLORD

PRINTED IN U.S.A